Crisis Prevention and
Prosperity Management
for the World Economy

Volumes in the *Turbulent Waters* series by Ralph C. Bryant

*Turbulent Waters: Cross-Border Finance
and International Governance*

Articulates a pragmatically sound vision of the evolution of international governance for the world economy and financial system, which is outgrowing its political structure.

Crisis Prevention and Prosperity Management for the World Economy
PRAGMATIC CHOICES FOR INTERNATIONAL FINANCIAL GOVERNANCE, PART 1

Advocates faster progress in reforming the international financial system, with emphasis on improving international efforts to prevent crises and manage prosperity.

Prudential Oversight and Standards for the World Financial System
PRAGMATIC CHOICES FOR INTERNATIONAL FINANCIAL GOVERNANCE, PART 2

Provides details on the background of prudential oversight and standards, progress made thus far, and unresolved issues that must still be addressed.

Crisis Management for the World Financial System
PRAGMATIC CHOICES FOR INTERNATIONAL FINANCIAL GOVERNANCE, PART 3

Offers a careful exposition of issues facing those managing financial crises, including an emphasis on needed enhancements in collective international management.

PRAGMATIC
CHOICES FOR
INTERNATIONAL
FINANCIAL
GOVERNANCE

PART ONE

Crisis Prevention and Prosperity Management for the World Economy

RALPH C. BRYANT

BROOKINGS INSTITUTION PRESS
Washington, D.C.

Copyright © 2004
THE BROOKINGS INSTITUTION
1775 Massachusetts Avenue, N.W., Washington, D.C. 20036
www.brookings.edu

Library of Congress Cataloging-in-Publication data
Bryant, Ralph C., 1938–
Crisis prevention and prosperity management for the world economy / Ralph C.
Bryant.
    p.   cm. — (Pragmatic choices for international financial governance ; pt. 1)
Includes bibliographical references and index.
ISBN 0-8157-0867-X (pbk. : alk. paper)
1. Capital movements. 2. International finance. 3. Financial crises.
4. International Monetary Fund. I. Title. II. Series.
HG3891.B788 2004
332'.042—dc22   2004017591

9 8 7 6 5 4 3 2 1

The paper used in this publication meets minimum requirements of the
American National Standard for Information Sciences—Permanence of Paper for
Printed Library Materials: ANSI Z39.48-1992.

Typeset in Adobe Garamond

Composition by OSP
Arlington, Virginia

Printed by IBT Global
Troy, New York

Contents

PRAGMATIC

CHOICES FOR

INTERNATIONAL

FINANCIAL

GOVERNANCE

PART ONE

Crisis Prevention and Prosperity Management for the World Economy

Introduction

My recent book, *Turbulent Waters: Cross-Border Finance and International Governance*, advocates faster progress in strengthening the international financial system (sometimes referred to as architectural reform). Most important, that book urges national governments and international organizations to upgrade the supranational surveillance of cross-border traffic regulations and of nations' macroeconomic, exchange rate, and balance-of-payments policies. Concurrently, they should streamline and strengthen intergovernmental lending intermediation for the liability financing of payments deficits.

In addition to surveillance and lending intermediation, *Turbulent Waters* identifies two other groups of reforms for enhancing the utilities infrastructure of the world financial system and strengthening the world economy. First, governments and international organizations should foster further major improvements in the prudential oversight of financial activity and in the associated design and monitoring of financial standards. Second, they should improve their cooperative management of financial crises. The enhancements needed include improvements in the contingent provision of emergency lending, in the handling of moral hazard difficulties, and in the involvement of private financial institutions in concerted lending.

All three types of reform—supranational surveillance and lending intermediation, prudential financial oversight, and cooperative crisis management—are needed. Each will reinforce the others. Each will help to strengthen the growth and resilience of the world economy and financial system.

The cooperative management of financial crises can be likened to the activities of a local fire department. A fire department is charged with extinguishing unexpected blazes, and international financial institutions may be charged with coordinating responses to unexpected financial crises. Surveillance at a supranational level of the economic and financial policies of national governments is akin to the activities at the local level of police departments, traffic regulators, and municipal agencies charged with licensing, inspection, public health, and safety standards. Supranational surveillance seeks to encourage compliance with international norms and intergovernmental agreements. It monitors cross-border traffic regulations. Surveillance is exercised in noncrisis and crisis conditions alike.

Traffic regulators discourage traffic violations. A major purpose of supranational surveillance is to inhibit individual nations from deliberately or inadvertently pursuing policies likely to cause economic disruption for other nations. Put the other way round, collective surveillance aspires to encourage preventive policies that are sound and neighborly.

Policymakers' concern with cross-border finance has been driven in recent years by the disruptions stemming from financial crises. Skillful crisis management is essential. Sound economic management in noncrisis conditions, however, is even more critical. Because choosing sound policies in normal times can substantially reduce the probability that crises will occur, enhancing the collective surveillance of national policies should have high priority. Intergovernmental lending intermediation to facilitate the adjustment of macroeconomic imbalances in national economies, most notably lending by the International Monetary Fund (IMF), can reinforce such surveillance, to the benefit of all.

More than anything else, in other words, architectural reform should emphasize the *prevention* of economic and financial crises. The primary preoccupation should be with encouraging healthy growth and financial stability—*prosperity management* rather than crisis management.

The reforms needed for crisis management and for supranational surveillance and lending intermediation presume central roles for the IMF and the national governments that are the predominant shareholders in the IMF. Reforms in prudential financial oversight, in contrast, involve numerous international organizations and consultative groups. One reason for differentiating prudential financial oversight from the macroeconomic dimensions of supranational surveillance and lending intermediation is its greater variety of institutions involved and the specialized complexity of their activities.

This essay augments and provides supporting detail for the analysis of collective surveillance and intergovernmental lending intermediation in *Turbulent Waters*. Supporting analyses for the other two areas of reform are contained in companion essays, *Prudential Oversight and Standards for the World Financial System* and *Crisis Management for the World Financial System*.

Collective Surveillance: Rationale and Basic Questions

The rationale for intergovernmental cooperation is straightforward and analytically sound. Decentralized national decisions that fail to take into account the cross-border spillovers from policy actions can produce welfare outcomes that are inferior to those that can be attained through informed collective action.

Inferior outcomes from decentralized decisionmaking are examples of situations in which negative externalities lead to market failures. If governments consult and bargain with one another cooperatively, they may be able to identify mutually beneficial adjustments of policy instruments that can offset market failures. Such adjustments may thereby permit nations to reach higher levels of welfare. Because cross-border economic integration has generated a growing variety and intensity of collective-action problems with cross-border dimensions, the rationale for intergovernmental cooperation is even more compelling in the first decade of the twenty-first century than it was half a century earlier.[1]

Efforts to cooperate are not invariably successful. Government intervention intended to remedy market failures can be counterproductive. In some circumstances, cooperative intergovernmental decisions can lead to government failures, thereby undermining rather than enhancing welfare. If intelligently pursued and not overly ambitious, however, cooperation

---

1. Bryant (2003), hereafter cited as *Turbulent Waters*, exposits the rationale for intergovernmental cooperation and the greater need for it when international economic interdependence increases (see especially chapters 3, 4, 7, and 8).

among national governments can often foster the common interests of their citizens.

When governments agree to make decisions cooperatively, they also need to ensure compliance with those decisions. The more ambitious the efforts to cooperate, the stronger the emphasis on compliance. The rationale for intergovernmental cooperation therefore comes with a corresponding rationale for *surveillance* of the policies of national governments. Establishing processes and institutions for surveillance facilitates compliance with international norms and intergovernmental agreements. Surveillance combines elements not only of *monitoring* but also of *enforcement*.[2]

The presumption in favor of supranational surveillance of national policies raises many difficult issues:

—Through which institutional venues—consultative groups, international organizations, or both—should surveillance be conducted? If several different venues are involved, how should surveillance activities be allocated among them?

—Should the surveillance of current account transactions (trade in goods and services) and the surveillance of capital account and financial transactions be conducted through separate processes and institutions?

—Should supranational surveillance focus on cross-border transactions and other external sector variables (for example, exchange rates) that pertain explicitly to several nations together rather than just a single nation? Alternatively, must surveillance pertain to all national policies—domestic as well as external—that can have significant influences on foreign nations?

—Can supranational surveillance of economic policies be underpinned by operational guidelines that are clearly and precisely specified?

—Is analytical knowledge about macroeconomic interactions among national economies sufficiently advanced to support effective surveillance?

—Do international organizations and intergovernmental consultative groups disclose sufficient information about their activities? Could disclosure during surveillance dialogues be so extensive as to compromise confidentiality when confidentiality is desirable?

—How should the policymakers of an individual nation choose an exchange-rate regime? Must the choice inevitably be restricted to the polar extremes of a "pure flex" (untrammeled floating) or a "hard fix" (a currency board arrangement or participation in a currency union)? Is there an opti-

2. *Turbulent Waters*, chapter 7.

mum or ideal exchange regime? Can the choice of regime be separated from decisions about other aspects of economic policy?

—Should the surveillance of macroeconomic policies and exchange rates be integrated with the surveillance of financial standards and prudential oversight?

—What general guidelines should prevail for capital account convertibility (freedom for money and capital to flow across national borders)? How should the IMF use these guidelines in its surveillance of national policies?

—Could individual nations and the world economy benefit not only from cautious supranational surveillance but also from a more ambitious, explicit *coordination* of national economic policies? If so, how might processes and institutions to nurture such coordination evolve?

—Does intergovernmental lending intermediation promote the smooth evolution of the world economy or should all lending—including any lending to national governments—be carried out by private financial institutions and financial markets? In particular, is it helpful for the IMF to have the authority to act as an intergovernmental lending intermediary to support its surveillance activities?

—Would it be preferable to narrow the IMF's mandate so that the focus of its surveillance shifts toward vulnerability to crises? Correspondingly, should the IMF lend only in times of financial crisis, or might it be helpful to lend in noncrisis circumstances?

—Should the IMF's surveillance efforts be restricted to a core area comprising macroeconomic policies, payments imbalances, and exchange rates? Should the IMF continue its recent trend toward focusing also on the surveillance of financial standards and prudential oversight of financial systems? The promotion of development and poverty reduction in member nations has gradually become a prominent IMF operating goal. Is that broadening of the IMF's original mandate a welcome evolution, perhaps one to be carried even further? Should the mandate be broader still, including, for example, the surveillance of labor standards and environmental standards?

—What is the appropriate size of aggregate IMF lending facilities? How much differentiation should there be among the different facilities? What interest rates and fees should be charged? What performance conditions ("conditionality") should be imposed on borrowing nations, in what manner?

—Which nations should be the main "clients" of the IMF? Should the IMF itself focus primarily on developing nations?

—What procedures and structures should underpin governance of the IMF? In particular, how should decisionmaking powers be allocated among the IMF's member nations?

Most of the questions in this list are contentious. It is not now possible to offer definitive consensus answers. Instead, this essay clarifies the questions, identifies the range of alternative views, and summarizes my own answers.

The adjectives *supranational* and *international* appear throughout *Turbulent Waters* and in this essay. To avoid confusion, the terms need to be carefully differentiated.

My approach to international financial governance seeks a middle ground between polar extremes. Hence even the adjectives I use to modify *collective governance* reflect a preference for taking the middle of the road. The governance optimists who favor sweeping institutional reform for the world in effect advocate genuine supranational collective governance, in the sense of governance over nations and authority over national governments. But with very few exceptions, genuine supranational governance is not politically feasible. It is not, at least not yet, even desirable. I have therefore been consistent in making recommendations for international rather than supranational collective governance.

In contrast, however, I often speak of supranational surveillance rather than international surveillance. *Collective surveillance* is a subset of the potential functions of international collective governance. The collective surveillance activities that exist or can realistically be envisaged today are weak precursors of more extensive and more muscular dimensions of collective governance. Yet even today's surveillance conducted by the IMF and other international financial institutions merits the adjective *supranational*. That use of language is appropriate because the nature and content of the surveillance inevitably require a perspective above the level of national governments.

But supranational in the context of surveillance definitely does *not* presume that those who exercise surveillance have significant independent authority to influence national governments. Quite the contrary. Surveillance in practice so far has been—and even when strengthened with incremental reforms in the near future will be—only tentative and shaped by "soft" rather than "hard" guidelines. The real exercisers of supranational surveillance are the national governments themselves. They choose to act collectively not because they agree to bend to the will of an independent authority above them, but because achieving their mutual interests requires cooperation.

The other context in which I use the adjective *supranational* is when referring to problems, as in "cross-border and supranational problems that require collective action by national governments." The literal meaning of supranational stems from the Latin *supra*, meaning "over" or "beyond" or "transcending." It would be misleading to speak of supranational governance in the sense of governance *over* (control of) national governments. But the nuances of supranational are appropriate when speaking of surveillance over national governments or of problems that transcend the level of nation states.

Venues for Intergovernmental Cooperation: General Considerations

In the first decade of the twenty-first century, the venues for collective action by national governments fall into two broad classes. National governments can interact through *consultative groups*. Or they can explicitly institutionalize their interactions and cooperation through *international* or *regional organizations*. Consultative groups serve as forums for cooperative interaction. They have no powers of their own. Meetings of a consultative group tend not to take place in a single, specific geographical location but rather to float over time from one locale to another, such as the capital cities of the participating governments. International or regional organizations are usually more than mere forums. These organizations typically have specific delegated powers, albeit narrowly circumscribed in most cases. An international or regional organization is headquartered in one specific geographical location or more, and most of its meetings occur at those locations.

In any given consultative group, typically a subset of national governments is involved. Many such groups are created by a limited cluster of governments so as to exclude other nations deliberately. In contrast, because of the political awkwardness of excluding particular nations once a collective decision has been taken to establish an actual organization, international or regional organizations tend to be inclusive rather than exclusive.

Intergovernmental consideration of a new regime environment must necessarily be tentative and informal at the outset of discussions. Episodic, top-level intergovernmental cooperation is therefore most likely to occur within a consultative group. Intermittent, lower-level types of intergovernmental cooperation, especially if they proceed beyond minimal gestures of mutual recognition to more ambitious cooperative efforts, often require some form of institutionalization to support collective decisionmaking. Lower-level cooperation therefore often is channeled through international or regional organizations. Indeed, the very existence of an international or regional organization presupposes prior top-level cooperation to establish an institution capable of sustaining ongoing, lower-level cooperation.[3]

The requirements for and availability of support resources are key differences between consultative groups and established organizations. The national governments participating in a consultative group typically do not allocate resources to the group itself. In fact, such groups operate with little or no collective administrative support. Often, for example, the group itself does not even have a supporting secretariat; each participating national government allocates staff and resources to backstop its own representatives, but typically no collective support exists for the group per se. Therefore, for consultative groups, issues about support resources either do not arise or are secondary.

In contrast, resource issues are a primary concern for international and regional organizations. Established organizations have permanent staff that must be paid, and often these organizations are given functions that require nonstaff expenditures. National governments therefore have to allocate resources to the organizations themselves. But how are the resource costs to be allocated among the member governments? This question is particularly acute for organizations whose activities require large operating resources. The size of the budget must be periodically agreed to, and then the total must be allocated among members.

Issues of relative power in established organizations are highly correlated with issues of how to share the burden of providing support resources. The relative powers of individual nations are most manifest in decisionmaking procedures, in particular in determining voting rights when decisionmaking entails a formal vote. Consultative groups often require unanimity in order to take a cooperative position. Seldom do such groups operate by taking explicit votes; therefore the issue of relative authority within a consultative group typically is suppressed rather than openly confronted. Like the issue of resources, the issue of relative authority and voting power inevitably has to be confronted more directly within an established organization. If an international or regional organization has been delegated significant powers, it will typically reach decisions through a weighted vot-

---

3. International regime environments, episodic top-level cooperation, and intermittent lower-level intergovernmental cooperation are discussed in *Turbulent Waters* (chapter 7).

ing procedure (or at least have such a procedure available) in which the most powerful nations have relatively larger shares of the total votes. Conversely, if such an organization operates by unanimity or consensus, it is less likely to be delegated significant powers.

The relative permanence of the venues is a further key difference between consultative groups and established organizations. New consultative groups can be easily created. Existing ones can be relatively easily disbanded. Because considerably more political effort and resources have to be expended to establish international or regional organizations, they are less likely to come into existence than consultative groups but more likely to be permanent once the initial inertia has been overcome.

Because a consultative group is merely a channel for cooperative interaction, does not acquire delegated powers or resources of its own, and may even be transitory, the issue of political accountability is less pressing than for a formal organization. Each national government is politically accountable for its participation in the intergovernmental group in much the same complex, controversial, and imperfect ways that the government is accountable for its domestic activities. An international or regional organization, in contrast, poses additional accountability issues. The national governments that established the organization in the first place are, to use the language of corporate governance, the shareholders. They appoint the management of the organization and exercise the votes that shape the organization's decisions. The organization is therefore, directly and powerfully, accountable to its member governments. But just as the modern literature on corporate governance distinguishes between the shareholders of and (more broadly) the stakeholders in a corporation, an international or regional organization can be perceived as having stakeholders in addition to its member governments. The workforce and suppliers of a private corporation are nonshareowning stakeholders. Some analysts have likewise perceived individual national citizens and their nongovernmental, civil society associations as nonshareowning stakeholders in international and regional organizations. These analysts have begun to argue that international and regional organizations should—somehow, to some degree—be accountable to "international civil society" as well as directly accountable to national governments.

For at least the first few decades of the twenty-first century, multiple and heterogeneous venues for intergovernmental cooperation will continue to be observed. Both consultative groups and established organizations will be needed. Both will persist. This heterogeneity is yet another manifestation of the messy, intermediate status of the world polity.

As the century progresses, the balance between the two types of venue is likely to tilt gradually toward international and regional organizations. Relatively more lower-level intergovernmental cooperation, in increasingly complex forms, will be required. It may seem natural and politically less contentious to delegate more of the associated responsibilities to government-like organizations with explicit cross-border mandates.

Yet not all political forces will foster that evolution. Controversially but inevitably, consultative groups and established cross-border organizations both will be dominated by the largest, wealthiest, most powerful nations. The governments of those nations will continue to find it easier to nurture their collaborative efforts by meeting in smaller, exclusionary consultative groups rather than openly and more inclusively through established cross-border organizations.

In the cross-border organizations themselves, it is true, the most powerful nations will have the largest voting shares—and the largest shares in the budget. But only if the most powerful nations confidently perceive the cross-border organizations as, on balance, decisively advancing their own interests will their governments shift the loci for intergovernmental cooperation toward those organizations. Smaller, less wealthy, less powerful nations will inevitably chafe at their exclusion from important consultative groups. They will continue to try to raise their relative shares and amplify their voices (but perhaps hope to raise their budget contributions less than proportionately?) in the cross-border organizations.

Institutional Dimensions of Supranational Surveillance

Issues about the institutional aspects of supranational surveillance arise in all areas of architectural reform of the world financial system, not merely those addressed in this essay. For example, emergency liquidity assistance in financial crises, if provided, is inevitably associated with surveillance and conditionality. Emergency lending may be arranged either through creditor nations acting through consultative groups or through the IMF or the Bank for International Settlements (BIS).[4] A multiplicity of institutional

---

4. *Turbulent Waters* (chapters 7, 10); Bryant (2004b), hereafter cited as *Crisis Management for the World Financial System.*

venues—consultative groups and international organizations—is involved in surveillance of financial standards and prudential oversight.[5]

Similarly heterogeneous and complex institutions are involved in the nascent supranational surveillance of all other types of economic policies. Consultative groups and international organizations both play key roles; the Group of Seven (G-7) has been the most influential of the former. Numerous other consultative groups, some transitory and some long lasting, have at times been significant. The IMF—particularly through its annual Article IV consultations and its surveillance of exchange rates—has played the largest role among international organizations in regard to macroeconomic and exchange-rate policies. But other international organizations have also been significantly involved. As supranational surveillance evolves further, issues about the allocation of responsibilities among the different institutional venues will become more salient and more difficult to resolve.

One issue about the allocation of responsibilities across institutions—whether to separate or integrate the surveillance of real sector and financial sector policies—is not controversial. More precisely, it has not been controversial in recent decades. A key function of surveillance is the monitoring and enforcement of traffic regulations for cross-border transactions. Because current account and capital account transactions are non-independent, a logical economic case can be made for conducting the surveillance of traffic regulations for trade in goods and services with that of capital account and financial transactions. In this area, however, politics has overruled economic logic. Governments have been reluctant to concentrate surveillance authority in a single international institution. By default, the consensus has been for separation rather than integration.

Since World War II, the rough consensus has been that the General Agreement on Tariffs and Trade (GATT) and more recently the World Trade Organization (WTO) should have most of the responsibility for monitoring and enforcing the traffic regulations for cross-border trade in goods and services. That consensus has also designated the IMF as the primary international organization for surveillance of capital flows and other cross-border financial transactions.

The Articles of Agreement of the IMF give limited responsibilities to the IMF for policing cross-border trade because of its responsibilities for over-

5. *Turbulent Waters* (chapters 3, 7, 10); Bryant (2004a), hereafter cited as *Prudential Oversight and Standards for the World Financial System*.

seeing *payments* for trade and other current account transactions. The Organization for Economic Cooperation and Development (OECD) and the World Bank also have limited roles in the supranational surveillance of trade transactions. But the responsibilities of other international organizations for surveillance of trade transactions are definitely secondary to those of the WTO.

In many ways, the collective governance issues involved in supranational surveillance of the traffic regulations for cross-border trade are similar to those for surveillance of macroeconomics and finance. Much could be said about how the role of the WTO is evolving in the monitoring and enforcement of international agreements on trade and property rights. But trade issues fall largely outside the scope of *Turbulent Waters* and of this essay. This essay will therefore not comment further on the WTO or discuss the evolution of supranational surveillance of trade.[6]

Evolution of Consultative Groups

For the foreseeable future, a few of the largest and most powerful nations will continue to meet alone in small groups. From the perspective of the nations excluded from these consultations, that fact is unfortunate. It is, nonetheless, a political reality. The G-7 venue, with its annual summit meetings and meetings of finance ministers—or a variant of the G-7 composed of similar countries—will survive for some time and is likely to be the primary locus of efforts by the largest nations to reach cooperative decisions about collective surveillance and other international financial issues.

Yet the G-7 will prove to be an unstable grouping over time. The evolution of political integration within Europe has already created significant tensions. Why, it is increasingly asked, should the four largest nations in the European Union—France, Germany, Italy, and the United Kingdom—be represented separately in the G-7 rather than collectively? Other European nations naturally resent their exclusion from the G-7, and complaints by Belgium, the Netherlands, Sweden, and Switzerland help to explain why the Group of Ten (G-10) was kept alive in the 1980s and 1990s even though the center of gravity of consultations among major nations had shifted overwhelmingly to the G-7.[7] Questions are sometimes raised about Canada's membership in the G-7 as well.

6. A volume edited by Krueger (1998) contains papers providing background about the WTO. Other background references about the WTO and GATT include Dam (1970), Hoekman and Kostecki (1995), Jackson (1997, 1998), and Collins and Bosworth (1994).

7. As of 2003, it was unclear whether occasional new tasks might be assigned to the G-10 in the future or whether the G-10 might instead atrophy further. *Turbulent Waters* (appendix) gives a brief history of the G-10, the G-7, and other consultative groups.

The checkered history of inclusion and exclusion of Russia from meetings of the G-7 illustrates the difficulties. Concerns about the dismantling of the former Soviet Union and developments in Russia caused the G-7 to consider including Russia in some fashion. A post-summit dialogue with the USSR and then with Russia began in 1991. Starting in 1994, the G-7 and Russia met as the "Political 8" in conjunction with the G-7 summit meetings. The 1997 and 1998 summits included still more extensive Russian participation. By the 1998 summit, numerous observers were referring to the G-8 or the G-7/G-8 rather than merely the G-7. In fact, however, Russia has not been a participant in financial and certain economic discussions at the summits. Nor has Russia's finance minister been included in the G-7 meetings of finance ministers that are held during the year apart from the summit.[8] Although the idea has been bruited to abandon the G-7 as a separate group and to have Russia participate in all meetings of a full-fledged successor G-8 group, that idea had not been accepted by 2004. For the time being, the G-7, not the G-8, is the more influential venue for financial and economic matters.

Moreover, China's size and importance in the world economy and its rapid growth in the 1990s make its exclusion from the G-7 or G-8 appear increasingly anomalous. The omission of nations as large as India and Brazil from key international consultations on financial and economic topics also is becoming more difficult to rationalize on objective economic grounds and even in terms of political power.

In September 1999 the G-7 finance ministers announced the creation of yet another consultative group of finance ministers and central bank governors, to be known as the Group of Twenty. The G-20 fulfilled a commitment made by the G-7 leaders at the June 1999 summit in Cologne, Germany, "to establish an informal mechanism for dialogue among systemically important countries within the framework of the Bretton Woods institutional system." The members of the G-20 include the seven members of the G-7 plus Argentina, Australia, Brazil, China, India, Indonesia, Mexico, Russia, Saudi Arabia, South Africa, South Korea, Turkey, and the European Union. It is still too early to tell whether the G-20 might eventually have significant influence as a consultative group in

---

8. At the time of the July 2000 summit meetings in Japan, for example, the G-7 finance ministers met separately without Russia prior to the Okinawa summit itself. Though a "G-8" communique mentioned some economic subjects, the G-7 rather than the G-8 issued the key economic and financial communiqué. Talbott (2002) discusses the major international security issues raised by Russia's political evolution in the 1990s and, in passing, describes the pressures to include Russia in G-7 summit meetings.

shaping key international decisions. Through the first half of 2004 the achievements and influence of the G-20 appeared modest at best.[9]

To summarize: issues of international financial and economic governance have so far been handled primarily through an intergovernmental institutional mechanism that leaves only minor roles and influence to smaller industrial nations and to all developing nations. The G-7 nations have met among themselves to discuss difficult international issues, forged a consensus when possible, and only then reached out to other nations to generate support for their decisions. In effect, the G-7 nations have presumed that the rest of the world should gratefully accept their decisions. Not surprisingly, and with justification, this posture has left outsider nations restive.[10]

Strong pressures to modify the consultative process and to give greater voice to nations excluded from G-7 consultations will surely increase over time. In recent years, prior to G-7 summit meetings, modest (and perhaps partly cosmetic?) steps were taken to arrange consultative sessions with government officials from developing nations and smaller industrial nations. Strengthening of the G-20 and alternative institutional innovations for including the less wealthy and less powerful nations seems likely. Greater legitimacy for collective international financial governance will not be possible unless further steps are taken over time to broaden participation in the decisionmaking process.

The International Monetary Fund: The Dominant Venue for Surveillance

Although topical, urgent surveillance issues are discussed bilaterally among the governments of the largest nations and within G-7 meetings,

9. In several respects, including its composition, the G-20 is a successor to a temporary consultative group formed in 1998 known as the Group of Twenty-Two. The managing director of the IMF and the president of the World Bank, as well as the chairpersons of the International Monetary and Financial Committee and of the Development Committee, participate in the G-20 discussions. The G-20 met for the first time in December 1999 and subsequently has held meetings annually. During the first half of 2004, several of the G-7 nations were rumored to be considering putting greater emphasis on meetings of the G-20. The G-20 dating from 1999 should not be confused with the Committee of Twenty that was active during the 1970s in the discussions of possible reforms of the international monetary system. See *Turbulent Waters* (appendix) for further discussion of the history of intergovernmental consultative groups.

10. Dani Rodrik (1999, p. 126) characterizes the situation as follows: "The current model is one in which the G-7 works out all the details and then conducts outreach to educate developing countries. The outcome of such a process will not only lack widespread legitimacy, it will also suffer from oversights arising from inadequate understanding of the developing countries' circumstances."

many aspects of surveillance require regular, continuing institutional input. Ongoing, lower-level cooperation does in fact constitute the bulk of collective surveillance activity. The IMF is the international financial organization that has most responsibility for surveillance of national economic policies. Accordingly, much of the following discussion is concerned with the IMF's mandate for surveillance and how it exercises that mandate.

The governance powers of the IMF are ultimately vested in its Board of Governors, which is composed of one governor and one alternate governor for each member nation. In practice, decisionmaking at the IMF occurs through its Executive Board. As of 2004, member nations were organized into twenty-four groups known as constituencies; the Executive Board was correspondingly composed of twenty-four executive directors, appointed or elected by the constituencies, plus the managing director, who serves as chairperson. The Executive Board typically meets several times during the week.[11]

The International Monetary and Financial Committee (IMFC) is the consultative venue most closely associated with the IMF's surveillance activities. The IMFC's predecessor, the Interim Committee, and more recently the IMFC itself (as well as the Development Committee, a counterpart to the IMFC for discussing development issues) have so far functioned primarily as venues for policy speeches and for signaling policy intentions. The G-7 nations, for example, have used the IMFC as a key platform for explaining to the wider international community cooperative decisions they have formulated earlier among themselves. In future years, the IMFC might conceivably acquire somewhat more importance as a locus for helping to shape key international decisions ex ante rather than merely discussing them ex post. As of 2004, however, that possibility seemed remote.

Over the longer run, the week-to-week decisionmaking of the IMF—and in particular, key decisions about guidelines and surveillance—could conceivably be vested in a new IMF body with greater powers than those of the Executive Board. Significantly, such an evolution was envisaged in the 1970s during the Committee of Twenty negotiations. The second amendment to the IMF Articles of Agreement adopted in 1978 provides explicitly for the establishment of a permanent and representative Council, to be composed of one Councillor appointed from each IMF constituency. Once activated, the Council was to succeed the Interim Committee. Unlike the

11. The Board of Governors delegates its powers to the Executive Board (except for certain reserved powers vested in the Board of Governors itself). The twenty-four constituencies of the board are discussed further toward the end of the essay.

Interim Committee and now the IMFC, which can only make recommendations, the Council would be a formal organ of the IMF and would have the authority to make decisions and exercise the powers of the IMF. By tacit agreement of both the industrial and the developing nations, the provisions for an IMF Council have remained inoperative. At the end of the 1990s, a few nations (most notably, France) suggested it might be timely to activate the Council, but so far that suggestion has not been widely supported.[12]

For the shorter run, the Executive Board will remain the key locus for the collective governance of surveillance decisions through the IMF, backstopped by discussions within and recommendations passed through the IMFC. Key decisions and recommendations will continue to be initially developed in non-IMF consultative groups such as the G-7.

Though the IMF has been and will continue to be the dominant locus for supranational surveillance, some aspects of surveillance activities have been and in the future will be channeled through the Bank for International Settlements, the World Bank, and the OECD.

The IMF and Other International Organizations as Traffic Monitors and Adjustment Referees

The designers of the IMF in the mid-1940s envisaged a function of collective surveillance that was, at least in its details, more implicit than explicit. In subsequent decades, however, national governments supported a modest strengthening and more explicit description of the surveillance responsibilities of the IMF (and of other international financial institutions as well).[13]

What Scope for Surveillance?

Which types of national policies should receive the greatest supranational surveillance? A first, superficially plausible reaction to this question would be to presume that surveillance should focus merely on cross-border transactions and on other external sector variables such as exchange rates and deficits or surpluses in national balances of payments. Those external sector variables are jointly determined by—"belong to"—the economies of several nations together. The appeal of this first reaction rests on the prag-

12. The clause providing for eventual activation of a Council is in schedule D, supplementing Article XII of the revised articles. For an early discussion of the Council, see Gold (1979a, 1979b).

13. *Turbulent Waters* (appendix, pp. 425–40) gives a summary of the historical background.

matic instinct that surveillance should not extend its reach unnecessarily into domestic matters and thereby raise fears about excessive infringement of national sovereignty.

Once examined, however, that initial reaction turns out to be economically illogical. (Political constraints are another matter, to be discussed below.) Given the marked increase in integration of the world economy and financial system, individual national economies are now more and more non-independent. They are like balls in a bowl. If one ball is moved, typically several other balls must move as well. That non-independence means that supranational surveillance needs to encompass all national policies having significant influences on other nations. In particular, the analytic logic of surveillance requires a focus not merely on compliance with cross-border traffic regulations but also on the cross-border consequences of domestic budgetary decisions made by fiscal authorities and of domestic monetary policy decisions made by central banks. Such domestic policies have marked, sometimes powerful, influences on foreign economies.

Views about the sustainability and appropriateness of an individual nation's external position invariably differ, especially those of the home and of foreign governments. Therefore views about the global pattern of imbalances and exchange rates also differ. But, ex post, there can be only one global pattern. Every exchange rate is two-sided. One nation cannot usually run a balance-of-payments surplus unless one or more other nations incur deficits.

These stark facts create a presumptive rationale for developing a *systemic perspective* to offset the inevitable biases in the perspectives of individual national governments. Systemic judgments about the sustainability and appropriateness of payments imbalances and exchange rates are notoriously difficult and inevitably rest on normative as well as objective criteria. Yet collective surveillance can try to identify ex ante inconsistencies in national policies and to foster cooperative reconciliation procedures among nations that would be mutually preferable to sequences of decentralized decisions. Inconsistencies in national policies typically lead to unexpected outcomes, including unwanted deficits or surpluses in national balances of payments or unwanted changes in exchange rates.

Consultative groups can to some degree develop the required systemic perspective. But that function is probably best performed by one or more international organizations. More ambitiously still, an international financial organization might be designated to act as an impartial referee for adjusting payments imbalances and as a forum and catalyst for coordinating nations' economic policies. *Turbulent Waters* labels such surveillance activities, for short, as the functions of *adjustment referee* and *coordination catalyst*.

The following analysis focuses on the content of and procedures for collective surveillance of macroeconomic policies and exchange-rate arrangements. Most of the discussion is about the IMF, given its central surveillance role. But the G-7 and international organizations such as the BIS and the OECD also are mentioned.

Surveillance of Exchange-Rate Arrangements

Even before the collapse of the Bretton Woods exchange-rate arrangements in the early 1970s, the IMF had little genuine leverage over its member nations' exchange-rate policies. The original IMF Articles of Agreement specified that a nation could not change its par value without the concurrence of the IMF. Typically, however, the IMF was informed of a change in a member's par value only hours before the change was to be publicly announced. The IMF could do little more than rubber-stamp the proposed change. The IMF's limited authority as a monitor of exchange rates was weakened still further by the economic turbulence of 1971–75 and the adoption of the new version of Article IV that went into effect in 1978.

The amended version of Article IV grants individual nations discretion in choosing an exchange-rate regime. It states that each member nation "undertakes to collaborate with the Fund and other members to assure orderly exchange arrangements and to promote a stable system of exchange rates."[14] (Note that the language specifies "a stable system of exchange rates" rather than "a system of stable exchange rates.") The amended version also preserves the principle that exchange rates are properly the subject of scrutiny by the IMF ("the Fund shall exercise firm surveillance over the exchange rate policies of members, and shall adopt specific principles for the guidance of all members with respect to those policies"). Nevertheless, the operative language of the amended Article IV authorizes nations to choose whatever exchange arrangements they wish. In effect, when adopting the second amendment to the IMF articles in 1978, member nations retreated from relatively well specified rules of the road to traffic regulations that were intended to be vague and much less constraining.

---

14. Section 1 of Article IV continues with a list of four associated obligations, but those are worded only in very general terms. (Two of the four vague obligations are quoted in succeeding footnotes.)

The greater vagueness in the amended Article IV is manifest in several ways. The IMF can make recommendations to its members, but it has no powers to make its recommendations binding. The IMF has the authority to adopt principles to guide its members with respect to their exchange policies. Yet "to guide" implies that a member's neglect of a principle is not automatically a breach of obligation. The conduct required of a member is not an obligation to achieve a specified objective but an obligation to make an effort to achieve that objective. The vague character of key obligations, moreover, makes it difficult to recognize by means of objective criteria whether a breach of an obligation has occurred.[15]

Following the negotiation in 1975–76 of the political compromises embodied in the revised version of Article IV, IMF staff began to develop guidelines for the "firm surveillance" of exchange-rate policies called for by the new Article IV. The Executive Board adopted a statement containing three "principles for the guidance of members' exchange rate policies" in April 1977. That policy document was periodically reviewed and supplemented by additional staff analysis. For example, in October 1997 the Executive Board reviewed methodologies for assessments of exchange rates and emphasized "that the IMF, as the central institution of the international monetary system, must continuously seek to strengthen its analysis and surveillance over exchange rate policies."[16] Yet the principles enunciated in the late 1970s continue to underpin the IMF's surveillance of exchange-rate arrangements. The three 1977 principles are worded as follows:

— A member shall avoid manipulating exchange rates or the international monetary system in order to prevent effective balance of payments adjustment or to gain an unfair competitive advantage over other members.

—A member should intervene in the exchange market if necessary to counter disorderly conditions which may be characterized inter alia by disruptive short-term movements in the exchange value of its currency.

---

15. There exists a deliberate imprecision, for example, in the passage in Article IV section 1(i) saying that each member shall "*endeavor to direct* its economic and financial policies *toward the objective* of fostering *orderly* economic growth with *reasonable* price stability, *with due regard to its circumstances.*" Article IV, section 1(ii) obligates a member—but notice the vagueness—to "*seek to promote* stability by fostering *orderly underlying* economic and financial conditions and a monetary system that does not *tend* to produce *erratic disruptions*" [emphasis added]. For a more detailed discussion of these points, see Gold (1984, vol. 2, "Strengthening the Soft International Law of Exchange Arrangements").

16. The quotation is from the IMF's *Annual Report 1998*, p. 44. Examples of the underlying IMF staff analysis include Clark and others (1994), Isard and Faruqee (1998), and Isard and others (2001).

—Members should take into account in their intervention policies the interests of other members, including those of the countries in whose currencies they intervene.[17]

The first of these guidelines repeats part of the general objectives contained in Article IV. The other two use concepts that elude objective, operational definition ("disorderly conditions," "disruptive short-term movements," "interests of other members"). The verbs in the guidelines are hortatory rather than obligatory ("should intervene" and "should take into account").

These soft principles derived from the vague provisions of Article IV do *not* constitute a genuinely firm basis for the "firm surveillance" of exchange rates. Given the messy, intermediate stage of evolution of the world polity, however, governments and the IMF are unlikely to be able to agree on guidelines for supranational surveillance that are clearer and "harder."

The IMF's Annual Article IV Consultations

Though the obligation of a member nation to consult with the IMF about its policies originally applied only to members availing themselves of the transitional arrangements of Article XIV, by the 1970s the IMF was conducting periodic (typically annual) consultations with all its members. Over time the process of annual consultations gradually acquired somewhat greater muscle and deeper analytical support.

Procedures for the annual consultations now entail extensive staff analysis of economic and financial developments in a member nation. An IMF staff mission makes a visit to the nation, collecting information and discussing the nation's policies with government officials. At the end of the visit, the mission generally prepares a concluding statement for discussion with the authorities. Thereafter the staff prepares a report and an appraisal. Additional reports often are prepared if the member happens to be currently borrowing from the IMF ("making use of Fund resources"). Most or all of the relevant documents are made available to the Executive Board.

The consultation process is completed by an Executive Board formal review, which usually occurs only a few weeks or months after termination of discussions between the member and IMF staff. At the end of the board's review, the chairman of the board summarizes the views expressed by the directors. This summing up, a written version of which was at one time

17. These principles are in the document "Surveillance over Exchange Rate Policies," which may be found in the IMF's *Annual Report 1977*, pp. 107–09, and in various printings of *Selected Decisions of the International Monetary Fund and Selected Documents*.

known as the "conclusions," is then transmitted to the government of the member nation.[18]

The IMF Executive Board supplements this systematic monitoring of developments in individual nations with periodic informal sessions on significant developments in selected nations and regions. Board meetings also occur periodically to review staff assessments of the economic outlook for and financial markets of the world as a whole. The most extensive and important of these assessments include the biannual forecasting and diagnostic exercise summarized in the *World Economic Outlook* (*WEO*) and an annual report, *International Capital Markets*.[19] The *WEO* and the capital markets report are key examples of IMF efforts to develop a systemic perspective that, when developed skillfully, can identify ex ante inconsistencies and problems in national policies and thereby signal the need for possible adjustments. Enhancements in these systemic analyses (discussed below) would further strengthen the supranational surveillance of macroeconomic policies, exchange rates, and payments imbalances.

As with the IMF's guidelines for exchange-rate arrangements, the guidelines underpinning its surveillance of overall macroeconomic policies tend to be soft rather than precise. An example of those guidelines, incorporating general principles rather than operationally usable benchmarks, can be seen in a declaration issued by the Interim Committee in September 1996 titled "Partnership for Sustainable Global Growth." That declaration has been referred to as the Eleven Commandments for making economic policy. One can grasp the general nature of the eleven points in the declaration from the following four examples. The committee, it says, "attaches particular importance to"

—Stressing that sound monetary, fiscal, and structural policies are complementary and mutually reinforcing: steady application of consistent policies over the medium term is required to establish the conditions for

---

18. The consultation procedures and significant developments in the process are discussed each year in the IMF's *Annual Reports*. See also Brau (1981) and Harper (1998). The formerly used term "conclusions" signified that the consultation process involves the exercise of *less* authority by the IMF than that exercised in connection with its regular "decisions" (the normal outcome when an item is placed on the board's agenda). Moreover, the conclusions were in theory the views of the managing director in his capacity as the chairman of the Executive Board rather than the views of the Executive Board (and hence the IMF) itself. These subtleties in procedure, which to an uninformed observer might seem a transparent fig leaf, in reality bore witness to the political sensitivities associated with the consultation process. (Formal decisions rather than mere conclusions continued to be required for member nations availing themselves of Article XIV.)

19. Beginning with the second quarter of 2000, the IMF also began to publish a quarterly review of developments and prospects for *Emerging Market Financing*.

sustained noninflationary growth and job creation, which are essential for social cohesion.

—Creating a favorable environment for private savings.

—Maintaining the impetus of trade liberalization, resisting protectionist pressures, and upholding the multilateral trading system.

—Improving the quality and composition of fiscal adjustment by reducing unproductive spending while ensuring adequate basic investment in infrastructure.[20]

Do the governments of member nations give substantial weight to the surveillance consultations conducted under Article IV? The degree of influence depends greatly on the particular country involved and its current circumstances. Important asymmetries, obvious but enormously consequential, exist among IMF member nations.

The primary asymmetry stems from the inevitable differences in the size and wealth of nations and hence in their relative political power. The IMF consults assertively with smaller members and leans on them heavily to consider changes in their policies if such changes seem appropriate. In contrast, the IMF tends to be less assertive with its largest and most powerful members and more hesitant to make recommendations for policy changes in their economies. The largest members are, after all, the dominant "shareholders" in the IMF. The IMF leadership and staff would be hopelessly naive and ineffective if they failed to recognize that.

A second dimension of asymmetry is significant. The IMF has considerably more potential leverage with members who are currently borrowing from the IMF or possibly contemplating borrowing in the near future. Conditionality is ineluctably associated with intergovernmental lending intermediation, as with all lending (discussed below). None of the industrial nations has been a borrower of IMF credit resources since the early 1980s. Hence the IMF influences the economic policies of developing nation members to a much greater extent than those of industrial nations.[21]

When IMF consultations bring to light differences between a member nation's government and the IMF, the resolution of the differences is fairly predictable. When a small nation and the IMF disagree, the small nation usually bends and falls into line. If one of the largest nations and the IMF disagree, the IMF typically falls into line. Some exceptions to these generalizations have occurred, but not many.

20. Interim Committee declaration of September 29, 1996 ("Partnership for Sustainable Global Growth"), reprinted in the *IMF Survey* for October 14, 1996, p. 327.

21. *Turbulent Waters* (appendix) summarizes the relevant history.

Article IV consultations extend, as in principle they should, across the entire range of a nation's macroeconomic policies. As noted above, surveillance cannot focus narrowly on payments imbalances and exchange rates alone.[22] Nevertheless, the IMF staff does use past and prospective changes in a member nation's balance of payments and exchange rates as key operational points of entry into dialogues with the national government. And, again, there is a de facto asymmetry among consultations with member nations. In practice, the IMF staff proceeds gingerly in its evaluation of domestic monetary and fiscal actions taken by its largest and most powerful members. Its evaluations of domestic policies of smaller members are relatively more fearless, especially if those nations are current or prospective borrowers of IMF resources.

Supranational Surveillance Conducted through Institutions Other than the IMF

Today the IMF is the predominant international financial organization conducting supranational surveillance. It was not always so. In the 1960s and 1970s, the largest and wealthiest nations had even less conviction than they do today that collective surveillance of their policies could be mutually beneficial. To the limited extent that they did engage in serious consultations about their exchange rates, external imbalances, and general macroeconomic policies, they did so through other venues, not through the IMF.

From the early 1960s, the Economic Policy Committee (EPC) of the OECD and its Working Party Three served as an institutional channel for the exchange of projections and policy ideas. The OECD staff began much earlier than the IMF to prepare an overview of the world "outlook" on aggregate demand and international trade. The focus of multilateral surveillance through Working Party Three was on payments imbalances. Efforts were made to judge the consistency of national projections—for example, whether the sum of ex ante national exports was approximately

---

22. The 1977 decision in "Surveillance over Exchange Rate Policies" (see note 17 above) recognized that "there is a close relationship between domestic and international economic policies." It also stated that the IMF's appraisal of a member's exchange-rate policies "shall be made within the framework of a comprehensive analysis of the general economic situation and economic policy strategy of the member, and shall recognize that domestic as well as external policies can contribute to timely adjustment of the balance of payments." These references and many subsequent ones thus indicate that member nations accept the principle that the appropriate scope for surveillance extends fully into "domestic" policies. Whether supranational surveillance in practice lives up to the rhetorical principle is another matter.

consistent with the sum of ex ante imports. A cautiously worded version of the OECD staff analysis has been publicly available since mid-1967 in the semiannual publication *OECD Economic Outlook*. In the 1960s and early 1970s, Working Party Three was arguably the most influential forum for surveillance consultations among the large industrial nations.

By the 1980s, however, the United States and several other large nations came to value consultations within the OECD less highly, in part because of the emergence of differences in the analytical views, real or perceived, of the OECD staff and key member governments. By the late 1970s, moreover, the annual economic summit meetings of the G-7 nations had become a focal point for discussing potential cooperation on domestic macroeconomic policies.[23]

As one looks ahead into the first decades of the twenty-first century, the prospective surveillance roles of the EPC and Working Party Three, and more generally of the OECD, are unclear. The G-7 governments appear to be schizophrenic about the functions of the OECD and how its responsibilities should be differentiated from those of other international organizations. The staff resources of the OECD are substantial, including expertise in the surveillance of macroeconomic policies, external imbalances, and exchange rates. Yet significant overlaps in function exist between parts of the OECD and the IMF and World Bank. For a few areas such as corporate governance standards, tax system competition, and tax havens, the OECD has a relatively clear mandate. But for surveillance of economic policies and some of the other broad functions of international governance, the OECD's mandate and responsibilities are not well defined. Additional nations such as Mexico and Korea have become OECD members, broadening its geographical mandate still further from its original historical rationale, which focused on Europe. OECD staff have sought to develop expertise on newly topical subjects—for example, the problems of population aging and of economies in transition from socialism to capitalism. The fact remains, however, that national governments have been slow to actively reconsider and reshape the OECD's responsibilities, in particular its role in supranational surveillance relative to the roles of the IMF, the BIS, and the World Bank.

23. James (1995) provides a historical account of the evolution of surveillance, covering both consultative groups and the international financial organizations.

The annual economic summits and associated meetings of finance ministers of the G-7 have continued to be an influential venue for consultations among the world's economically dominant nations. The G-7 meetings, however, lack a permanent staff secretariat and strong analytical support. Without more continuity and a stronger analytical foundation, the G-7 and other consultative groups are not as able to conduct effective ongoing surveillance as the established international financial organizations. That difference is an important reason why, in the second half of the 1980s and in the 1990s, the institutional pendulum swung back toward greater involvement of the international organizations, particularly the IMF.[24]

The Bank for International Settlements has a narrowly defined but still significant role in supranational surveillance. The BIS, an institution operated by and for the major central banks, jealously protects its activities from intrusion by finance ministries or other government officials. The independent status of the BIS derives from and reflects the increasingly widely accepted view that central banks should operate with a large measure of political independence.

The surveillance that occurs through the BIS is restricted to nations' general monetary policies, financial standards, and policies for prudential oversight of financial systems. The roles of BIS management and staff tend not to be as extensive as those sometimes played by the IMF and its staff in Article IV consultations. IMF staff, acting in the strongest fashion open to them, at times may be able to function as an adjustment referee or a coordination catalyst. A similar statement cannot be made about the BIS and its staff. Rather, the extensive consultations that occur through the BIS monthly meetings constitute peer-group mutual surveillance among the major central banks.

The World Bank's activities in lending to individual developing nations require periodic analysis of and judgments about virtually any of those nations' economic and financial policies. The World Bank therefore is to some degree inevitably engaged in the business of supranational surveillance. Because both the IMF and the World Bank are institutions with surveillance functions, delicate issues arise about differentiating their respective responsibilities and forging an appropriate division of labor.

---

24. Beginning in the 1980s, the finance ministers of the G-7 nations began to include the managing director of the IMF in part of their consultative sessions. This step opened up an influential and confidential channel through which analysis by the IMF staff could be transmitted to key decision-makers in G-7 governments.

Soft or Hard Guidelines?

The IMF's Articles of Agreement, its principles for the surveillance of exchange rates, the Interim Committee's "Eleven Commandments," and numerous other IMF documents rhetorically support the surveillance function. Yet there exists a softness in their legal underpinnings. The documents do not clarify operational objectives or provide clear-cut guidelines for how surveillance should be conducted. The rhetoric calls for "firm surveillance." But in practice what can "firm" really mean in a messy, intermediate world polity? Underlying that question is the issue of what lawyers refer to as the relative merits of soft law and hard law.

Where social consensus exists, it is argued, hard law often is to be preferred. Suppose, for example, that traffic regulations on city streets were deliberately designed to be vague. It would then be unclear which drivers have the right of way in particular circumstances. Hence traffic police could not themselves decide unambiguously how traffic regulations should be enforced. In the absence of clear authority to impose their own judgment, the police might have little choice but to withdraw to the sidewalks, exhorting drivers to behave well but leaving the resolution of disputes and accidents to those directly involved. Disputes and accidents would be more frequent than they would with stoplights and clearly designed regulations. Similarly, the referee in a football match could not make sound rulings and fairly adjudicate disputes if the rules of the game were left unclear. Such situations demand hard, not soft, law.[25]

In principle, supranational surveillance of nations' economic policies could be more effective if it could be underpinned by hard rather than soft traffic regulations. When underlying operational guidelines are fuzzy, the monitoring required for collective surveillance is bound to be less than "firm." The adjustment referees will have only limited ability to enforce compliance. Because of the fuzziness of the operational objectives, they may not even be able to judge whether particular nations are in or out of compliance in the first place. They can monitor only with difficulty. They can only exhort, not enforce.

In particular, the IMF's surveillance of macroeconomic policies and exchange rates is severely limited by the softness of the definition of "good behavior" of nations and of their underlying obligations. Analogous limita-

25. For discussion of the distinction between hard law and soft law in international governance, see Abbott and Snidal (2000) and Abbott and others (2000).

tions apply to surveillance through the BIS and the OECD and even more to surveillance discussions within the G-7 and other consultative groups.

As one illustration, consider the numerous shifts in exchange-market intervention policies of the United States in recent decades and the difficulties of applying supranational surveillance to them. In the fall of 1978, U.S. monetary authorities adopted a highly activist posture to mitigate depreciation of the dollar. By 1981, with a different administration in power, a completely hands-off stance was adopted. In 1985, after excessive appreciation of the dollar and after a change in the leadership of the U.S. Department of the Treasury, a somewhat activist policy was again implemented. Several further shifts in policy stance occurred in the last half of the 1980s and in the 1990s. The intervention policy of the United States became, if anything, even less transparent in the 2001–03 period.

Despite large variations in U.S. intervention policy and major controversies inside and outside the United States about what the U.S. policy stance ought to be, the numerous shifts in policy were deemed consistent with IMF guidelines. Because of the vagueness of the guidelines (for example, "countering disorderly conditions, if necessary") and the inability of the U.S. authorities, the IMF, or anyone else to define clearly what constitutes "disruptive short-term movements" in dollar exchange rates, no effective way existed to apply collective surveillance. Some of the shifts in the U.S. stance probably had significant effects on other nations, some favorable, others not. European nations and Japan strongly lobbied the U.S. authorities for or against intervention. U.S. intervention was sometimes cooperatively managed with the nations whose currencies were directly concerned. The IMF, however, was at best tangentially involved, and essentially only after the fact, in an effort to analyze the consequences.

Numerous additional illustrations could be given. At one time or another, controversies arose about the policies of Japan, the United Kingdom, Germany (prior to European monetary union), and the European Union itself regarding intervention in the exchange markets. By 2003 the exchange regime and intervention policies of the People's Republic of China had become a source of controversy. The softness of the definitions of "good behavior" for national budgetary and monetary policies, and hence the difficulties of conducting surveillance of those policies, is still more striking.

One should not be hasty, however, in drawing inferences about this situation. Yes, clear-cut—"hard"—guidelines for supranational surveillance would be, other things being equal, preferable to soft guidelines. But other things are far from equal. Severe obstacles impede the design and use of hard guidelines.

A yearning for hard law should be tempered by pragmatism. When social consensus does not exist, hard law is frequently unattainable. Society often may have to choose between no law or soft law—between no traffic regulations or fuzzy traffic regulations, between no guidelines at all or guidelines that enunciate principles but fail to facilitate clear monitoring and firm enforcement.

Law and guidelines that are hard rather than soft cannot be developed in the absence of substantial agreement about an underlying analytical framework. When objective analysis generates consensus in diagnosing a problem and identifying measures to alleviate it, progress in formulating hard guidelines and clear policies may be possible. Consensus on an appropriate analytical framework is typically a necessary (though not a sufficient) condition for designing hard guidelines to underpin collective action. Without agreement about the appropriate framework, however, no foundation exists for generating the wider social consensus necessary for hard guidelines.

Policymakers and their advisers have limited knowledge about the functioning of their own national economies. Their understanding of how national economies interact to generate regional and global economic outcomes is even more imperfect. At the international financial organizations, the analytical understanding of macroeconomic interactions among national economies is, though perhaps slightly better, still highly uncertain. This analytical ignorance—for brevity, *model uncertainty*—is the single greatest impediment to sound policymaking within national governments and to the development of firm guidelines for effective supranational surveillance.

National policymaking and supranational surveillance are both bedeviled by the prevalence of competing analytical models of how national economies interact with each other. Analysts at international organizations trying to clarify the interactions and ex ante inconsistencies among national economies, like national policymakers trying to formulate alternative policies, must employ some sort of analytical model that connects policy actions to expected outcomes. But several rival models will invariably exist, often embodying significantly different analytical views and having conflicting implications. Analysts and policymakers will accordingly be uncertain about which of the competing models represents the least inadequate approximation of the "true" model (the actual relationships that will determine actual outcomes in the real world).[26]

26. For a more extensive discussion of model uncertainty, see Bryant (1995, chapter 7).

Model construction is the initial step in creating some piece of analytical machinery to shed light on issues of policy interest. Model evaluation is the process through which a model is systematically assessed to determine whether it can achieve the objectives for which it has been constructed and to judge its performance according to theoretical and empirical criteria thought to characterize a "good" model. Model improvement is the process through which efforts are made to remedy the inadequacies of individual models and to promote convergence among competing models. If the processes of model evaluation and model improvement worked ideally, inconsistencies across models would be gradually eliminated and a single model would become the encompassing, consensus model for a particular analytical purpose.

But the processes of model evaluation and improvement do not work ideally. At best they do not work quickly. Analysts and policymakers therefore confront the thorny problem of model selection, of choosing from among the array of alternative models currently in existence and deciding how to use them most felicitously. The competing claims of rival models and the other dimensions of model uncertainty would not vex policymaking and supranational surveillance so greatly if analysis could safely downplay uncertainty. But good analysis cannot. In any practical policymaking or surveillance situation, uncertainty should be explicitly taken into account when formulating and implementing decisions.[27]

The macroeconomic models that pose the greatest analytical difficulties and that are most uncertain are those that attempt to study the interaction among multiple national economies. Such models are, of course, what is required as an analytical foundation for supranational surveillance.[28] Note, too, that the traffic regulations and supranational guidelines for adjustment that are applicable to national *domestic* policies are even more difficult to formulate than those for cross-border transactions. Yet such traffic regulations and guidelines are needed for effective supranational surveillance.

Insufficient understanding of the macroeconomic interactions among national economies is a fundamental obstacle in its own right. It also helps to explain why it has not been possible to reach intergovernmental consensus on more specific traffic regulations for cross-border transactions and

27. The importance of incorporating information about uncertainty into analytical and policy decisions was stressed by Brainard (1967). Many subsequent researchers confirmed and refined his original line of inquiry. For applications to intergovernmental cooperation, see, among numerous others, Ghosh and Masson (1994).

28. For an introduction to existing multination macroeconomic models and some of the analytical problems they confront, see Bryant, Hooper, and Mann (1993, chapter 1).

on firmer rather than soft guidelines for refereeing adjustments in national macroeconomic policies. Political support for attempting to develop less soft guidelines for supranational surveillance will remain weak until improvements in analytical knowledge can be made.

On balance, the prospects over the shorter run for clearer guidelines for supranational surveillance are not bright. Harder guidelines are certainly a worthy aspiration for the longer run. Without stronger analytical underpinnings and harder guidelines for surveillance, no international institution can act truly effectively as a traffic monitor, an adjustment referee, or a coordination catalyst. Yet soft, rather than hard, guidelines are the only feasible possibility for the time being.

Improving Analytical Foundations

Because improving analytical understanding of macroeconomic and financial interactions among national economies is a prerequisite for better national policymaking and for enhanced supranational surveillance, one might think that this fundamental point would be emphasized in discussions about reforming the international financial architecture. Surprisingly, it seldom receives attention. National governments, even those of major nations, have taken little direct interest in promoting such improvement. Nor have they put pressure on international institutions to make it a high priority for staff work. Such efforts as have been made have been sponsored by individual central banks, individual groups within international institutions, or research or academic institutions.

The paucity of analytical support for intergovernmental consultations and supranational surveillance has been more pronounced than can be explained solely by the inadequacies of existing knowledge. The series of annual G-7 summits and finance ministers' meetings have had less continuity and institutional infrastructure than consultations conducted through the IMF, the BIS, or the OECD. G-7 meetings have not been backstopped by consistent staff support. The G-7 governments have not wanted to establish a new secretariat to support the G-7 process, and at the same time they have been unwilling to allow existing international organizations such as the IMF to become actively enough involved to play that role.[29]

---

29. The extent to which the managing director and staff of the IMF have been involved in preparatory analysis for G-7 meetings and in the meetings themselves has been discussed by Crockett (1989), Solomon (1991), Dobson (1991, 1994), Fischer (1994), and Goldstein (1995).

Explicit government support for improving the analytical underpinnings of supranational surveillance will probably remain anemic in the short run. But it should be strengthened over the medium and long runs.

A key feature of such support would be the establishment of an international staff group charged with the collective task of improving analytical knowledge and diffusing that knowledge more widely. The IMF (or perhaps some combination of the IMF, the World Bank, the BIS, and the OECD) is the most logical institutional locus for this staff support. The new support staff, both general and special, could be incorporated into the IMF research department or lodged in a newly created IMF department. An inferior alternative would be to establish a secretariat for the G-7 and to include the analytical staff as part of that secretariat.[30]

Policymakers and the public in general do not find the analytical foundations of policymaking a sexy subject. But over the longer run, building more solid foundations is the only reliable way to improve policy debate and to render policy decisions and supranational surveillance more robust to error. Refining and enhancing the processes of model evaluation and model improvement is the ultimate answer to the problem of competing models.[31]

By tradition and comparative advantage, society looks to the academic community to discover new knowledge and to rebuild analytical foundations. For cross-border macroeconomic interactions, as in general, the academic community can and should play an important role in improving analytical foundations. But policymakers cannot count solely on the academic community to make sufficient progress on its own. Most academic researchers have limited knowledge of the ways in which unresolved ana-

30. Several keen observers of international consultations argue for more active use of the IMF and its staff rather than creation of a competing G-7 secretariat. For example, see Dobson (1994), Solomon (1991), Fischer (1994), and Goldstein (1995). I share that judgment, both about general staff support for the backstopping and monitoring of G-7 consultations and in particular for the location of a special support staff charged with strengthening the analytical foundations for intergovernmental cooperation on macroeconomic stabilization policies.

31. Dobson (1991, p. 146), speaking about the multicountry macroeconomic models available for assessing the linkages among economies in an internally consistent manner, observes that "few ministers or deputies are enthusiastic about this kind of work. They tend to distrust quantitative sophistication of this kind, even as an aid to judgment, preferring to rely on their accumulated experience and back-of-the-envelope knowledge about linkages. But this kind of work is needed to build a better shared technical understanding of the connections across economies, which eventually will feed upward into the deputies' briefings." Solomon (1991, p. 110) also points to the need for more explicit government support of "an ongoing research program on some of the unresolved analytical problems concerning coordination." Fischer (1994, p. 164) emphasizes the need for the IMF "to ensure that the analytic quality of its staff remains very high, and is indeed enhanced."

lytical issues surface in policy discussions. Without sustained contact with the policy community, researchers are much less likely to condition their research in ways that are helpful to policymakers. Even more important, the incentives and rewards for advancement in the academic community inhibit academics from giving priority to the analytical needs of policymakers. Their fellow academics accord much higher praise—and give much greater weight in decisions about university appointments—to new theoretical wrinkles published in prestigious academic journals than to thoughtful efforts to refine empirical models by better application of existing analytical knowledge. Even the small group of academic economists who develop forecasting and simulation models for use in policy analysis are reluctant to devote their limited resources to model validation and model evaluation. Few academics hand out kudos to researchers who do the hard work of identifying the deficiencies in existing analytical frameworks or who carefully try to remedy inadequacies in existing data sources. To complement and supplement academic research, policymakers therefore need to make adequate resources available for officially commissioned research to strengthen supranational surveillance.

Two types of research should be commissioned from support staff lodged in the IMF. One, the responsibility mainly of the general support staff, would focus on topics figuring prominently in discussions about current policy or policy in the immediate future. Analyses of controversial aspects of the current economic outlook, for individual economies or the world system, would typically dominate the work. The second type, the responsibility of the special support staff, would have a longer horizon. Projects would be chosen because of their potential importance as building blocks for improving analytical foundations, not because they could be expected to have an immediate payoff.

As an example of the longer-horizon type, the special support staff would be charged with careful evaluation of the strengths and weaknesses of alternative national operating regimes for domestic monetary and fiscal policies. Such research would also seek to develop alternative specifications of presumptive guidelines for supranational surveillance of the regimes. The research would begin with quite simplified specifications of regimes and guidelines before more complex and realistic alternatives could be examined. Model evaluation and comparison would inevitably be at the core of this work.[32]

32. This research would be, in effect, an intensification of the "rule analysis" discussed in Bryant (1995, chap. 4) and Bryant, Hooper, and Mann (1993).

As a second example, the special support staff could be charged with defining and estimating alternative concepts of equilibrium exchange rates and of equilibrium interest rates (national and global). What normative and analytical assumptions have to be specified if policymakers wish to identify an exchange rate deemed to be in "equilibrium"? Essentially the same analytical issues are at stake in determining when a nation's exchange rate is "misaligned" or "overvalued" or "undervalued." How can policymakers tell when a nation's real interest rate (or "the global" real interest rate) is too high or too low? Under what circumstances might a policymaker conclude that an exchange rate or an interest rate should be judged "excessively variable"?

Analysts have great difficulty in supplying nontautological answers to these questions. A carefully defined equilibrium rate must be characterized as a dynamic time path rather than a single value. Any specific calculation of an equilibrium path necessarily makes use of normative assumptions and therefore cannot be "neutral" about policymakers' goals. Moreover, estimates of equilibrium paths, for exchange rates or interest rates, are inescapably contingent on the particular theoretical or empirical model with whose aid the estimates are derived. Because estimates are both goal contingent and model contingent, multiple useful calculations of equilibrium paths may exist. Analysts and policymakers have only begun to clarify the relevant concepts and empirical procedures, despite their clear importance in supporting national policy decisions and supranational surveillance.[33]

Collection and publication of statistical data, for both national economies and the global economy, is an important collective good supplied by international institutions. The process of data collection and publication always demands rethinking and improvement. Even within nations the quality and availability of data leave much to be desired. As regional economies and the world economy become still more integrated, the demand for reliable and consistently compiled data will increase further. International institutions should play a catalytic role in meeting this need.

Policymakers and their advisers must be the primary advocates of enhancing analytical support for supranational surveillance. But in a mod-

---

33. Preferably, the general concept of equilibrium paths for exchange rates and interest rates should not by definition exclude certain types of policy action or embody certain policy goals to the exclusion of others. The status of analytical understanding of equilibrium exchange rates is reviewed in a volume edited by John Williamson (1994); see, among other contributions, Artis and Taylor (1995), Stein and others (1995), Driver and Wren-Lewis (1997), and Hinkle and Montiel (1999). For the evolution of the analytical techniques used by IMF staff, see Artus and Crockett (1978), Artus and Knight (1984), Goldstein (1984), Clark and others (1994), and Isard and Faruqee (1998).

est way there exists an epistemic community of individuals outside of governments and international organizations—for example, in academic institutions—who also try to advance theoretical and empirical knowledge about cross-border macroeconomic interactions. Farsighted policymakers have a clear interest in nurturing this community, encouraging it to play an active role in developing analytical knowledge, and in applying that knowledge to supranational surveillance.

Dissemination of Information: Transparency versus Confidentiality

Surveillance consultations raise delicate and controversial issues of *confidentiality*. Dialogues between a government and the IMF in an Article IV consultation, for example, may not be frank and meaningful without the assurance of confidentiality. Effective surveillance requires extensive access to a government's data, analyses, and projections. Yet that information often is politically sensitive or market sensitive. If the government does not have the assurance that the IMF will protect the confidentiality of sensitive information, the IMF will not be given sufficient access. Understandably, governments prefer to decide for themselves what information and policy advice is, and is not, made available to the world public.

Transparency—dissemination of information about the procedures, conclusions, and differences of view involved in surveillance—is the opposite side of the coin. Disclosure of relevant, accurate information contributes to the efficient allocation of resources by ensuring that economic agents have enough information to identify risks and to distinguish the circumstances of one enterprise, or one nation, from those of others. Disclosure shapes market expectations and thereby often reinforces the effectiveness of sound government policies. The beneficial effects of information disclosure are no less important in enhancing the effectiveness of supranational surveillance.

The dilemma is that transparency and confidentiality must be traded off against each other. Because of the beneficial effects of transparency, confidentiality should be restricted to circumstances in which the balance of benefits and costs argues strongly against information disclosure. To gain the benefits of confidentiality, transparency and full disclosure of information sometimes must be limited. This general dilemma, found in many aspects of life, arises in an acute form in the supranational surveillance of nations' economic policies.

In the very early years of their existence the international financial institutions were not notably forthcoming in their disclosure of information.

The governments that had created them, the shareholders to whom the institutions were directly accountable, did not push for wide dissemination of detailed information about their activities. There was a keen sensitivity to preserving the confidentiality of interactions among member governments. Some outside observers accordingly perceived the institutions as aloof and opaque, even secretive.

The documents from the IMF's Article XIV and Article IV consultations with member governments are a revealing illustration. Until the 1980s, all the documents were considered confidential. A member nation might itself have occasionally leaked a favorable report. But any breach of confidentiality was frowned upon and the IMF itself never made the documents publicly available. Most other reports and analyses conducted by the IMF, especially staff analyses of economic developments and policies in particular member nations, were likewise unavailable to the general public.[34] A similar state of affairs existed at the BIS, the OECD, and the World Bank; most staff analyses and documents, especially those associated with sensitive surveillance of nations' policies, were not placed in the public domain.

Happily, in recent decades views on the appropriate balance of confidentiality and transparency among both the international organizations and many of their member governments gradually shifted. Most notably, the international financial organizations substantially increased the quantity and quality of information about the supranational surveillance of national policies that they made available. This evolution was especially marked in the last years of the 1990s and in the early 2000s. The shift in attitude was pronounced at the IMF, but it occurred at the BIS, the World Bank, and the OECD as well.

As late as 1994, most background reports, papers, and staff appraisals associated with Article IV consultations were still treated as confidential.[35] In the fall of that year, however, the IMF began to make publicly available some of the less sensitive documents, for example, the staff reviews known as Recent Economic Developments.[36] Then in May 1997 the IMF Execu-

---

34. Research papers published in the journal *IMF Staff Papers* were an important exception.

35. There were some exceptions. For example, an early change occurred in 1984 in conjunction with a multiyear rescheduling of Mexico's external debts arranged between the Mexican authorities and the advisory group representing the commercial banks lending to Mexico. As part of the 1984 agreement, the IMF agreed to enhance its Article IV consultations with Mexico. Among other things, it agreed to prepare reports and hold Executive Board discussions twice rather than once per year. It was also understood that Mexico itself could, and would, make IMF reports available to its commercial bank creditors. This action established the precedent that analyses prepared in connection with Article IV consultations could be made available outside the member governments themselves.

36. For discussion, see Fischer (1994) and Goldstein (1995).

tive Board began to issue Public Information Notices (PINs) at the conclusion of many Article IV consultations. The PIN for a member's consultation gave a background description of the economic situation at the time of the Article IV consultation and provided the Executive Board's assessment of the situation as reflected in the chairman's summary of the board's discussion. Release of a consultation's PIN was voluntary rather than mandatory; the member government made the decision. In the fiscal year ending in the summer of 2003, a PIN was issued for five-sixths of the annual consultations (106 of 127).[37] In fiscal 2003, 136 Article IV consultations were held and PINs were issued for 117 of them.[38]

Further significant changes in the IMF's disclosure of information began in 1999, when a pilot program experimented with publication of the staff reports associated with Article IV consultations.[39] Member governments could voluntarily approve release of the staff report prepared during their consultations. By August 2000 the Executive Board judged the pilot program on balance to have been successful and approved a general policy of voluntary publication of Article IV staff reports and staff supplements.[40] In 1999 the IMF also decided in favor of a presumption for publication, again on a voluntary basis, of the key documents prepared in connection with member nations' borrowing from the IMF—their "use of Fund resources" (UFR).[41] By August 2000, the Executive Board adopted a policy presuming publication of almost all the main documents associated with a member's use of IMF resources. For Poverty Reduction Strategy Papers (PRSPs), the presumption went even further: if the member government would not agree to have its PRSP published, IMF staff would not recommend endorsement of the document by the Executive Board.[42]

In still another set of developments bearing on transparency, the IMF commissioned several external evaluations of different aspects of its opera-

37. IMF (2000f, p. 17). The IMF compiles and publishes the consultation PINs for member nations in a publication, *IMF Economic Reviews*, first produced in May 1998.

38. IMF (2003d, pp. 5–6).

39. For example, the IMF extended its use of PINs to issue releases covering IMF Policy Papers and numerous other IMF documents. IMF policy on access to its archives was changed, shortening the period of confidentiality from the previous twenty years to five years.

40. By the spring of 2000, fifty-eight member nations had volunteered to participate in the pilot project and some forty staff reports had been published. For fiscal year 2003, ninety-seven staff reports were published out of the total of 136 consultations held.

41. These key documents include the Letters of Intent and Memoranda of Economic and Financial Policies, known as LOIs/MEFPs, and Policy Framework Papers (PFPs). The August 2000 policy of voluntary publication also applies to so-called combined Article IV/UFR staff reports.

42. A summary of the status of "transparency progress" as of 2000 is provided in the IMF's Public Information Notice 00/81, September 20, 2000. For an update as of 2003, see IMF (2003d, chap. 7).

tions, including an evaluation of IMF surveillance.[43] By 2000 a decision had been taken to establish an independent evaluation office in order to enhance the IMF's accountability. By 2003 the office had prepared and published several extensive studies, including reports on the prolonged use of IMF resources, the role played by the IMF in capital account crises, and the role of fiscal adjustment in IMF-supported programs.[44]

The BIS, the World Bank, and the OECD also significantly enlarged the amount of formerly confidential material that they release to the general public. The websites for these organizations, like that of the IMF, make it easy to obtain a wide range of information not only about the organizations themselves but also about their member nations. For example, the BIS now makes available many of the reports and staff papers prepared under its auspices. Extensive documentation is released about the activities of the Basle Committee on Banking Supervision. The World Bank has increased by an order of magnitude its disclosure of papers and reports, including many documents sensitively related to its lending to individual nations. In 1998, for example, the World Bank began to publish its key Country Assistance Strategy reports.

Many commentators do not seem to be aware of the expansion in the availability of information about international organizations and their nascent efforts at supranational surveillance. The striking fact, however, is that major improvements have been made in the transparency and accountability of international financial institutions. Considerable further progress is possible, and desirable. Nevertheless, the progress that has already been made should at least be recognized.

Has the recent emphasis on disclosure and accountability perhaps been too strong? In the trade-off between confidentiality and transparency, has confidentiality been compromised in instances when it would have been constructive and desirable? Most close observers do not perceive significant worrisome effects. Even the IMF Executive Board has taken a relatively relaxed attitude, concluding in September 2000 that "the candor of consultation discussions and reports to the Board had generally not been significantly affected." To be sure, Executive Board members expressed a range of views, including some dissent.[45]

43. See IMF (1999a). The other external evaluations included reports focusing on IMF research and the formulas for determining IMF quotas; see IMF (1999a) and IMF (2000d).

44. IMF, Independent Evaluation Office (2002, 2003a, 2003b, 2003c).

45. On the positive side, "several Directors considered that the prospect of publication had, in fact, served to improve the quality and analysis of consultation discussions and staff reports." On the other side, however, "several Directors thought that the risk of loss in candor might materialize over time. . . .

On balance, I believe that the benefits of greater disclosure and transparency have substantially outweighed the costs and risks. Sentiment has even changed enough to produce a shift in nuance about how "voluntary" publication, or the presumption in favor of publication, should be interpreted. Whereas voluntary publication was once interpreted to mean publication only if a nation's authorities requested it, many now think that it should imply publication unless the authorities explicitly object.[46]

As far as I know, no observers have claimed to identify instances in which the release of the IMF's or other international organizations' analyses of a nation's economy or disclosure of communications with the national government have created significant moral hazard. In theory, extensive IMF disclosure could lead a nation's foreign investors and creditors to rely on the IMF to issue warnings and identify risks instead of undertaking their own risk analysis. At worst, participants in world financial markets might presume that the IMF has a moral obligation to extend financial assistance to a nation deemed to be in good health and, conversely, no obligation to provide assistance to nations failing to heed IMF advice; such market views might contribute to excessive capital inflows in "safe" nations and unwarranted outflows and financial turbulence in nations where the IMF identifies problems. But so far at least, this concern seems theoretical rather than practical.

On the benefits side of transparency, the inevitable asymmetry in supranational surveillance—the fact that large and powerful nations feel much less pressure to comply with recommendations than small nations that borrow from international financial organizations—can be somewhat mitigated by extensive disclosure of information and analysis. At its best, supranational surveillance can never be completely evenhanded: the powerful will always, alas, be better able to get away with questionable behavior than the meek. But extensive disclosure can foster better accountability—even among the powerful, even among the very largest nations. A strategy of "name and shame" may be the most potent recourse available to the meek. Wisely used, it can certainly enhance the surveillance activities of international organizations.

The extent and nature of requests for modifications to staff reports suggested that concerns that a trend toward negotiated documents might emerge over time were not wholly misplaced and should be guarded against." The quotations are from IMF Public Information Notice 00/81, September 20, 2000.

46. This difference in nuance was emphasized in the G-22's *Report of the Working Group on Transparency and Accountability* (Group of Twenty-Two, 1998).

Remember, too, that a name-and-shame strategy can be an effective tool for the world community in dealing collectively with smaller "renegade" jurisdictions. If a nation refuses altogether to comply with reasonable world minimum standards for prudential oversight of its financial systems and for the prevention of money laundering and tax evasion, the name-and-shame recourse is likely to be the best course of collective action available.[47] Just as police cannot allow criminals to be the sole judge of their own behavior, the world community cannot permit the government of a renegade jurisdiction to decide exclusively on its own what information it will and will not make publicly available. Doubts may exist about which organizations can legitimately speak on behalf of the world community. Just as police power can be misused, the ever-present asymmetry of political power among nations can be abused in international relations. Large nations may wrongly use the "world community" umbrella to impose their narrowly conceived interests on smaller nations. Nevertheless, a few nations in the world may at times behave like renegades. In such instances, the world community can justifiably use disclosure of information about inappropriate behavior as a device to change it.

The Individual Nation's Choice of Exchange Regime

The analysis so far has emphasized a systemic perspective. Because the IMF's guidelines for surveillance are soft, however, and because the amended Article IV leaves the choice of exchange regime and exchange-rate policies to the discretion of each nation, it is necessary to address exchange-rate issues from the perspective of the individual nation as well.

The subject of exchange regimes pervades debates about reform of the international financial architecture. Many commentators regard the choice of exchange regime as the single most important policy choice to be made by a nation's government. A few go even further to presume that if a nation makes the supposedly all-important choice of exchange regime correctly, then other national choices and other dimensions of architectural reform pale into virtual insignificance.

Yet the preoccupation with exchange regimes is misguided. Exchange regimes and exchange-rate policies receive disproportionate emphasis relative to other, still more important dimensions of a nation's economic and financial policies. The paragraphs that follow summarize the more balanced approach that an individual nation should adopt in choosing an

47. For further discussion, see *Prudential Oversight and Standards for the World Financial System.*

exchange regime and integrating that regime into its overall macroeconomic policy.

The beginning of wisdom is to recognize that just as *any* exchange regime
is afflicted by inevitable uncertainty, no exchange regime—none—can insulate a nation from financial turbulence and economic misfortune. If a
nation's domestic macroeconomic policies and the prudential oversight of its
financial system are inadequate and are expected to deteriorate rather than
improve, for example, financial institutions and investors in the rest of the
world will sooner or later lose confidence in the nation and its government.
Financial institutions and investors within the nation also will eventually
turn skittish, often before world financial markets do so. If national macroeconomic policies are seriously faulty, no conceivable exchange regime can
protect the nation from hellish economic consequences.

Moreover, even if a nation's own policies are basically sound, unexpected
adverse shocks—originating either at home or in the rest of the world—can
severely buffet the national economy and financial reservoir. Fundamentals
contagion effects by themselves may be sufficient to spook the world financial markets, causing them to lose confidence that the nation can weather
the storm without disruptive policy changes. Because world financial markets and cross-border investors in a national economy are especially prone
to informational cascades and herding behavior, pure contagion effects may
add to the turbulence. In such adverse circumstances, no conceivable
exchange regime can come close to insulating and protecting the nation's
economy.

The more open a nation's financial reservoir is to the rest of the world,
the greater is its vulnerability to unsound national policies and unexpected
adverse shocks. In particular, the fewer restrictions and frictions there are
to inhibit cross-border financial transactions, the greater is a nation's potential exposure to worldwide informational cascades and herding behavior and
hence to financial contagion, both fundamentals and pure. Complete freedom for cross-border financial transactions will certainly undermine any
regime that pegs exchange rates. Yet complete freedom can also facilitate
severe turbulence within an exchange regime that permits untrammeled
flexibility in the exchange rate. Any conceivable exchange regime can be
temporarily overwhelmed in stormy conditions, the more so if there are no
cross-border or cross-currency "breakwaters" on capital flows.

A nation's choice of exchange regime is not a matter of indifference. Not
all regimes are equally vulnerable in the face of unexpected adverse shocks.
Depending on the circumstances, particular exchange regimes will lead to

more trouble more rapidly. Some exchange-rate policies more than others will exacerbate skittishness and capital flight when national policies are inadequate and deteriorating.

An especially reliable way for an individual nation to get into bad trouble is to implement a peg for the exchange value of its currency when prospective developments may subsequently require it to change the pegged rate.[48] If the circumstances of a nation argue for its adoption of currency board arrangements or even ultimate membership in a currency union, choosing to peg the exchange rate could be the appropriate regime even in stormy weather. Most nations, however, aspire to have some degree of autonomy in setting domestic monetary policy. If the monetary authorities in such a nation risk pegging the exchange rate "for the time being," that gamble can prove to be very costly if the peg subsequently has to be abandoned, typically in crisis conditions. The different variants of the pegging choice are especially problematic for nations that permit a wide measure of freedom for cross-border financial transactions.

Virtually every nation that experienced severe financial problems in the Asian financial crises of 1997–98 had been, formally or informally, pegging its exchange rate prior to the onset of its crisis. Had the crisis-afflicted nations permitted earlier and more gradual flexibility for movements in their exchange rates, they would have had less difficulty in coping with their large adverse shocks and would probably have incurred smaller costs from traumatic breakdowns in their exchange regimes.

Again, however, one should not disproportionately emphasize the choice of exchange regime. No variant of a floating exchange rate can prevent trouble if domestic policies are badly out of whack or if foreign financial markets lose confidence. Nor should one imagine that some particular exchange regime is "optimal" across all circumstances for all nations. Good exchange-rate policy is highly dependent on the context in which it is implemented. For an individual nation, no single regime may be best at all times and in all circumstances. There certainly is no single regime that will prove ideal for all nations at all times and in all circumstances.

---

48. As in *Turbulent Waters*, I use loose language here in referring to "the" exchange rate for a nation's currency rather than the plural, "exchange rates." This simplification, usually not misleading, is short-hand for the idea of a weighted-average measure of the nation's many bilateral exchange rates with each foreign currency of any significance in the nation's cross-border transactions. When a national government "pegs" its exchange rate, it announces that it will fix the value of the national currency against some major foreign currency (or a weighted basket of foreign currencies), subject perhaps to small day-to-day fluctuations within a narrow band.

In recent years conventional wisdom and journalistic commentary moved away from this eclectic position. It became increasingly popular to argue that the only viable options for a nation's exchange regime are the two extremes: either the pure flex of a free float or the hard fix of an irrevocable peg through a currency board or currency union. That assertion, often labeled the "vanishing-middle" or "corner-solution" view, contends that the entire middle ground of intermediate exchange regimes—the different variants of *managed floating* or *managed pegging*—is unsustainable and bound to disappear in the short or medium runs.

The shift in conventional wisdom toward the vanishing-middle view was encouraged by Barry Eichengreen's articulation of the position in his study for the Brookings Integrating National Economies series.[49] Lawrence Summers, deputy secretary and then secretary of the U.S. Treasury in the Clinton administration, essentially endorsed the view. Other significant endorsements included those by Jacob Frenkel (formerly the economic counselor at the IMF and then the governor of the Bank of Israel), an influential report by a Council on Foreign Relations task force, and the report to the U.S. Congress of its International Financial Institution Advisory Commission. Here is a representative, albeit unvarnished, statement of the position:

> [I]n a world of increasingly mobile capital, countries can either allow their currencies to float or fix them irrevocably, for instance through currency boards. They can even go further and attempt currency union. But the muddled middle ground, so popular in the years when capital was less mobile, has been wiped out by technological innovation and policy liberalization.[50]

49. Eichengreen (1994). When I was editing Eichengreen's book for the Brookings series, I tried— without notable success—to persuade him to back away from the strong line that all intermediate regimes were unsustainable. His views appeared to be mellowing somewhat as of 1999–2000, as can be seen in Eichengreen (1999a). The pragmatic Eichengreen, vintage 1999, seems to me more persuasive than the corner-solution Eichengreen, vintage 1994. The corner-solution Eichengreen is still apparent, however, in Eichengreen (1999b, pp. 103–06).

50. Statements by Summers on the subject include his testimony to the Senate Foreign Relations Subcommittee on International Economic Policy and Export-Trade Promotion on January 27, 1999; remarks at Yale University on September 22, 1999; remarks at the London Business School on December 14, 1999; and his testimony before the full Senate Foreign Relations Committee on February 29, 2000. Jacob Frenkel's endorsement was given in a luncheon speech at an IMF conference in Washington in May 1999. See also Council on Foreign Relations Independent Task Force (1999) and International Financial Institution Advisory Commission (Allen Meltzer, Chairman) (2000). The quotation is from an article by Zanny Minton Beddoes in *Foreign Affairs* (1999, p. 9).

The vanishing-middle view about exchange regimes emerged with particular intensity as part of a regional debate in emerging market nations, especially in Latin America. One set of corner-solution proponents argued that emerging market nations must allow their currencies to float freely. Advocates of the opposite corner solution argued that many if not all emerging market nations should abandon their own national currencies and instead unilaterally adopt the strong currency of a major nation; most of these advocates recommended unilateral adoption of the U.S. dollar (often referred to as the "dollarization" of the emerging market economy). A few advocates preferred the European euro (especially for European nations outside the European Union) or, if the emerging market nation was in Asia, possibly the Japanese yen.[51] The polarization of views was especially prominent in Latin American debates. Ricardo Hausmann, for example, observed that "both sides seem to accept that there can be no middle ground, no halfway arrangement between allowing a currency to float freely and bolting it down completely."[52]

The newer conventional wisdom about the vanishing middle, despite its influential adherents, is not persuasive. The yearning for a single, ideal set of exchange-rate arrangements, even for one individual nation, is misguided. The hypothesis that the intermediate middle ground is bound to disappear in the short or medium runs does not rest on sound theoretical foundations. Nor is it well supported by empirical evidence.[53] Salvation is not simple. Again, no exchange regime can insulate a nation from financial

51. Dollarization or "euro-ization" are in essence the *currency union* extreme of the spectrum of exchange regimes. But of course there is an enormous political difference between joining a currency union and participating in its management versus unilaterally adopting the currency of a major foreign power (the United States or the European Union) *without* any voice in the monetary policy of the power or in the exchange market management of the currency. (See below for further discussion.)

52. Hausmann (1999). Other contributors to the recent Latin American debate include Calvo and Reinhart (2001, 2002), Sachs and Larrain (1999), and Rojas-Suarez (2000).

53. A decade and a half ago I criticized the yearning for a single, ideal set of exchange-rate arrangements and went on to observe: "The two traditional policy views about fluctuations in exchange rates, the minimum-variance position and the untrammeled-market position, are each analytically deficient. In itself, variability in exchange rates is neither good nor bad. Neither its presence nor its absence makes sense as an *objective* for most nations' macroeconomic policies." Bryant (1987, p. 161); also Bryant (1980a,1980b). For cogent recent analyses that support an eclectic position and criticize the corner-solution view, see Frankel (1999) and Williamson (2000). Masson (2000) and Jadresic and others (2001) review empirical evidence that casts doubt on the view. The summary position of the IMF's research department as of April 2000 endorsed an essentially eclectic rather than corner-solution view; see Mussa and others (2000, p. 36). That view of the research department, however, may not have been fully accepted in other parts of the IMF.

turbulence and economic disruption if its macroeconomic and prudential oversight policies are unsound.

Open economy textbooks have for decades exposited the difficult choices facing an individual nation in terms of an "impossible trinity." The simplified expositions assert that a nation cannot simultaneously achieve the three objectives of *exchange-rate stability, financial autonomy*, and *full financial integration with the rest of the world*.[54] The insight stressed in the textbooks is that the three objectives are mutually incompatible. Any two of the three may be attainable. Full financial integration with the rest of the world and exchange-rate stability could be realized if the nation were to join a currency union and give up an independent monetary policy. Financial autonomy and exchange-rate stability could be achieved if the nation were to erect barriers to prevent cross-border financial transactions. If the exchange rate were allowed to fluctuate freely, it might be possible to have financial autonomy and complete freedom for cross-border capital flows. But the three cannot all be attained together. The more the nation strives to attain any two of the three, the more it must surrender its aspirations to simultaneously achieve the third.

The impossible trinity of textbook discussions seems at first blush to support the recently popular view that intermediate exchange regimes are bound to be unsustainable. Lawrence Summers, for example, invoked the textbook exposition:

> [T]he core principle of monetary economics is a trilemma: that capital mobility, an independent monetary policy, and the maintenance of a fixed exchange rate objective are mutually incompatible. I suspect this means that as capital market integration increases, countries will be forced increasingly to more pure floating or more purely fixed exchange rate regimes.[55]

The argument is reinforced if one believes that nations will be unable or unwilling to resist a worldwide tendency toward financial market integration (in other words, choose not to maintain effective inhibitions to

54. Full financial integration with the rest of the world implies complete freedom for cross-border financial transactions. Financial autonomy permits the nation to enjoy substantial economic and financial independence from the rest of the world, in particular to have its central bank pursue an independent monetary policy. Exchange-rate stability avoids disorderly fluctuations in the external exchange value of the nation's currency, which, other things being equal, helps to avoid disorderly fluctuations in financial prices in general.

55. Summers (1999a, p. 326).

cross-border financial transactions). It seems to follow that individual nations must either surrender financial autonomy or surrender exchange-rate stability.

On careful examination, however, the textbook catechism is not compelling. Nowhere is it convincingly written that nations must be purist in their goals. For example, rather than striving for the whole loaf of financial autonomy and the whole loaf of exchange-rate stability, a nation can in principle surrender some of both goals and thereby aim at getting half a loaf of autonomy combined with half a loaf of stability. Alternatively, instead of trying for untrammeled financial autonomy and complete freedom for cross-border financial transactions, the nation could seek half a loaf of autonomy and half a loaf of financial integration with the rest of the world. More generally, rather than striving for full attainment of any two of the three objectives, the nation may be better off aiming for some mix of all three.

The underlying strategy characterizing most managed-float or managed-peg exchange regimes is precisely a halfway policy. It seeks to satisfy some fraction of the fluctuating exchange market demands for the national currency with increases or decreases in the nation's official reserve position but also to satisfy the remaining fraction with adjustments in the exchange rate itself. More generally, when a nation chooses some variant of an intermediate exchange regime, it may surrender some part, but not the entirety, of all three goals of exchange-rate stability, financial autonomy, and financial market integration with the rest of the world. The nation may thereby pragmatically choose a compromise combination of the three that is preferable to any of the purist choices.[56]

Furthermore, a nation need not treat the choice of exchange regime as a once-and-for-all decision. The political climate and the stability of governance institutions may change, for better or worse. The relative weights of other nations as trading and financial partners may gradually shift. Correlations of national income with the incomes of particular trading and financial partners can increase or decrease. Shifts may occur over time in the relative importance of different types of unexpected adverse shocks. Considerations such as these can change the relative advantages and disadvantages of alternative exchange regimes.[57]

56. Both Frankel (1999) and Williamson (2000) point out the inadequacy of inferences drawn from a simplified textbook exposition of the impossible trinity. Both advocate, in effect, "interior solutions" rather than one of the "corner solutions" which expositions of the textbook diagram commonly stress.

57. Frankel (1999) and Masson (2000) thoughtfully explore this line of thinking. Masson's analysis explicitly treats nations' regime choices in terms of the likelihood of their transiting from one regime to another.

For example, over the last half-century national governments within Europe have altered their views of the desirability of participating in efforts to enhance Europe's financial integration. Those shifts reflect changes in the relative weights of the perceived benefits and perceived costs, both political and economic. France and Germany were committed to the project of a European monetary union (EMU) by the early 1990s. Earlier, in the era of Charles de Gaulle and Konrad Adenauer, the net benefits on both economic and political grounds seemed quite different. By 2000, Denmark's exchange regime closely shadowed the nascent EMU and kept the Danish kronor stable against the euro. Yet Denmark, a member of the European Union, was not willing to join the monetary union because of political doubts among a majority of its citizens. As of 2004, Sweden and the United Kingdom were still hesitating on both economic and political grounds. Norway, not a member of the European Union, was following a managed floating regime with no preannounced path for the exchange rate; as of 2004, Norway was not considering joining the EMU project. Hungary, however, appeared eager to join the EMU as well as the European Union. Poland, another nation joining the European Union in May 2004, probably perceived the pros and cons of EMU membership as more evenly balanced. The way different European nations perceive the benefits and costs of membership in EMU will change further as the twenty-first century progresses.

In some very long run, the world may well have a much smaller number of separate national currencies and separate exchange rates than exists now, in the early years of the twenty-first century. The idea of a few common currencies for large regions—conceivably, in the longest of long runs, even a single common currency for the entire world—might be seriously debated by policymakers as well as academics. But before a small number of currency unions could gradually become an actuality, a legion of difficult issues would have to be resolved.[58] Such an evolution would entail a wholesale revision of collective international governance for regions composed of many countries and, ultimately, for the world as a whole. It would mean

58. The long-run evolution of currency unions could occur in several ways. One process might involve individual smaller nations unilaterally choosing "dollarization" (or "euro-ization") of their currencies but without the large central nation whose currency is chosen perceiving itself as the center of gravity of a formal currency union (and hence without granting the smaller dollarizing countries a voice in its monetary policy and prudential oversight policies). A very different process, and one fraught with even more political difficulties, would entail groups of countries establishing a formal currency union in which by agreement all members of the union have a voice in common monetary and prudential oversight policies.

political integration at least as much as monetary, financial, and economic integration!

Over the short and medium runs, policymakers and analysts in nations not already in a currency union or contemplating a move to a currency union or currency board arrangements need to retain a supple mindset about exchange regimes. They should avoid decisions that make the exchange rate itself rigid; the exchange rate should be able to adjust as circumstances change. Nor should they yearn for some optimum regime to be preferred for all times and circumstances. And they should not allow themselves to be convinced that intermediate regimes will inevitably prove unsustainable.

Such cautious eclecticism has a downside. It presumes a modicum of competence and communication skills on the part of the nation's policymakers. That modicum cannot be taken for granted in every nation. If the discretionary aspects of regime choice are handled poorly, moreover, such mismanagement can contribute to rather than mitigate financial turbulence.

Whatever the exchange regime chosen, policymakers should avoid augmenting uncertainty by lack of clarity about what their exchange-rate policy actually is. The risks that an unclear exchange-rate policy will augment uncertainty are greater for intermediate regimes than for the polar extremes of a hard fix or a free float. Unskillful and unclear management of an intermediate regime, leading to volatile expectations that the regime may have to be altered, is probably the worst of all possible outcomes.

A hard-fix currency board and an unmanaged, pure-flex regime are simpler to describe than many intermediate regimes. And they probably are simpler for the public to understand. Because the public can verify that policy is what the monetary authorities say it is, simple regimes may be somewhat more credible than complex managed regimes. Simple regimes may therefore be less liable, other things being equal, to engender destabilizing expectations.[59]

If the management of a managed float or managed peg regime is entirely discretionary with little announced indication of how discretion will be exercised, market expectations will have an uncertain policy anchor. When that occurs, the potential problems of herding behavior, contagion, and multiple equilibria, which can afflict any exchange regime, have a higher probability of emerging. Policymakers adopting an intermediate exchange regime therefore should explain clearly why they believe the chosen regime

---

59. The "verifiability" of exchange regimes is discussed by Frankel, Schmukler, and Serven (2001).

is suited to their nation's current circumstances and what principles and guidelines will govern their management of it.[60]

Some amount of constructive ambiguity is inevitable about whether a change in a nation's exchange regime might occur sometime in the longer run. Policymakers cannot credibly assert that their current regime choice will always be the appropriate choice. But neither should they make statements implying that the regime choice is continually being actively reconsidered. Uncertainty about pressures on the nation's exchange rate and balance of payments is always present, regardless of the exchange regime. Uncertainty about whether the regime itself may soon be changed will add to those pressures; at worst, such uncertainty can feed unstable expectations about the future and trigger destabilizing asset shifts into or out of the nation's currency.

Unfortunately for living the easy life, a nation's choice of exchange regimes is invariably fraught with difficulties. Private sector expectations can be fragile and unstable. Self-fulfilling expectations have the potential to generate bad as well as good equilibria. Faulty government policies and incompetence in government are not as rare in this world as one could wish. If unsound policies are followed, adverse private sector expectations are sure to be generated. Government failure and the potential for market failure then interact.

Again, all exchange regimes suffer these difficulties to some degree. A poorly managed intermediate regime is vulnerable to speculative attack and herding behavior when adverse shocks occur; it is virtually certain to experience financial crisis if domestic macroeconomic policies are seriously erroneous. Even a well-managed intermediate regime can be buffeted by speculative attack in the face of adverse shocks; it too is likely to be undermined by crisis when domestic policies are erroneous. But the polar exchange regimes are not crisis proof. Both untrammeled flexibility and a hard-fix currency board can suffer from speculative attack following adverse shocks. Both will experience crisis if domestic policies get badly off track.

Complete freedom for cross-border financial transactions can certainly undermine any exchange regime that attempts to peg exchange rates if the nation pursues autonomous financial policies. But such freedom greatly complicates life for any other exchange regime—including the corner solution of untrammeled flexibility. For some nations, breakwaters inhibiting

---

60. Williamson (2000) criticizes variants of managed floating in which policymakers do not announce their objectives or their rules for the regime's management. He advocates formal intermediate regimes in which policymakers announce a reference exchange rate or a monitoring band.

cross-border capital flows may provide modest buffering, and their benefits may exceed costs. But if and when a case exists for maintaining breakwaters, typically it will not turn decisively on the nation's choice of exchange regime, whatever that choice may be.[61]

The general conclusion is that a nation's policymakers should avoid preoccupation with the choice of exchange regime and ensure that decisions about the exchange regime are made jointly with decisions about the rest of the government's macroeconomic and financial system policies. The manner and degree of exchange-rate variability are important. But they are not, in themselves, the policy issues of overriding importance. The highest priority should be placed on developing sound macroeconomic policies (budget policies and domestic monetary policy) and ensuring high financial standards and competent prudential oversight of the financial system. If the nation can get its macroeconomic and financial system policies right, any one of several alternative exchange regimes might be satisfactory.

The analysis now turns from the choices facing individual nations and returns to options for conducting supranational surveillance. Judgments about the appropriate degree of freedom for cross-border transactions critically influence options for the supranational surveillance of macroeconomic policies and exchange rates. The following discussion therefore focuses on international guidelines and monitoring of cross-border financial transactions.

Guidelines for Cross-Border Financial Transactions

Most economists and many policymakers have long presumed that border restrictions on trade in goods and services should be limited, if not eliminated altogether. The reasoning is familiar. If a nation's residents could not trade with foreigners, the pattern of national spending would have to match slavishly the goods produced at home. As long as relative prices differ at home and abroad, however, a nation's residents can unambiguously improve their consumption possibilities by exchanging goods with foreigners. Furthermore, such exchange gains can be augmented by production gains. Production gains result when the structure of production in a nation becomes specialized along the lines of *comparative advantage*. Resource and factor endowments are used more efficiently when production is specialized, permitting the nation to sell domestic production at

61. Financial breakwaters are described and discussed in *Prudential Oversight and Standards for the World Financial System*.

favorable relative prices abroad, which in turn raises national consumption possibilities still further.

Because of cross-border transactions, a nation's residents thus can enjoy higher standards of living—time paths for their consumption that are higher, better adapted to their particular preferences, and not rigidly tied to the peculiarities of their geographical circumstances—than would otherwise be possible. What is true for the individual nation is true for the world as a whole. Cross-border transactions among nations permit a more efficient allocation of world resources than would otherwise occur and thereby increase world consumption possibilities.

The potential gains from cross-border transactions can be very substantial. The gains may be proportionately larger for small nations and nations with relatively poor endowments of natural resources. The gains from some types of cross-border transactions are no doubt much more consequential than those from others. But there is a strong presumption that nations can, and in practice do, enjoy sizable benefits.

That is not to say that each resident in each nation invariably benefits. Practical observation and economic theory agree that particular individuals or particular factors of production can be harmed. For example, firms and workers producing goods and services that are displaced by increases in competitively priced imports can experience losses. Sectors of a nation's economy specializing in particular goods that are becoming obsolete because of technological innovation or changes in consumer preferences can suffer losses as resources are diverted from those sectors. Business and financial interests are the driving force behind cross-border transactions and are usually better placed politically to influence policies affecting such transactions. Individuals whose values or well-being are partly in conflict with business and financial interests may believe, sometimes justifiably, that their values or well-being are adversely affected, in relative if not absolute terms.

Nor can it be justifiably claimed that each nation, on balance, invariably benefits from all the cross-border transactions conducted by or with its residents. Because of externalities and market failures, not every move toward liberalized cross-border transactions is invariably beneficial. Nor does every imposition of new restrictions unambiguously reduce welfare. Interpersonal comparisons of well-being are problematic, and aggregative comparisons between nations even more so. Assertions about the welfare of entire nations or the world as a whole are therefore inescapably controversial.

These important caveats notwithstanding, scholars widely believe that the gains from cross-border transactions are substantial. There is virtually no scholarly support for the argument that a typical nation can improve its standard of living by a wholesale movement toward autarky.

Protectionist forces are politically powerful in most nations. In practice, virtually all nations restrain trade in goods and services in some ways. Nonetheless, a presumption for relatively free trade prevails. Restrictions on trade declined significantly in the second half of the twentieth century.

Traditional expositions of the gains from trade focus on transactions in goods and services. In theory, there exists a similarly strong presumption in favor of freedom for cross-border financial transactions. As with trade in goods, trade in financial services yields exchange gains and production gains. Changes in cross-border assets and liabilities, moreover, are a necessary counterpart of goods and services transactions. Benefits associated with cross-border financial transactions accrue to both the "importing" and the "exporting" nations.

Notwithstanding the arguments from theory, the presumption for unfettered cross-border flows of money and capital is more contentious and much less widespread than the presumption for free trade in goods. Therefore substantial controversy exists about the traffic regulations that should govern restrictions on capital account transactions. Similarly, little consensus exists about what general guidelines for cross-border capital flows should be used by international financial organizations in their surveillance of national policies.

It is a striking fact that opinions and policy stances about the benefits and costs of cross-border capital flows oscillated back and forth over the course of the twentieth century. The norms of the gold standard, accepted in the later decades of the nineteenth century and in the early 1900s, strongly favored liberalized capital movements. But World War I, the turbulent 1920s, and especially the worldwide Great Depression soured many observers on the supposed benefits of free capital movements (and even free trade). The most widely accepted economic analyses of the 1920s and 1930s identified "disequilibrating" capital flows as a prime cause of the unfavorable economic performance during those years. Virtually all nations emerged from World War II with extensive exchange and capital controls ("separation fences") at the border. The predominant postwar attitude was suspicion of capital flows and hence support for government policies to restrain them.[62]

The architects of postwar international monetary arrangements believed that freedom to engage in cross-border financial transactions would be

62. See, for example, the influential study by Nurkse and others (1944).

undesirable. They welcomed capital flows representing direct payments or receipts for current account transactions and those closely associated with direct investment. They gave some encouragement to long-term capital exports, especially direct investments, from nations with a strong external economic position. But they feared and recommended restraining other types of capital flows, particularly those motivated by short-run differentials in interest rates or the prospect of capital gains from changes in exchange rates. Writing in 1941, John Maynard Keynes insisted that "nothing is more certain than that the movement of capital funds must be regulated."[63] In a 1944 speech supporting the plans to create the IMF, Keynes argued:

> We intend to retain control of our domestic rate of interest, so that we can keep it as low as suits our own purposes, without interference from the ebb and flow of international capital movements or flights of hot money. . . . Not merely as a feature of the transition, but as a permanent arrangement, the plan accords to every member government the explicit right to control all capital movements. What used to be heresy is now endorsed as orthodox. . . . Our right to control the domestic capital market is secured on firmer foundations than ever before, and is formally accepted as a proper part of agreed international arrangements.[64]

Even the government of the United States, which had the fewest restrictions on capital movements at the border, shared the belief that many types of capital movements were disruptive and should be discouraged. The IMF Articles of Agreement embodied such attitudes and policies. Extensive separation fences for financial transactions—high breakwaters—were the accepted norm. It was presumed that financial instability was a *national* problem and could be quarantined within a nation's borders.[65]

63. Keynes (1980a, pp. 30–31).
64. Keynes (1980b, pp. 16–17).
65. The American experts were more guarded than Keynes and the British. They observed, "It would be incorrect to assume that most capital exports are prohibited under the Fund's provisions or that the policy of the Fund with respect to capital exports requires the maintenance of exchange controls or exchange restrictions in all or even the majority of cases. A careful examination of the Fund proposal will reveal that most capital exports can probably take place freely, and only in a minority of cases will exchange restrictions have to be imposed." Nevertheless, they too argued that "the flow of capital from one country to another seeking political and economic security, or speculative profit, is frequently undesirable. . . . It is not the purpose of the Fund to facilitate such capital movements." Horsefield and others (1969, vol. III, pp. 176, 178). For a fuller discussion of views in the 1940s, see Gold (1977, pp. 7–30).

As the second half of the twentieth century progressed, however, many governments started to lower the fences separating their financial systems. In 1958, following postwar reconstruction, many European nations restored convertibility for current account transactions. Those policy actions inevitably undermined the early postwar distinction between current account payments, which were welcome, and capital account transactions, which were not, and in turn loosened government restraints on capital flows generally. Some new capital controls were imposed in the 1960s, most notably in the United States. Germany imposed some new controls on capital inflows in the early 1970s. Viewed in retrospect, however, the predominant trend among the industrial nations was to reduce or eliminate such restrictions.[66]

The pendulum of opinion also gradually swung the other way. Prevailing sentiment drifted toward a less unfavorable view of cross-border capital movements. Increasing emphasis was placed on their possible benefits. In the first decade or two after the onset of floating among the major currencies in 1973, the potential risks of destabilizing capital flows seemed less worrisome. Many governments also came to doubt the administrative feasibility of controlling capital flows, whatever the potential benefits and costs.

By the 1990s, the salience of border breakwaters, especially in the industrial nations, was altogether different from what it had been at mid-century. Most policymakers in the United States and almost all private sector participants in U.S. financial markets argued strongly against all forms of breakwater. The U.S. government began to lean on other major nations, and even emerging market nations, to reduce their remaining controls on domestic as well as international financial transactions. Many nations were in any event doing so.[67]

Some industrial nations—for example, France, Italy, and especially Japan—were still less than ardent advocates of freedom for international capital movements. But those nations too experienced increasing difficulty in maintaining their separation fences. France and Italy ultimately aban-

66. The United States had eliminated all of its 1960s restrictions on capital outflows by 1974. Major oil-importing nations relaxed their controls on capital inflows after the first big oil price shock in 1973–74.

67. The United Kingdom eliminated its remaining exchange controls in 1979. In 1981 Germany removed restrictions on nonresidents' purchase of domestic bonds and money market instruments. By the mid-1980s the British and German governments had become advocates of unfettered capital flows. During 1984 the United States, the United Kingdom, Germany, and France abolished withholding taxes on interest income paid to nonresidents.

doned their restrictions in the 1990s. The case of Japan is especially interesting. Japan relaxed its border restrictions on capital movements at a pace that was markedly slower than the average for all industrial nations. Even in Japan, however, formal exchange controls ended in the early 1980s. By the mid- and late 1980s, the Japanese government had agreed, under pressure from the United States, to significant liberalizations of its other restrictions on capital flows. Further liberalizations occurred in the 1990s.

A majority of developing nations retained some form of breakwaters for cross-border financial transactions. Even some of them, however, had significantly eased earlier restrictions. Argentina, Chile, and Mexico, for example, experimented with relaxing or abandoning some restrictions in the 1970s and 1980s. In contrast, Brazil and Colombia kept their exchange and capital controls more or less intact through that period. By the 1990s, still more developing nations followed the trend toward relaxation. Many emerging market nations in the early and mid-1990s enthusiastically (albeit prematurely) embraced the idea that foreign financial funds should flow freely into and out of their financial reservoirs.

The apogee of the drift toward relaxation was reached in 1997 just as the Asian financial contagion was beginning. At the September 1997 annual meetings of the IMF and World Bank, the Interim Committee adopted a statement requesting the IMF Executive Board to complete work on a draft amendment to the IMF Articles of Agreement focusing on the orderly liberalization of capital movements. The draft would have made the liberalization of capital movements one of the purposes of the IMF and would have extended the IMF's jurisdiction by requiring member nations to assume "carefully defined and consistently applied obligations" with regard to capital account liberalization.

In the early years of the twenty-first century, the pendulum of opinion about cross-border restrictions on capital flows was once again reversing. The Asian financial crises in 1997–98 and the generalized financial crisis that followed the Russian devaluation and default in 1998 vividly reminded everyone that financial funds can rush for the exits in troubled times even more rapidly than they can pour in during good times. In policy and academic circles, and especially in emerging market and other developing nations, suspicion of unfettered capital flows was renewed and their benefits and costs were being reevaluated.

Such reevaluations were needed. From the perspective of the individual nation, prudent use of breakwater measures for cross-border financial transactions can be a sensible component of an overall national strategy.

Breakwaters may be especially helpful for nations whose financial systems are at early or middle stages of evolution relative to those of the largest industrial nations. An individual nation has no good reason to select the extreme option of the "Golden Straitjacket" as its policy toward economic and financial openness.

Just as with the choice of exchange regime, policymakers should be eclectic and pragmatic about their nation's financial integration with the rest of the world. Typically neither of the extremes, neither the Golden Straitjacket nor the "Great Wall," is appropriate. National policymakers should seek a compromise combination of the goals of financial autonomy, integration with the rest of the world, and exchange-rate stability that is most appropriate for the nation's circumstances. They should transparently articulate that strategy to their citizens and to foreigners. And they should be prepared to adjust the compromise combination to suit the nation's current and prospective needs if circumstances change greatly.[68]

Individual nations that choose to maintain financial breakwaters must do so judiciously. Going overboard with the Great Wall position will usually prove ineffective and deny important net benefits to the nation even if the barriers are effective. Yes, breakwaters tend to erode more rapidly than was once true, when communications and financial technology were more limited. Yes, financial institutions and markets often can innovate faster than the nation's government can increase its monitoring and administrative capacities to maintain the breakwaters. Yes, breakwaters that rely on discretionary administrative decisions rather than market-based measures create major opportunities for corruption. Nations whose financial systems are not already extensively connected to foreign institutions and markets have, other things being equal, somewhat greater potential for successfully maintaining breakwaters. Yet even this potential tends to erode as time passes and financial development proceeds.

Important though they are, the preceding qualifications do not nullify the main point. Some types of financial breakwaters are viable. Some provide modest friction and modest protection. One example is the imposition of reserve requirements on short-term liabilities of the domestic offices of financial institutions to foreign depositors and investors. Another is a cross-border capital withholding tax. Some prudential restraints that influence

68. The extreme options of the Great Wall (a high and impermeable separation fence for financial transactions) and the Golden Straitjacket (fully liberalized cross-border transactions) are discussed in *Turbulent Waters* (chapters 4 and 11) and in more detail in *Prudential Oversight and Standards for the World Financial System*. The term "Golden Straitjacket" originated with Thomas Friedman (1999).

cross-border financial transactions, though not breakwater measures per se, are sound regulations that deserve to be a permanent part of the structure of financial supervision and regulation. An important example is setting upper limits on the net open foreign exchange positions of financial institutions.[69]

International traffic regulations for cross-border financial transactions should respect the diversity of nations' circumstances and needs. Just as Article IV of the IMF Articles of Agreement gives an individual nation wide latitude to choose an exchange regime appropriate for its circumstances, the world community and the IMF should give a nation wide latitude to choose which breakwater measures, if any, it believes are suitable. National discretion and experimentation are desirable. Precise traffic regulations recommending extensive or complete liberalization of capital flows are not desirable and not politically feasible.

In effect, the world community should want traffic regulations and international guidelines for cross-border capital flows to be "soft law." Surveillance of capital flows would be similar in spirit to the IMF's existing soft guidelines for surveillance of exchange regimes. More specifically, the IMF might enunciate some general principles, similar to its 1977 exchange regime principles.

Rough principles to guide an individual nation's choice of financial breakwaters have been identified.[70] Refinements of those principles, adjusted to accommodate a world perspective, could constitute IMF guidelines about capital flows and capital account convertibility. The principles might state, for example, that a nation's government should give substantially higher priority to its overall financial standards and prudential oversight policies than to its breakwater measures per se; that breakwater measures should not be used as a substitute for sound national macroeconomic policies, for a well-chosen exchange regime, for maintenance of a strong international investment position, or for competent supervision and regulation of the financial system generally; that breakwaters should rely when possible on market forces rather than on direct administrative controls and should be designed as well as possible to limit opportunities for regulatory capture or corruption; that nations typically are better advised to design breakwaters to try to moderate unwanted capital inflows than to try to stem unwanted capital outflows; and that breakwater measures designed

---

69. The measures identified in this paragraph are discussed in *Prudential Oversight and Standards for the World Financial System*.

70. See again *Prudential Oversight and Standards for the World Financial System*.

to be transitional may prove more viable than measures intended to be permanent. These recommended IMF principles would explicitly acknowledge the diversity among nations and thus indicate that surveillance of an individual nation would focus on its particular circumstances and the specifics of its particular policies.

IMF surveillance of capital flows based on such guidelines would, it is true, be fuzzy. It could not be "firm surveillance" in the sense of establishing clear operational guidelines that would be uniformly applicable across all nations. But, just as with the other dimensions of supranational surveillance, soft rather than hard guidelines are the only feasible possibility for the short and medium runs.

It follows from the preceding discussion that a formal amendment of the IMF's Articles of Agreement to modernize its provisions for capital flows is unnecessary, at least for the shorter run. Such an amendment was under consideration in 1997, as noted above, but interest has now waned. The existing language in Article VI is out of date and in some ways unbalanced. But neither the IMF itself nor individual governments are seriously constrained by that language.[71] Obtaining international agreement even for soft guidelines of the sort just suggested will prove to be difficult. It would probably be impossible to secure agreement on a formal and precisely written revision of Article VI and the other articles concerned with cross-border capital flows.[72]

As the pendulum of opinion about cross-border restraints on capital flows again swung back toward the center in the last few years, the views of the governments of the largest nations moved toward the posture and general guidelines recommended here. The international organizations themselves, including the IMF, moderated their official positions to indicate greater sympathy toward a judicious use of breakwaters by emerging markets and developing nations.[73]

71. The current version of Article VI, section 1 of the IMF Articles of Agreement, forbids the IMF to make its lending resources available "to meet a large or sustained outflow of capital" and states that "the Fund may request a member to exercise controls" to prevent such use of IMF resources.

72. The main thrust of the draft amendment to the IMF Articles of Agreement considered in 1997 was to encourage eventual worldwide freedom for cross-border financial transactions. However, the draft amendment would also have provided for transitional arrangements analogous to those in the original Article XIV (chapter 7). Thus individual nations would have been able to maintain financial breakwaters during a (perhaps lengthy?) transition period even while the IMF would have been legally mandated to encourage general worldwide liberalization of such transactions. For a helpful collection of essays commenting on the pros and cons of the 1997 proposed amendment, see Fischer (1998).

73. For the now moderated position of the IMF, see Fischer (1998, 1999). The Financial Stability Forum's Working Group on Capital Flows (2000) included the following passage in the executive sum-

Use of Financial Sector Assessments in Broader Surveillance of a Nation's Economic Policies

The establishment of agreed minimums for financial standards and the prudential oversight of national financial systems is a critical component of a nascent utilities infrastructure for the world financial system. International standards require effective monitoring. External assessments are required to supplement self-assessments.[74]

Should self-assessment and external assessment of an individual nation's financial system be an integral part of the overall surveillance of the nation's economic policies? If so, which international financial organization should incorporate these assessments into the surveillance and how should it be carried out? For the shorter run, the main practical issue is whether the IMF should integrate the evolving international reports on the observance of standards and codes (ROSCs) and on financial sector assessment programs (FSAPs) into its annual Article IV consultations with individual member nations. An analogous question is how the ROSCs and FSAPs should be used by the World Bank (and even the regional development banks) in making decisions about lending to individual nations.

The international financial organizations and most national governments have recently adopted the position that the IMF should definitely be *using* (incorporating) the ROSCs and FSAPs as inputs in its overall surveillance of a nation. Similarly, the notion that the World Bank should be using the reports as an input into its lending decisions is uncontroversial.[75] The more difficult questions concern which organization or organizations should have primary responsibility for actually *conducting* the various assessments incorporated in ROSCs and FSAPs.

---

mary of its spring 2000 report: "In certain circumstances, such controls [on capital inflows] could be considered if they have a prudential element and, therefore, fit into a risk management framework. The costs and benefits of such controls should be assessed relative to the costs and benefits of alternative means of achieving the same objectives. If controls on inflows are to be implemented for prudential reasons, they are likely to work best when they are temporary and apply broadly, and when they are implemented in an environment of sound macroeconomic policies and a strong external position."

74. The points discussed in this section are covered in greater detail in *Prudential Oversight and Standards for the World Financial System*.

75. For example, in the September 2000 report of the IMF's managing director to the IMFC on progress in strengthening the architecture of the international financial system and reform of the IMF, it is stressed that "IMF surveillance needs to take into account the extent to which standards are observed as part of efforts to evaluate whether members' institutional structures and policy practices are consistent with economic and financial stability" (IMF, 2000e, paragraph 36).

The thorny issue here is how to allocate assessment and surveillance responsibilities across the numerous international financial organizations. Some analysts would prefer the IMF to be the dominant institution for surveillance of all standards, supervisory procedures, and economic policies of individual nations and the global system. They would even recommend that the IMF staff itself have primary responsibility for preparing and publishing comprehensive assessments. But others demur. Although they endorse the IMF's use of assessments prepared by other organizations as inputs into the general surveillance process, they do not want IMF staff to have exclusive or even primary responsibility for all dimensions of conducting financial system assessments.

The cooperation between the IMF and the World Bank through their joint Financial Sector Liaison Committee continues. Some progress seems to have been made in developing a "shared ownership" approach to the preparation of ROSCs whereby "different institutions take primary responsibility for undertaking assessments in different areas."[76] Nonetheless, some differences of view about appropriate responsibilities appear to exist among the institutions, especially between the IMF on one hand and the Bank for International Settlements, Basle Committee for Banking Supervision, International Organization of Securities Commissions, and International Association of Insurance Supervisors on the other. The evolutions of international assessment procedures and of IMF general surveillance seem likely to result in heightened tensions about the allocation of responsibilities among all the international financial institutions.

The use of assessments of financial standards and financial systems in surveillance is challenged by the trade-off between transparency and confidentiality discussed earlier in general terms. Both the IMF and the World Bank as monitoring institutions face that familiar dilemma. Ample disclosure of information about a nation's financial system and the market discipline that results are beneficial features of prudential oversight and supranational surveillance. The better the disclosure and transparency of a financial system, the lower the ultimate probability of severe financial turbulence. Yet it is difficult for the IMF and the World Bank to serve as a confidential policy adviser to a member nation while simultaneously publishing frank and critical judgments about the member's adherence to international standards and codes of good practice. Some governments may support the release of the ROSC and FASP for their nation despite critical

---

76. IMF (2000e, paragraph 37).

findings because they believe that release of the information will send a positive signal to world financial markets. But other governments may fear that the financial markets will punish their nation if their financial sector assessments are publicly released. The most appropriate trade-off varies from one nation to another, and it will vary over time as a nation's financial system evolves.

Explicit Coordination of National Macroeconomic Policies?

The feasible types of supranational surveillance discussed so far are relatively modest. Could the world economy and financial system benefit from explicit *coordination* of the macroeconomic policies of large nations? Coordination, especially if activist, is a much more ambitious form of intergovernmental cooperation.[77]

Examples of attempted coordination of macroeconomic policies are few and controversial. As intergovernmental cooperation evolves further, however, the governments of the largest nations may give more attention to the possibilities for explicit coordination. If so, supranational surveillance will then be increasingly called on to serve as a *coordination catalyst* as well as a monitor for traffic regulations and a systemic adjustment referee.

Coordination is not a synonym for altruism or benevolence. Coordination does not require national governments to have common or even compatible goals or demand that some governments sacrifice their goals to the goals of others. Nations' goals typically are not identical. The natural presumption is that each government gives primacy to the welfare of its own citizens. Coordination merely implies the self-interested mutual adjustment of national behavior. The potential for large gains from coordination may well be greatest when national goals are inconsistent and discord is high.

Coordination of macroeconomic stabilization policies should not be confused with "harmonization." The two are fundamentally different. One would not normally expect coordinated national monetary and fiscal policies to be harmonized. With coordination, for example, national governments do not necessarily adjust policies in the same direction, with every government contracting or every government expanding. If asymmetric disturbances hit their economies, sound policymaking and effective coordination typically require governments to do different things.

77. *Turbulent Waters* (chapter 7).

The size of potential gains from explicit coordination of macroeconomic policies is uncertain and, of course, context dependent. Some theoretical and empirical research suggests that often the potential gains may be modest. But the existing evidence is inconclusive because available estimates are sensitively dependent on the analytical models and ancillary assumptions used to study the issues. The presumption that coordination may yield potential gains is stronger for coordination among larger economies than among smaller economies. Sizable systemic externalities are more likely to result from, say, fiscal or monetary actions taken by the United States or Japan than from actions taken by Denmark or Portugal. Other things being equal, the nations whose economies are largest should worry most about the cross-border spillovers stemming from their economies and should be most alert to the potential gains from coordination.

Some analysts argue that the risks and costs of possible government failures resulting from ambitious efforts at coordination could outweigh any potential benefits. One line of argument, for example, asserts that efforts to coordinate policies may deflect the attention of national governments from higher-priority (domestic) policy choices or give governments incentives to delay policy actions they ought to be taking regardless of international considerations. Some even see international negotiations and bargaining as a smoke screen, enabling a government to blame foreign governments for its own failure to take responsible action. A second line of argument asserts that intergovernmental cooperation, especially activist coordination, can reduce rather than increase welfare if the interests of nations excluded from the coordination exercise are ignored.

Other analysts believe that the potential benefits deserve as much emphasis as the potential risks. Although the possibility that coordination could produce undesirable outcomes for excluded parties has to be taken seriously, the argument about deflected priorities is less convincing. Yes, governments can and do engage in short-sighted and obfuscating behavior. But the preferred remedy for the risk of deflected priorities is to straighten out the erring policymakers rather than forgo the benefits of coordination. The problem is analogous to a problem that a doctor may have when prescribing medication: there is a risk that some patient may swallow an entire bottle of aspirin, but that risk is not considered a valid reason to forgo prescribing aspirin completely. Proponents of international coordination do not regard it as a substitute for sound domestic policies. Rather, they ask whether efforts to coordinate policies among nations can facilitate the selection of domestic policies that are more sound than they otherwise would have been.

On balance, a presumptive bias toward attempting coordination is warranted in selected circumstances. If wisely conducted, such attempts by national governments can plausibly be expected—in many, though admittedly not all, circumstances—to advance the common interests of their citizens.

Belief in subsidiarity as a principle for collective governance supports a favorable bias toward coordination of national policies. Subsidiarity is the presumption that the decentralized allocation and exercise of political authority is to be preferred in the absence of compelling reasons for centralization.[78] The presumption for subsidiarity is a safeguard inhibiting national governments from trying to coordinate stabilization policies with excessive zeal. When governments respect subsidiarity as a guideline, actual coordination will be attempted only when strong evidence suggests that cross-border spillover externalities are causing major difficulties and that a feasible adjustment of national policies will improve the macroeconomic outlook. Analysts in the IMF and other international financial organizations who aspire to catalyze effective supranational surveillance should likewise be guided by the principle of subsidiarity.

Though the governments of major nations should be alert to possible opportunities for mutually beneficial coordination, the analytical uncertainty about macroeconomic interactions among their economies, stressed earlier, severely limits feasible opportunities. Successful explicit coordination of macroeconomic policies cannot occur to a greater extent in the future—and the IMF and other international financial organizations cannot serve more effectively as a catalyst for coordination—in the absence of enhanced analytical knowledge as a foundation for the process.[79]

Evolution of Macro-Surveillance for the World Economy

Despite present shortcomings in analytical knowledge and political will, there is merit in imagining a future when the analytical foundations for supranational surveillance and policy coordination will be much stronger.

78. *Turbulent Waters* (chapter 4).

79. All the observations in this section are discussed more extensively and carefully in Bryant (1995). That book reviews historical experience and the analytical literature about intergovernmental cooperation, with an emphasis on the more ambitious forms of cooperation that seek explicit coordination of national stabilization policies.

An evolutionary vision for enhanced macroeconomic surveillance foresees a slow but steady intensification of intergovernmental cooperation among major nations on their macroeconomic policies, exchange rates, and payments imbalances. Consultations about the current and prospective world economic outlook would be gradually augmented. The consultations would be backstopped by an international secretariat responsible for administrative and analytical support. As a result, governments would be helped much more than at present to identify potentially fruitful opportunities for activist coordination.[80]

Each participating government would submit periodic projections of a *baseline outlook* to the international secretariat. The frequency of the projection rounds and meetings associated with them could vary, but it might be two or three times a year. At a minimum, the G-7 governments and the G-7 central banks would be involved. The nature of the consultations and projections within each nation (involving the fiscal authority, the central bank, and other government agencies) would of course vary.[81]

The baseline outlook prepared by each government would assume no departures from its macroeconomic policies presently in force or, alternatively, could incorporate policy changes already decided on or very likely to be made. Each national projection would be derived with the aid of one or more analytical frameworks (models) that try to be internally consistent. Each government would be willing to—and would—exchange information about its models and projection methods. An individual government would concentrate most on projecting the key macroeconomic variables pertaining to its own economy. But each government would be free to submit projections for other economies if it chose to do so.

The international secretariat would provide its own baseline projection of the outlook for each major nation or region. The analytical support staff in the secretariat would make its own models and projection methods trans-

---

80. I omit here the obviously important question of whether the institutional venue for the secretariat would be the IMF, the BIS, the OECD, the G-7, still another consultative group, or some combination of these venues.

81. Delicate, controversial issues of central bank independence and the allocation of responsibilities for economic policy within governments have so far inhibited deeper involvement of central banks in G-7 consultations. But more extensive involvement by central banks would greatly improve the quality and relevance of the consultations. A key way to improve within-nation coordination is to strengthen the interactions between the fiscal authority and the central bank in preparing the baseline outlook. Possibly, although not preferably, a nation's fiscal authority and central bank could submit separately prepared versions of the baseline outlook.

parent to national governments. And it would function as a clearinghouse for the exchange of models and projections among governments.[82]

A wide range of quantity and price macroeconomic variables—for domestic real sectors, domestic financial sectors, balances of payments, and international markets—would be projected and reported in each baseline outlook. Some projections would be made for higher-frequency (monthly) data as well as for quarterly and annual data. Those preparing the projections would employ best-practice analytical techniques to render the projections for each frequency internally consistent. The actual instruments of each nation's monetary and fiscal policies and, of course, the ultimate target variables of national policies would feature most prominently. But key intermediate indicator variables also would be included. Treatment of exchange rates in the projections would be, no less so than now, a delicate matter. A politically safe approach would be to have all participants assume that real effective exchange rates (or, within arrangements such as the European monetary union, nominal exchange rates) would remain unchanged from the values prevailing in a period just prior to preparation of the projections. If mutual trust was high enough and confidentiality could be maintained during the process, it would be analytically preferable to project the paths of key exchange rates endogenously.

The international secretariat would play a key role in evaluating the different versions of the baseline outlook. For example, the secretariat would prepare a systematic comparison of the new baselines prepared for the current projections round, pointing out inconsistencies among the nations' and the secretariat's versions. The secretariat would also systematically compare the ex ante outlooks submitted in the preceding round with updated information about ex post actual outcomes. An integral task of the support staff associated with this process would be to identify analytical puzzles and gaps in knowledge that warrant further clarification and research.

Another vital component of this evolutionary process would be *what-if* simulations. Such simulations, judiciously chosen to shed light on issues of current relevance, would examine the consequences of changing this or that policy instrument. Similarly, simulations would be prepared to predict what would happen if one or another type of nonpolicy shock were to occur. Changes in macroeconomic variables resulting from these hypothetical policy and nonpolicy alterations would be measured and compared

82. The IMF's *World Economic Outlook* and the *OECD Economic Outlook* as published in the 1990s are prototypes for the baseline outlooks of the international secretariat. Similarly, the surveillance in G-7 consultations in the 1990s is a precursor of the intensified surveillance I envisage here.

with the baseline outlook. Such what-if scenarios would be prepared, at a minimum, by the international secretariat. Ideally, national governments also would prepare them, especially for changes in their own policy instruments but even for changes in other governments' policy instruments and for various nonpolicy shocks. Differences in models would of course lead to differences in the answers to the what-if questions. No attempt would be made to suppress differences attributable to model uncertainty. On the contrary, the range of differences would be the focus of attention in the consultations and would be important grist for the mill of the analytical support secretariat, suggesting problems with the differing models or properties needing clarification.

The baseline outlook projections, some of the most relevant what-if scenarios, and the evaluations prepared by the secretariat would be examined in periodic meetings of national policymakers and preparatory meetings of their deputies. The consultations would also involve frank exchanges of information about individual governments' goals. Efforts would be made to classify differences in the baseline projections and what-if scenarios according to whether they were due to differences in identification of initial conditions (current positions of the national economies), differences in national goals, differences in preferred analytical models, or differences in assumptions about expected future nonpolicy shocks.

The cooperative exercise envisaged here could sometimes give rise to activist coordination of policies. Examination of the what-if scenarios would in any event keep the participating governments alert to possibilities for mutually beneficial coordination at the same time that they focused on differences among models and the risks of making errors because of model uncertainty. If the process worked well, a creative tension would be maintained and participants would continually try to balance beneficial opportunities against the possibilities for counterproductive consequences. In effect, lookouts would be posted to watch for market failures and government failures alike.

A plausible by-product of this strengthened process for ongoing consultations would be some convergence in the analytical understandings brought by policymakers to the consultations. Preferred models for describing national economies and cross-border spillovers could become less diverse. One can even imagine that some convergence might eventually occur in the way government officials articulate national goals and identify common goals.

A rudimentary variant of the long-run vision sketched here could conceivably be tried in the medium run. In limited respects, it is even possible to interpret G-7 discussions in the 1990s as hesitantly groping in this direction. The most important element missing from actual experience has been the supporting role of a proactive international secretariat charged with catalyzing the process. Putting greater muscle into such a process will of course be contingent on continuing advances in the base of analytical knowledge underlying it.

If one peers through a very dark glass into the distant future, one can imagine intergovernmental economic cooperation and supranational surveillance on a greatly enhanced scale. The possible creation of federalist supranational institutions for the world, for example, could conceivably become a subject for serious debate. The explicit harmonization of some national economic policies might be politically feasible and hence would require evaluation of the associated costs and benefits. The political economy of the messy, intermediate world would be messier still, but international collective governance would have evolved much further. Speaking loosely, the center of gravity of many functions of collective governance might have drifted much further above the national level to the level of regions or the world as a whole.

More concretely, the number of separate national currencies still in existence might be much smaller. Coordination of national monetary policies might evolve into adoption of regional monetary policies or even a "world" monetary policy as national financial systems became very much more integrated than they are today. For many nations, to aspire to maintaining an independent national monetary policy and financial breakwaters at the nation's borders might seem an anachronism. How to manage exchange rates among the separate currencies still in existence would become an issue of first-order importance. Fascinating institutional possibilities would gain salience. People might ask, for example, whether the IMF (or an entirely new institution?) should evolve into a world central bank, and whether such a bank should be politically independent of other supranational federalist institutions and of national governments.

Fiscal policies in that far-distant time would be even more complex and multilayered. One would still observe national governments deciding upon and implementing national budgets. Even under such conditions, one would not speak of the explicit harmonization of national (and local) budgetary policies but rather of their coordination. Many layers of fiscal policies would still be subject to the presumption in favor of subsidiarity, accommodating diversity in preferences, and tying governance and the provision of public goods to different political jurisdictions in which differing preferences are manifested. But of course analysis and debate would also have to focus on the budgets of the regional and supranational institutions and their interdependence with lower-level fiscal policies and with regional or world monetary policies.

Even to allude to these imaginative hypotheses is to underscore the fact that they will arise only in the distant future. For the time being, it is sensible to focus aspirations for the coordination and supranational surveillance of macroeconomic policies on what might be accomplished during the next decade or two. Within that time frame, the key goals for major governments should be to perceive more clearly their collective interest in establishing adequate analytical support for international macroeconomic surveillance and to give supporting groups sufficient resources and authority to foster that collective interest.

Lending Intermediation among National Governments: General Considerations

In the sections that follow, the emphasis shifts from the function of supranational surveillance itself to the function of intergovernmental lending intermediation in support of surveillance. I first summarize some general analytical points about intergovernmental lending intermediation because those points are poorly understood and too seldom remembered in current discussions. Then I focus on intergovernmental lending through the IMF and the interrelationships between IMF lending and IMF surveillance of nations' economic policies.

The possibility that a national government experiencing financial crisis might borrow from other national governments is straightforward in concept. But national governments might also borrow from or lend to each other in times not troubled by financial crises. Furthermore, national governments might establish an international financial organization to act, in noncrisis as well as crisis circumstances, as a lending intermediary to facilitate the liability financing of payments deficits. National governments did of course establish just such an institution, the International Monetary Fund, in the middle of the twentieth century.

To fix ideas about this function for intergovernmental cooperation, recall first some general observations that apply to crisis and noncrisis circumstances alike. An individual nation faces difficult choices about how to cope with external payments imbalances. When imbalances are likely to persist, the nation's government will, later if not sooner, be forced to focus more on adjustment than on financing. Changes in the nation's exchange rate often may be part of a required adjustment. Over the shorter run, however, the government can try to cushion some types of shocks by using official financing as a supplement to adjustment. For temporary imbalances, official financing may even seem preferable to immediately adjusting policies since such adjustments might subsequently have to be reversed. Financing that takes the form of asset financing—drawdowns of the government's external assets—can be better controlled by the home government. But asset financing may not be possible in some circumstances. If financing is to be used, it may therefore have to be liability financing—increased borrowing from abroad by the home government.[83]

When a nation's overall deficit is liability financed, one or more nations that have an overall surplus necessarily acquire the counterpart loan claims. Such borrowing could be handled entirely through bilateral arrangements between lenders in particular surplus nations and the deficit nation's government. (The foreign lenders might be governments, or they might be private financial institutions extending credit on commercial or quasi-commercial terms.) Rather than relying on bilateral arrangements, however, the government in the deficit nation might find it advantageous to have some or all of the liability financing channeled through a multilateral international institution established to expedite such transactions.

If it is established, a multilateral lending intermediary does not alter the essential economic facts of liability financing: funds supplied by lenders resident in surplus nations will be loaned to the borrowing nation in deficit. And such lending, whether from private creditors or governments, will inevitably be accompanied by performance conditions and lending terms that constrain the freedom of maneuver of the debtor nation.

Yet a multilateral intermediary may permit more flexibility in the lending from surplus to deficit nations than would otherwise be possible. When the foreign lenders to a deficit nation are governments rather than private creditors, additional dimensions of intergovernmental cooperation come into play. As a formal matter, moreover, the deficit nation's government incurs liabilities to the international intermediary rather than direct liabilities to the creditor governments in surplus nations. Similarly, surplus nations' governments hold claims on the intermediary rather than direct claims on the borrowing nation's government.

---

83. *Turbulent Waters* (chapter 6) explains the trade-off between adjustment and financing of payments imbalances and the distinction between asset financing and liability financing.

Numerous variants of a multilateral intermediary can be imagined. Alternative criteria could be devised for determining which nations participate. The rights of participating nations to borrow when in deficit and their obligations to lend when in surplus could be specified in a variety of different ways. Numerous provisions could be agreed on to govern the particulars of lending operations—for example, the performance conditions to be satisfied by a deficit nation before it would be permitted to borrow.

Similarly, a multilateral intermediary could acquire the resources it lends in different ways. One possibility would be to have participating national governments irrevocably transfer certain amounts of standard reserve assets to the intermediary at the outset of its operations. A second possibility would be to have participating national governments commit themselves on a contingency basis to make certain amounts of standard reserve assets available to the intermediary as needed for its lending operations. A third possibility, economically very similar to the second, would be to have each participating nation transfer to the intermediary a certain amount of funds in its own currency with the understanding that the intermediary can lend the participant's currency to liability-financing deficit nations when the participant itself is in a strong balance-of-payments or a strong reserve position. Under any of the three preceding possibilities, the amounts of resources made available by individual participating nations might be made in accordance with "subscription quotas," the relative sizes of which could be proportional to the relative economic sizes of the participants (as measured by, for example, populations, gross national products, exports). Still a fourth possibility would be to authorize the intermediary to borrow funds selectively, when needed for its lending operations, from individual nations having strong balance-of-payments or reserve positions. The borrowed funds could supplement those obtained from subscription quotas or, in another variant, could constitute the sole source of funds. In practice, today the IMF obtains the bulk of its resources through the third of these four methods, with smaller amounts coming from borrowed funds.

Differences among the possible variants of a multilateral intermediary could significantly determine the amounts and timing of its lending. The details of the obligations of participating national governments to lend to the intermediary when in balance-of-payments surplus or in a strong reserve position would obviously determine whether the intermediary could be generous or alternatively would have to be cautious in extending credit to the national governments of deficit nations. An intermediary obtaining resources through quota subscriptions would have greater assurance about

its lending ability—and could take correspondingly bolder lending initia-
tives—than an intermediary that had to rely on intermittent selective
borrowings.

Intergovernmental lending intermediation facilitates the liability financing of payments deficits. Such liability financing might at first blush seem
to be conceptually separable from efforts to encourage adjustment of those
deficits. In practice, however, the financing of deficits through a multilateral intermediary cannot feasibly be divorced from encouraging policy
actions to promote adjustment.

As in all arms-length lending arrangements, a home government wishing to finance an overall deficit by borrowing will become involved in
consultations and then negotiations with prospective creditors. The subject
of possible performance conditions, in some form, will invariably arise in
those negotiations. In particular, any potential acquirer of the prospective
loan claims will express a judgment about the appropriateness of financing
the home nation's deficit. The prospective creditors also will seek assurances
that, following any required adjustment actions, the inappropriate portion
of the deficit will be eliminated (and, eventually, reversed). Prospective
adjustment and the capacity of the borrowing nation to repay are—
inescapably—preoccupations of the lenders in bilateral arrangements for
liability financing between a deficit nation and creditors in surplus nations.
Use of liability financing therefore necessarily subjects the borrowing
nation's government to conditionality (performance conditions) imposed by
foreign lenders. Even so, the ability to arrange liability financing may sometimes cause the borrowing government to accept, if not positively embrace,
the creditors' imposition of conditionality.

There is no reason to expect creditors' preoccupations with conditionality to be less salient—indeed, they may be more important—if liability
financing of a deficit is arranged through a multilateral lending intermediary. Nations in surplus or expecting to be in surplus will not support the
intermediary's operations—after all, the lending is conducted on their
behalf—unless they are assured that the loans are accompanied by appropriate performance conditions and satisfactory repayment provisions.
Invariably, therefore, a multilateral intermediary will be compelled to act as
an adjustment promoter, not merely as an originator and curator of loan
claims.

Because the interests of debtor and creditor nations diverge, differences
in judgments are virtually inevitable about the sustainability of individual
nations' balance-of-payments positions and the appropriateness or inap-

propriateness of particular values for exchange rates. Unavoidably, therefore, a multilateral lending intermediary will become enmeshed in reconciling the differences in normative judgments held by the national governments that are its lending and borrowing participants.

Why do governments of prospective surplus nations participate in multilateral organizations like the IMF rather than restrict liability financing of deficits to direct bilateral intergovernmental transactions? Indeed, why do governments themselves choose to act as lenders? Why not leave financing of payments deficits entirely to private capital flows?

The general answer to these questions is analogous to the answer to the question of why a government, in a purely domestic context within a nation, might establish a government lending intermediary. National governments may believe that market imperfections in the world financial system, such as information asymmetries influencing private lenders' willingness to lend to nations in overall deficit, could inhibit the smooth flow of financial funds between surplus and deficit nations. By establishing an intergovernmental mechanism for the liability financing of payments deficits, governments might hope to offset such market failures and thereby enhance the efficiency of the world financial system. This motive for government involvement in cross-border financial intermediation is of course controversial, just as is direct government lending intermediation within a nation.

A particular motive underlying the participation by governments of prospective surplus nations is the belief that negotiations with a borrowing government can be handled more efficiently if lending governments coordinate their judgments and decisions. For example, potential creditor governments may believe that they can more easily negotiate appropriate performance conditions and repayment terms if they work together through a single intermediary. Similarly, they may believe that deficit nations' compliance with performance conditions can be more effectively monitored through a multilateral organization. The government of a surplus nation concerned about criticism of its own imbalance and its own policies might also perceive political advantages to participating in a multilateral lending process.

What induces the governments of deficit nations to participate? A variety of motives may be relevant here, too. Deficit nations' governments may believe that their potential access to liability financing will be greater, more assured, or available on less costly terms than it would be if they rely on bilateral governmental arrangements or borrow from private foreign markets. They may hope that the involvement of surplus nations in a multilateral lending intermediary will expose those nations to pressures to adjust their surpluses. They may regard the activities of a multilateral lending intermediary as a means of partially mitigating the hegemony of a single large surplus nation or a dominant group of surplus nations.

If sufficiently farsighted, individual national governments may recognize that their nation may not be accurately characterized over a long period as primarily a surplus or primarily a deficit country. That perspective would be especially appropriate if payments imbalances in the world economy were on average adjusted reasonably promptly and smoothly. In such a world, deficits and surpluses would alternate or revolve over time. Neither deficits nor surpluses would be "permanent." Nor would exchange rates be persistently misaligned for long periods.[84]

Notice that the generalizations in the preceding paragraphs make no distinction between—in fact, they apply equally to—crisis and noncrisis conditions. Lending intermediation among governments, in particular the lending activities of an international financial organization acting as a multilateral intermediary, may be initiated during times of crisis. If so, the lending may be regarded as emergency financial assistance and analyzed as part of the function of crisis management. If the lending occurs under noncrisis conditions, its purpose may better be described as crisis prevention rather than crisis management.

Lending Intermediation and Surveillance by the IMF

Lending intermediation by the IMF, especially in noncrisis circumstances, has become controversial in recent years. A basic question lurks beneath the surface of the controversies: should the IMF be in the business of lending intermediation at all? Some market enthusiasts, greatly impressed by the functioning of financial markets and the growth of cross-border finance, have argued that virtually all lending in the world—including specifically any borrowing by government entities—should be conducted by and for the account of private sector economic units. These enthusiasts emphasize that the private sectors of national economies are the overwhelming source of savings in the world financial system. From that correct observation, they go on to conclude that the only appropriate role for governments is to provide an infrastructure within which strong and sustainable private sec-

---

84. The statements about deficits and surpluses in the text apply, of course, to overall payments imbalances. They do not apply to current account imbalances. See *Turbulent Waters* (chapter 6) for definitions and discussion.

tor lending can flourish. They therefore argue that governments themselves should not lend. Some with stiff convictions on this matter even conclude that intergovernmental lending routed through international financial organizations such as the IMF should be prohibited.

On one level, criticism of noncrisis lending intermediation by the IMF is readily understandable. Within a nation with a well-developed financial reservoir, one does not normally expect a government institution to act as a financial lender to private borrowers in noncrisis times. If such a government-run intermediary were to subsidize its domestic lending, for example, by charging below-market interest rates (even if the rate includes a market-related risk premium), its activities would be especially controversial. In an analogous way, noncrisis lending to a national government by the IMF can be criticized as "unfairly" competing with private lending. If the borrowing government has access on some kind of terms to private capital in foreign financial systems, the IMF lending can be criticized as "unwarrantedly cheap" financing to the nation at below-market cost.

But analysis must go beyond such observations. The untrammeled-markets position—that all lending to all borrowers in all circumstances should be conducted solely by private sector creditors—is badly misguided. At a minimum, proponents of that extreme view fail to acknowledge that emergency lending in financial crises, either within nations or to the governments of entire nations, cannot reasonably be left to financial markets and private financial institutions alone.

Rationales for intergovernmental lending intermediation in noncrisis periods are less straightforward. They are more controversial. But they certainly exist. One general argument for government involvement in lending activities is that in some circumstances borrowers may not have access to private credit and financial markets because of market imperfections and externalities. Government lending may then be able to induce matches among borrowers and lenders preferable to those that would otherwise prevail, offsetting the market failures and enhancing the efficiency of the financial system. Government lending may be able to achieve social goals by reallocating financial resources. Government lending may aim at inducing a redistribution of income and wealth.

One of the rationales for IMF lending intermediation is a special case of the market imperfections and externalities argument. Information asymmetries and political factors strongly influence private lenders' willingness to lend to nations in overall deficit. In some circumstances, the smooth flow of financial funds between surplus and deficit nations may be undermined even when the borrowing nation has a sound case for the liability financing of its deficit. In such circumstances IMF lending intermediation can contribute to the efficiency and stability of the world financial system.

A second rationale deserves equal emphasis: IMF lending intermediation can support and reinforce the IMF's surveillance of nations' policies, exchange rates, and payments imbalances. Creditor nations may be better able to negotiate repayment terms and appropriate performance conditions for lending to deficit nations if they work together through a lending intermediary such as the IMF. At the same time, the access of debtor nations to liability financing for their deficits may be greater, more assured, or less expensive if they borrow from the IMF. The powers for adjustment promotion that are associated with the conditionality of its lending therefore can facilitate the IMF's role as an adjustment referee for payments imbalances and exchange-rate misalignments.

Again, however, there is an inherent asymmetry in the powers for adjustment promotion that accompany IMF lending. Those powers are integrally derived from the IMF's imposition of conditionality. The IMF does not lend to the governments of surplus nations and therefore has no comparable way to exert pressure on them to adjust their surpluses. Hence the IMF's lending intermediation function is a single-edged, not a double-edged, sword in its support of the IMF's surveillance function. Conditionality can only constrain deficit nations.

Because of the asymmetry, lending intermediation cannot be regarded as a *necessary* accompaniment to the IMF's supranational surveillance. It certainly cannot be regarded as *sufficient*. Surveillance would be lopsided and thus ineffective if it were applicable solely to deficit nations and could be conducted only in association with IMF lending. The IMF's ability to impose conditionality in conjunction with its lending to deficit nations is therefore a desirable, but not essential, handmaiden to surveillance.

To drive home the point that supranational surveillance is needed and that ways must be found to make it effective in the absence of IMF lending intermediation, one need think for only a few seconds about the economic policies of the wealthy industrial nations. Conventional wisdom asserts that these nations will "never" again borrow from the IMF in their credit tranches, thus continuing their nonborrowing behavior that dates from the mid-1970s. I am more agnostic about that prediction than most. I can at least imagine occasions in the distant future when exchange-rate variability might be markedly less than it is today and when industrial nations might therefore again choose to borrow from the IMF for the liability financing of payments deficits. But the conventional wisdom is surely correct for the shorter run. The case for subjecting wealthy industrial nations to supranational surveillance is, as argued earlier, at least as strong as that for smaller and developing nations. Therefore the world community should nurture IMF procedures and mechanisms for surveillance that apply to all nations and that are *not* contingent on IMF lending intermediation.

The rationales for government-to-government lending through the IMF are sound in principle. IMF lending can, *when the particular circumstances are appropriate*, make a significant contribution to the efficiency and stability of the world financial system. Careful analysis is needed to assess different views about definitions of "appropriate."

Recent controversies about the IMF, if not concerned directly with IMF lending intermediation, stem from related disagreements about what the IMF's mission ought to be. More accurately, the debate is fueled by differences of view about the IMF's possible *missions*. The term *mandate* is convenient shorthand for the variety of missions that are now or potentially could be assigned to the IMF. Some participants in debates about the IMF would like to narrow its mandate and curtail its lending accordingly. Other participants, with heterogeneous motives, argue for broadening the IMF's mandate and therefore augmenting its lending powers.

Should the IMF's Mandate Be Narrowed to Crisis Vulnerability?

Consider first views that the IMF's mandate should be narrowed. The most influential voices suggesting this change recommend that the IMF concentrate on the prevention of crises and, should crises nonetheless occur, on their amelioration. The IMF, assert these voices, should focus narrowly on the external vulnerability of national economies and financial systems and the prevention of "modern capital account crises." The spotlight of IMF surveillance would shift to crisis vulnerability. IMF lending would be confined to crisis or precrisis situations.

Narrow the Focus of Surveillance?

To focus only on situations of actual or threatened crisis, the IMF would first have to be able reliably to distinguish crisis from noncrisis circumstances. Yet in practice that distinction is murky. The line between crisis and noncrisis situations should presumably be drawn so as to include on the crisis side of the line a "precrisis" period when a crisis is brewing but has not yet struck. The precrisis period is when timely IMF surveillance or lending might prevent the crisis, or at least reduce its adverse consequences through anticipatory crisis management. To recognize the need for including a precrisis period in the definition of crisis, however, is to reveal the severity of the identification problem. How long may a precrisis period last? What criteria can be used to differentiate precrisis circumstances that have a sizable probability of turning into an actual crisis from modestly problematic circumstances that probably will not develop into a crisis?[85]

The analytical difficulties are acute. But some techniques exist to help analyze the external vulnerability of a nation's economy and financial system. Indeed, efforts to monitor and assess aggregated risk and liquidity exposures are a crucial component of a prudent overall strategy for managing a nation's financial openness. The IMF itself has made progress in developing such techniques for its own surveillance of nations' economies. Progress also has been made in collecting and disseminating the data needed as a foundation for such analyses.

Because of the rapid expansion and increasing sophistication of cross-border finance, the need for improved analyses of nations' external vulnerability and of the causes of capital account crises has acquired greater importance. National governments themselves need to enhance their capacity to conduct such analyses. It would certainly be helpful for IMF staff to improve their ability to identify sources of external vulnerability at an early stage and to propose timely corrective measures in surveillance consultations. Such observations are not controversial; they even command consensus.[86]

What is controversial is whether the IMF should actually narrow the focus of its surveillance to the point that noncrisis aspects of a nation's situation and policies receive markedly less attention than in the past. Some influential advocates of an emphasis on crisis vulnerability do appear to go that far. For example, in 2000 the U.S. secretary of the treasury spoke of a "new paradigm for surveillance." He advocated "a new focus in the IMF's surveillance on vulnerabilities to modern capital account crises" and "more effective means of preventing crises, through stronger surveillance, more focused on preventing the policies that enabled a panic in financial markets." This new focus would include "a revolution in transparency that will make surprises less likely; development of international codes and standards . . . ; [and] more systematic incorporation of indicators of liquidity

---

85. Distinguishing emergency and preemergency circumstances from nonemergency situations is essentially the same problem described with different words.

86. For further discussion, see *Prudential Oversight and Standards for the World Financial System.*

and balance-sheet risks in IMF surveillance reports." Emerging market economies would be encouraged to pursue "safer policies," and the IMF would become "better-equipped for modern crisis response." The managing director of the IMF appointed in 2000, Horst Kohler, also spoke sympathetically of tilting IMF surveillance toward a greater focus on nations' vulnerability to crisis.[87]

Advocates of radically narrowing the IMF's mandate to focus on crisis vulnerability alone would actually reduce the surveillance attention paid to nations' policies during "normal" periods or in circumstances in which the threat of a capital account crisis seems small. One can imagine "new-paradigm" Article IV consultations with a member nation in which IMF staff develop and systematically use indicators of vulnerability to liquidity and balance-sheet risk but devote little attention to analysis of the ongoing soundness of fiscal and monetary policies. An alternative, less radical variant would entail an increase in the staff resources devoted to studying external vulnerability that would reduce the *relative* but not the *absolute* importance of the analysis of general macroeconomic policies.

The radical interpretation of a new paradigm for surveillance focused on crisis vulnerability would be an unwise evolution. Analytical techniques for appraising crisis vulnerability are far from foolproof. Even with further analytical progress, these techniques will remain highly uncertain. The operational murkiness of separating crisis and precrisis circumstances from noncrisis situations, not to mention the rapidity with which an economy can move from the noncrisis to the crisis side of the line, argues strongly against emphasizing vulnerability to crisis to the exclusion of other aspects of surveillance. An actual contraction in the scope of IMF surveillance might free up a modest amount of staff resources. But the contraction could seriously unbalance the IMF's overall appraisal of national economic and financial policies. The IMF should enhance its surveillance of vulnerability to capital account crises without weakening the other, noncrisis aspects of IMF surveillance that have been slowly developing stronger legs in recent years.

Lend Only When Crisis Threatens?

If one or more nations experience an actual financial crisis, especially if the crisis threatens contagion and systemic turbulence, there certainly may be a case for IMF involvement in crisis management and, as part of the

---

87. Lawrence Summers, speech of September 20, 2000; see also his speech to and post-meeting press conference at the April 16, 2000, meeting of the IMFC. Kohler's comments are in IMF (2000e).

collective management, for emergency IMF lending. That conclusion is not at question here. The question here is whether all other IMF lending should be aimed specifically at reducing crisis vulnerability.[88]

The difficulty of differentiating crisis and precrisis from noncrisis situations is, as just discussed, a serious obstacle to narrowing the focus of IMF surveillance to crisis vulnerability. It would be a still more formidable obstacle if the IMF were to try to restrict its lending intermediation solely to situations of actual or threatened crisis.

Language on this matter can be slippery. All IMF lending is in some sense concerned with fostering economic prosperity, therefore with preventing crises, and therefore with reducing vulnerability to crises. And in some loose sense, prosperity management of all sorts can help to reduce the probability of crisis and vulnerability to crisis. But to speak in that loose manner begs the operational question. To define crisis vulnerability and crisis prevention very broadly would make it impossible to rule out IMF lending of any type. The intent of those wishing to curtail IMF lending is to define circumstances in which the IMF would *not* lend because the circumstances do not conform to their narrower concept of crisis vulnerability.

The proponents of a narrower lending mandate also typically emphasize the principle, summarized above, that IMF lending should not substitute for private finance.[89] That principle, too, is relatively noncontroversial on a general level. The difficulty comes in giving the principle operational content. Developments in a nation's economy that are adverse but do not constitute a crisis can quickly turn into precrisis and then crisis circumstances if additional unexpected adverse shocks occur. The transformation from a noncrisis to a precrisis situation can occur especially promptly if the national government's policies change and the financial markets suddenly perceive those policies not as satisfactory but as irresponsible.

If the IMF were to refrain from lending to national governments except under conditions in which it could be unambiguously demonstrated that private finance would never be forthcoming, little or no IMF lending would

---

88. General issues about the IMF's appropriate behavior in times of financial crisis are analyzed in detail in *Crisis Management for the World Financial System*.

89. An influential statement of this principle occurs in a December 1999 speech of U.S. Treasury Secretary Lawrence Summers: "Official finance should be a backstop, not an alternative, to private sector finance." "The IMF should be in the front line of the international response to financial crises" but "should not be a source of low-cost financing for countries with ready access to private capital, or long-term welfare for countries that cannot break the habit of bad policies." "The IMF must be a last, not a first, resort—and its facilities and approaches should increasingly reflect that." Summers (1999d); see also (1999c). More assertive and less qualified expressions of this view include Calomiris (1998a, 1998b) and the International Financial Institution Advisory Commission (2000).

occur in noncrisis conditions. The IMF would not use its lending powers and the associated conditionality to prevent crises at early stages. But after tensions had built up and become widely recognizable, at which stage private investors often would already have started to flee for the exit together, the IMF would then be called on to make major emergency loans.

The difficulties should not be overstated. Analyses of a nation's external vulnerability can sometimes point the way to sharp, clear conclusions well before a financial crisis begins, which can then justify IMF decisions to lend that are narrowly and proximately focused on preventing a capital account crisis. Such cases, however, are likely to be infrequent. If the IMF were to restrict its lending merely to clear-cut cases of that sort while refusing to lend when diagnoses are murky and crisis prevention potential is less certain, the total amount of IMF lending would be significantly curtailed. That outcome, of course, is what some proponents of a narrow IMF mandate wish to achieve.

My view is that it is neither practical nor desirable to try to sharply separate crisis and precrisis lending from more general crisis prevention and nonemergency lending. IMF lending can sometimes be helpful to a nation and the world financial system even in circumstances when no crisis obviously threatens or when current crisis vulnerability is judged to be low. I therefore see little merit in trying to restrict the IMF's operational mandate to cover only crisis vulnerability, narrowly defined.

The overriding purpose of both IMF surveillance and IMF lending intermediation should be to foster prosperity management and crisis prevention, broadly conceived. Prosperity and stability in the world system require individual nations to pursue sound policies in good times and bad. Some national governments lag well behind others in adopting sound policies and in helping to integrate their nations as responsible units in the world economy and financial system. If a nation has a payments imbalance that appears to justify IMF lending, if it wants to borrow from the IMF even though it cannot say (and of course does not want to say) that a crisis is likely, and if the conditionality associated with IMF lending can raise the probability that the nation will pursue improved policies, it will usually be preferable for the IMF to lend sooner rather than wait until a crisis can be shown to be imminent.

IMF lending and the associated conditionality of course bring in their train some risks and dangers. The lending can be counterproductive. Individual member nations might try to make excessive or overly prolonged use of IMF financial resources. The IMF can make mistakes in judgment. But no convincing case has been made for a wholesale narrowing of the size or frequency of IMF lending.

IMF lending can occur through a variety of facilities. Differentiation of those facilities is desirable depending, among other things, on the speed of response required of the IMF. If an imminent or actual crisis requires emergency lending, the IMF and other parts of the official creditor community should be able to respond very rapidly. Such situations constitute the "full counterattack" or "risky counterattack" scenarios identified and discussed in the companion essay *Crisis Management for the World Financial System*. The IMF took steps in 1997–99 to create additional procedures and loan facilities—the Supplemental Reserve Facility (SRF) and Contingent Credit Lines (CCL)—that enable it to react rapidly in severe crisis circumstances. In contrast, if a nation's situation and its approach to the IMF for a lending package are not driven by actual or imminent crisis, the timetable for discussions with the nation can and should be more relaxed.

The development of the SRF represents a helpful strengthening of the IMF's lending capacities. Transparency of the IMF's operations is promoted by differentiating the crisis-oriented SRF facilities from the other types of IMF lending. Strong support for the SRF and its differentiation from other types of lending, however, in no way constitute an endorsement for narrowing the IMF's mandate to crisis vulnerability, nor for restricting IMF lending to narrowly defined crisis or precrisis circumstances.

Should the IMF's Mandate Be Broadened?

Countering the voices proposing a narrowing of the IMF's mandate, numerous diverse critics argue that the IMF's mandate is not broad enough. Such critics urge the adoption of one form or another of a still more ambitious, expanded agenda. The opponents of a broader mandate worry that "mission creep" already has undermined the IMF's capacities for surveillance and lending intermediation in its core areas of macroeconomics and cross-border finance.

The current debates about the IMF's purposes and objectives are taking place against a historical background of de facto broadening of the IMF's mandate after the mid-1970s. The original mandate emphasized the monitoring of cross-border traffic regulations for trade and capital flows, lending intermediation to facilitate the adjustment of payments imbalances, and a minor role for surveillance of macroeconomic policies and exchange rates. With the demise of the Bretton Woods exchange-rate arrangements and the onset of larger payments imbalances caused by higher oil prices, national governments pushed the IMF to pay more attention to the promotion of sustainable economic growth. Critics of the IMF in the 1970s and 1980s complained that IMF lending programs were short-sighted and excessively preoccupied with payments imbalances. Member governments—developing nations especially, but with the assent of the largest industrial nations—urged the IMF to take a longer-run view and to shape its programs to support structural reforms that would foster growth and development in poorer nations.

Numerous IMF programs and lending facilities were created with the intent of fostering growth and development. These included the Compensatory Financing Facility, the Buffer Stock Financing Facility, the Extended Fund Facility, the Supplementary Financing Facility, the Policy on Enlarged Access, and the Extended Structural Adjustment Facility. The interest rates and charges for borrowing under several of these facilities tended to be "concessional"—substantially less than those for other IMF lending. The Poverty Reduction and Growth Facility (PRGF) was established in 1999 to replace the Extended Structural Adjustment Facility, again with concessional interest rates. Together the IMF and the World Bank launched in 1996, and modified significantly in 1999, a Debt Initiative for Heavily Indebted Poor Countries (HIPCs), which provides grants to qualifying members to help reduce external debt burdens.

The IMF is thus now deeply involved in promoting growth, supporting structural adjustment, and reducing poverty in developing nations. In many of its lending activities, the IMF has become an intermediary extending longer-term loans to a subset of the world's nations that tend to have a persistent demand for development finance, not merely a temporary need for the liability financing of an overall payments deficit. This emphasis on lending to developing nations is a substantial departure from the original vision for the IMF framed at the middle of the twentieth century.[90]

Expansion by the IMF into the areas of growth promotion, structural adjustment, and poverty reduction greatly blurred earlier notions of how responsibilities would be allocated between the IMF and the World Bank. The World Bank originally was charged with addressing longer-term and structural aspects of promoting economic growth and development. To the extent that either institution had an explicit mandate to focus on

90. The appendix to *Turbulent* Waters summarizes recent IMF history and describes the variety of lending facilities. De Vries (1985, 1987) and Boughton (2001) document the broadening of the IMF's mandate into the areas of development promotion and poverty reduction.

income distribution issues and promote poverty reduction, it was the World Bank, not the IMF.

In a quite different expansion of its mandate, at the end of the 1990s the IMF became increasingly involved in the surveillance of financial standards and prudential oversight of financial systems.

Some enthusiasts for international governance would go still further in expanding the IMF's mission. They recommend that the IMF use international environmental standards as a component of its surveillance of national policies. Others, especially concerned with labor markets and working conditions for the world's poor, recommend that the IMF help to monitor and even enforce international labor standards.

Individuals and groups often push the IMF to become engaged in a wider range of issues for political reasons. The conditionality that accompanies IMF lending to a nation's government gives the IMF some leverage over national policies. Other international organizations—for example, the World Health Organization, the International Labor Organization, and the World Trade Organization—provide little or no direct financial assistance to national governments and therefore do not have comparable leverage. Legislators and interest groups, especially those based in creditor nations, therefore may think that they can better achieve their own objectives if they can succeed in lobbying the IMF to incorporate performance conditions related to those objectives into IMF programs. Political pressures on the IMF to engage in other issue areas also can originate within the borrowing nations themselves. Domestic residents with reform agendas, for example, may regard the negotiations between the government and the IMF as an opportunity to get their particular reforms adopted, even if their reform measures, however desirable for the longer-run benefit of the nation, are not especially pertinent to the problems giving rise to lending negotiations with the IMF.

How should politically sensitive issues about the IMF's mandate be resolved? Will the world community benefit, especially developing nations and the world's poor, if the IMF is deeply engaged in trying to address development and poverty problems? Should the IMF become directly involved in the surveillance of labor standards or environmental standards? Alternatively, would the IMF better serve world welfare if it resisted pressures to incorporate more and more performance conditions in its lending programs when such conditions are not directly related to the financial and macroeconomic purposes that are the primary rationale for IMF lending?

A wise evolution of international collective governance requires specialization of function among international organizations and consultative groups. If the mandates of institutions are unclear or overlapping and if mission creep occurs over time at some or all of the institutions, the result can be a confusing duplication of responsibilities, unclear lines of accountability, and diminished effectiveness.

Within nations, specialization of function is a hallmark of government. Municipal fire departments are charged with fighting fires and overseeing measures to prevent fires, but not with ensuring the safety of the local water supply or collecting tax revenue. If the police were asked to directly monitor and enforce every type of regulation in a society, they would have an impossible job. Even if they could carry out such extensive responsibilities, the police force might become too large and powerful. A nation's central bank sets general monetary policies and usually participates in the maintenance of the utilities infrastructure for the financial system. But the central bank is not asked to oversee public health policies, the distribution of welfare payments, or the operation of bankruptcy courts. Specialized inspectorates with detailed technical knowledge are assigned responsibilities for ensuring safe working conditions, vetting new drugs, monitoring air pollution, and so on.

Specialization of function in principle should be no less applicable to international levels of collective governance than to the various levels within nations. If anything, the arguments supporting specialization are stronger at levels of governance above the nation state. Ideally, each individual international institution should focus on only a few responsibilities. Asking any one institution to perform too wide a range of activities could thwart its effectiveness in meeting its primary goals. Mission creep, particularly if it occurs at many institutions, is likely to lead to confusion and costly duplication of effort.

When guidelines about specialization in governance are applied to the IMF, the presumption is that the IMF should concentrate on a core set of responsibilities assigned to it alone. Other international institutions should defer to the IMF in its areas of core competence. Correspondingly, the IMF should be discouraged from straying significantly outside its core areas into issues that are the primary responsibility of other institutions.

The logical core areas for the IMF's mandate, still today as half a century ago, are cross-border finance and macroeconomics. A fuller description would include payments imbalances, exchange rates, cross-border barriers, macroeconomic policies, and financial sector policies (financial standards and prudential oversight of financial systems). Financial sector policies were not a prominent component of the original Bretton Woods vision but, as discussed, a case can be made for including them today.

If the IMF becomes deeply engaged in areas outside its area of core competence, it risks spreading its staff resources too thinly and undermining its leverage for conducting systemic macroeconomic surveillance. Looking back over the last several decades, one can empathize with the pressures on the IMF to become more involved in fostering economic growth, structural adjustment, and poverty reduction in developing nations. Yet that de facto expansion of the IMF's mandate may not have been in the best long-run interests of developing nations, creditor nations, or the IMF itself.

Promoting growth and structural adjustment and facilitating reduction in poverty should be the primary responsibility of the World Bank and the regional development banks. (A nation's government itself has the ultimate responsibility within a nation.) Those objectives should be not a primary responsibility of the IMF but regarded as outside its area of core competence.

It is a corollary of this perspective that the division of labor between the IMF and the World Bank should be clarified. The two organizations should, of course, cooperate closely. Both have responsibilities for surveillance of policies within individual nations. The World Bank as well as the IMF must pay attention to the effects of World Bank lending on a nation's macroeconomic and exchange-rate and balance-of-payments outcomes. The IMF as well as the World Bank must assess the effects of IMF surveillance and IMF lending on a nation's growth and on its longer-term structural and social policies. To insist that the two organizations cooperate closely, however, is not to argue that the two share identical mandates. The comparative advantage of the IMF is in cross-border finance and macroeconomics. The activities of the IMF should be shaped by its competence in those core areas. The comparative advantage of the World Bank is in growth promotion, poverty reduction, and structural economic reform.

Though the preceding observations identify the right principles for determining the two institutions' respective mandates, pragmatism requires one to recognize that a clear-cut specialization of functions for the IMF and the World Bank is not now possible. Consider just the single controversial issue of the IMF's Poverty Reduction and Growth Facility. In principle, there is no compelling case why a concessional financing facility with this purpose should reside in the IMF given that the World Bank makes similar loans and that the World Bank should have primary responsibility for shaping programs with these purposes. Other things being equal, it would be preferable for a single PRGF-like facility to be lodged in the World Bank, with the World Bank's decisions supported by the IMF's macroeconomic and financial expertise. Yet it would be complicated to transfer the PRGF to the World Bank: the IMF would lose immediate control of the resources, there might be difficult implications for the IMF's grant funds supporting the HIPC debt initiative, and so on. Regardless of the merits of functional specialization, the IMF's Poverty Reduction and Growth Facility is likely to continue to reside in the IMF.[91]

Pragmatism also counsels against challenging political symbols unnecessarily. On behalf of all its member nations, the IMF should believe, and should state publicly, that economic growth and poverty reduction are vitally important goals of the world community. The IMF must be careful not to send inadvertent signals that can be misinterpreted as implying that it is disinterested in the effects of its policies and actions on long-run growth, structural reform, and social justice. It would be unwise for the IMF to be perceived as "withdrawing" from the task of poverty reduction.

One can and should believe that the goals of reducing inequity and poverty in the United States are vital for the health of the nation without also concluding that the Federal Reserve System must be charged with those goals. Analogously, it would augur better for an efficient evolution of international collective governance if over time the World Bank could be more clearly and unambiguously assigned the leading role in promoting growth, structural reform, and poverty reduction. The IMF does not have to be charged with leadership in those areas just because men and women of good conscience agree that those goals are important.

The case for extending the IMF's mandate into areas such as the surveillance of international labor and environmental standards is even weaker. Here again, the issue is not the inherent worthiness of international labor and environmental standards as goals of national public policy or goals for the world community. Not at all.

Some proposed international labor standards are reasonable, others not. Unfortunately, some proponents of international labor standards suggest that real wages should promptly be equalized across national borders. Some union activists in the United States, for example, argue that real wages in developing nations ought to be brought up to the level of real wages in the United States. Failing such equalization, they argue, imports from low-

91. The IMF's managing director and deputy managing director, as well as the U.S. Treasury Department, all went on record in the summer of 2000 in defense of retaining the PRGF in the IMF. See IMF (2000e), Fischer (2000), and U.S. Department of the Treasury (2000).

wage countries should be restricted. Many proposals for the speedy equalization of real wages across borders turn out in practice to foster blatant protectionism that would harm labor in developing countries and would be detrimental to mutually advantageous cross-border trade. But international labor standards need not be framed so as to have predominantly protectionist effects. Labor standards in many developing countries are weak and should be strengthened. It is certainly a worthy goal to design nonprotectionist international labor standards and to encourage surveillance of them by some international organization.

Soundly designed international standards to protect the environment are likewise a worthy aspiration. Lax standards regarding the use of natural resources and air and water pollution have created serious problems for individual nations and the world as a whole. Differences in environmental standards across nations can influence trade flows. Differences across nations often require international discussion and intergovernmental cooperation to foster needed adjustments. To be sure, it is problematic to insist that environmental standards be harmonized across nations at the highest levels prevailing in the wealthiest industrial nations. Such insistence frequently masks protectionist motives. But world *minimum* standards often are desirable and may well be negotiable. Surveillance of environmental standards by one or more international organizations will surely be a growing feature of international governance later in the twenty-first century.

Again, however, the relevant issue about labor and environmental standards for the IMF is whether such responsibilities should be included in its mandate. The principle of functional specialization argues against inclusion. The contention that the world community should encourage surveillance of well-designed international labor and environmental standards, valid in itself, does not constitute a persuasive argument that the IMF should be charged with that task. It makes more sense to allocate those surveillance functions to international organizations or other forums with specialized competence in labor market or environmental issues. The IMF should not be assigned an agenda bloated with every important world economic problem. The IMF can be more effective and the world better served if the IMF focuses on its core competence in cross-border finance and macroeconomics.[92]

92. The position I summarize in the text has gained increasing support in recent years. For example, the problem of IMF mission creep and recommendations to avoid a further broadening of the IMF's mandate are discussed by, among others, a group of outside experts in a report, *External Evaluation of IMF Surveillance* (IMF, 1999a), and the Council on Foreign Relations Independent Task Force (1999). Williamson (2000) reviews a number of contributions to the debate on reform of the international financial architecture and discerns a consensus that mission creep is a concern. Goldstein

IMF Lending Facilities

The IMF implements its lending in a variety of ways. Details of the lending operations raise technical and specialized issues, most of which can be suppressed for the purposes of this essay. The discussion that follows concentrates on issues of general importance.

What Range and Variety of Lending Facilities?

The types of lending facilities—their variety, and their different characteristics—depend, of course, on the scope of the IMF's mandate. Because its mandate expanded over time, the IMF drifted into creating several new lending mechanisms to supplement its more traditional facilities.

Regular facilities for IMF lending differ significantly from *concessional facilities*. Interest rates, fees, and other terms associated with the concessional facilities are significantly lower or easier to meet than the terms of regular facilities. Within the regular lending facilities, the mechanisms for *fast-turnaround emergency lending* differ in important ways from those for *longer-fuse lending arrangements*, in which the periods for negotiation and disbursement are more protracted.

As of 2004 the concessional facilities included the Poverty Reduction and Growth Facility and the grants made under the Debt Initiative for Heavily Indebted Poor Countries. The fast-turnaround facilities for emergency lending were the Supplemental Reserve Facility and the Contingent Credit Lines. Regular lending arrangements with a longer fuse typically took the form of Stand-By Arrangements (SBAs) in the credit tranches of quotas or borrowings under the Extended Fund Facility (EFF). Less important lending facilities included a Compensatory Financing Facility and arrangements for providing emergency assistance for natural disasters and post-conflict situations.[93]

Longer-fuse borrowing under an SBA or the EFF differs from emergency borrowing primarily in the length of time required for negotiation

---

(2000a) likewise urges the IMF to keep to its core competence and "do less so that it can do it better." The International Financial Institution Advisory Commission (2000) expresses strong views about the IMF's mandate; for discussion of that report, see Williamson (2000) and U.S. Treasury Department (2000).

93. Following the changes made in regular IMF lending facilities during the year 2000, another distinction is sometimes made between "core" facilities (SBAs, the EFF, the SRF, and the CCL) and "non-core" facilities (the first credit tranche, the Compensatory Financing Facility, and emergency assistance for natural disasters and post-conflict situations). For a more detailed overview of IMF lending facilities and policies, see the IMF annual reports—for example, IMF (2000f, chapter 6; 2003d, chapter 4).

and preparation. For example, if a national economy runs a payments deficit that develops gradually and does not appear likely to trigger a capital account crisis and contagion effects, approaching the IMF for a lending package might result in four to six months of discussions. If the problem is complex and recommended policy adjustments prove controversial, the length of time between an initial request and final approval might extend even to twelve months or more. In contrast, if a quick-spreading financial crisis threatens, the IMF and the official creditor community may be called on to react within a few weeks, perhaps even just a few days. The amount of emergency lending required also is likely to be much larger than for nonthreatening payments imbalances. In a typical noncrisis standby arrangement, some 50 to 100 percent of the IMF quota for a borrowing nation might be disbursed each year. Emergency lending packages triggered by financial crises, such as those to Mexico in 1995 and to Thailand and Korea in 1997, were much larger relative to quota and were approved in just a few weeks after the initial request. A very large loan, the largest in the IMF's history, was made to Brazil in 2002.[94]

Standby arrangements are the central facility for IMF lending; most of the IMF's financial assistance in its first five decades was provided through this mechanism. SBAs are designed to deal with balance-of-payments problems of a relatively temporary or cyclical nature. Prior to September 2000, SBAs were to be repaid within three and a quarter to five years. The EFF, first introduced in 1974, is intended for member nations with medium- or longer-term balance-of-payments difficulties resulting primarily from structural problems. The EFF provides for longer repayment periods—prior to September 2000, the period was four and a half to ten years—thereby taking into account the need to implement structural reforms, which can take longer to implement and take full effect.[95]

The amount of funds available to a member nation under an SBA, together with borrowings (if any) under an EFF arrangement, is normally limited to 100 percent of its quota annually, with a cumulative limit of 300 percent of quota. The IMF can extend these limits in exceptional circumstances, most notably if some of the borrowings occur under the SRF.

---

94. Boughton (2000, pp. 275–76; 2001).

95. The length of an SBA is typically twelve to eighteen months, although there is no required minimum and the period can be extended to a maximum of three years. The length of an EFF loan typically is three years, with the possibility of extension to a fourth year.

Members borrowing through an SBA or an EFF pay an interest rate proportional to and slightly above the market-related special drawing right (SDR) interest rate.[96] Disbursements of funds under both an SBA and an EFF are phased in over time subject to conditionality (performance clauses) regarding the nation's policies; the policy conditions necessary for IMF support through the EFF include implementation of structural reforms.

The IMF's capacity to conduct fast-turnaround emergency lending is relatively recent. The SRF, established in 1997 and streamlined in 2000, permits rapid disbursement of funds, possibly for much larger amounts than those available under an SBA or the EFF. Disbursements of SRF loans are expected to be made within a period of one to one and a half years, with the possibility of extension for up to one more year. SRF loans are initially subject to the same market-related interest rate charged for SBAs and the EFF, plus an additional surcharge; if the loan remains outstanding for more than one year, the surcharge is increased further in six-month steps.

The Contingent Credit Lines facility, created in April 1999, was envisaged as a precautionary line of defense against crises. Usable only if demanding eligibility and prequalification criteria could be met, the CCL was contentious from the outset. As with the SRF, access to the CCL was to be determined separately from access to regular SBAs or to the EFF. Commitments under the CCL could be in the range of 300 to 500 percent of a member's quota. If borrowing actually took place after a CCL commitment was in place, the repayment obligations and the charges were to be the same as those under the SRF. The CCL was discontinued in 2003 (see below).

Concessional lending through the PRGF, as already discussed, is the post-1998 successor to various earlier types of lending to developing nations motivated primarily by IMF involvement in growth promotion, poverty reduction, and structural reform. Borrowing arrangements under the PRGF require the member nation to design a poverty reduction strategy, "formulated in a participatory manner involving civil society and developmental partners." The strategy must be spelled out in a poverty reduction strategy paper, produced by the borrowing member "in cooperation with the World

---

96. For 1999–2000, the IMF standard rate of charge was 113.7 percent of the SDR interest rate. IMF lending also bears a relatively small service charge (0.5 percent) and a small commitment fee (0.25 percent). The income earned by the IMF from the small premium of the IMF rate of charge for lending over the SDR interest rate is used by the IMF to cover operational and administrative expenses and to achieve a target amount of net income to add to its reserves.

Bank and the IMF"; that paper describes the government's goals and macro-economic and structural policies for the three-year program to be supported by PRGF resources and associated external financing. PRGF loans carry the very low interest rate of 0.5 percent per year and are repayable over ten years with a five-and-a-half-year grace period on principal repayments.

This brief overview is sufficient to indicate the considerable complexity of the various IMF lending facilities. One might well ask whether this complexity is justified. Would it be possible to simplify by combining all the nonconcessional lending into a single facility?

Nations are heterogeneous in many ways, including the types of balance-of-payments difficulties they may experience. Given the heterogeneous nature of balance-of-payments adjustment problems, different forms of conditionality, different lengths of repayment periods, and perhaps even different interest charges will sometimes be appropriate. For example, the issues arising in crisis or precrisis circumstances need to be handled with different procedures, and greater speed, than when a financial crisis does not appear to threaten. Because the duration of one member's balance-of-payments needs differs from another's, imposing a single maturity for all lending could force some borrowing members into an undesirable Procrustean bed. If the IMF could not reasonably differentiate the different circumstances of borrowing members ex ante (prior to its decisions on lending), the case for multiple facilities would be weak. But in many instances such ex ante differentiation, though difficult, has been possible.[97] Despite the appeal of simplification, therefore, the idea of forcing all IMF lending into a single facility with uniform terms does not on balance seem wise.

Some thoughtful observers of the IMF have argued for simplifying the regular lending into just two facilities, one for crisis and precrisis circumstances and the other for noncrisis needs. Other observers defend the existing variety of facilities. As a form of noncrisis lending, the EFF has defenders and critics, inside as well as outside the IMF. The CCL facility for emergency lending was especially controversial. Critics wanted it not to be used, hoped it would atrophy, and recommended that all crisis-related lending be folded into a revamped SRF. Those who had favored its creation regarded the conceptual distinction between the SRF and the CCL as important and wanted to keep the CCL alive. The most debated issue

97. This issue of ex ante differentiation, and some evidence, are discussed in IMF (2000b, 2000c).

about the CCL was whether prequalification is workable in practice and whether its advantages outweigh its disadvantages.[98]

The most important longer-run question about the range of IMF lending facilities concerns the concessional PRGF and the grants to HIPCs. As argued already, it would be preferable for the IMF to concentrate on its core competence in macroeconomics and finance. If over time the World Bank is gradually to assume a still more dominant leadership role on issues of growth promotion, poverty reduction, and structural reform in developing nations, the PRGF in the IMF should progressively assume a less important role. Eventually, the PRGF might disappear altogether.

Issues about Interest Charges, Repayment Terms, and Conditions of Access

No matter what the type of facility, IMF lending is intended to be temporary. Article I of the IMF Articles of Agreement lists as one of the IMF's basic purposes "To give confidence to members by making the general resources of the Fund *temporarily available* to them under adequate safeguards" [emphasis added]. Even for the concessional facilities and the regular lending arrangements designed for longer-term structural problems, therefore, the IMF specifies guidelines for repayment periods and seeks to ensure that those guidelines are met.

Earlier in the IMF's history, executive directors debated at length whether interest charges for IMF lending should be related to market interest rates. From the IMF's inception through 1974 and even from 1974 to 1981, schedules of fixed charges prevailed. As new lending facilities were created, the number of schedules proliferated and the system of charges became unwieldy and nontransparent. Although the schedules were occasionally changed, the charges did not vary with market interest rates and tended to be substantially below even short-term market interest rates in the largest IMF creditor nations.

By the end of the 1980s, the debate had been won by those who believed that the IMF's charges should vary in proportion to market interest rates. A simplified system of IMF charges, with a single interest rate for regular (nonconcessional) lending, was introduced in 1981. And in 1989 that single rate was linked directly to the variable interest rate on the SDR. (The SDR interest rate is a weighted average of short-term interest rates prevail-

---

98. For the range of views on the CCL, see, for example, Goldstein (2000a), Williamson (2000), Council on Foreign Relations Independent Task Force (1999), International Financial Institution Advisory Commission (2000), and U.S. Department of the Treasury (2000).

ing in the United States, United Kingdom, France, Germany, and Japan.) The post-1989 rate for nonconcessional lending is still subsidized relative to the terms that member governments could obtain by borrowing on their own directly from private financial institutions or in private world capital markets. But the IMF rate of charge now at least fluctuates in proportion to market interest rates so that the size of the subsidy component varies little over time. (The market-related borrowing terms of the IMF's regular facilities, of course, depart very much less than those of the concessional facilities from the terms available in private financial markets.)

Notwithstanding the changes in IMF lending made in the 1980s, a general issue about interest charges and repayment terms continues to be contentious. Do borrowing member governments make "excessive" use of IMF financial resources because the interest charges are too far below market interest rates, because there is excessive leniency in enforcing the obligation to repay loans, or perhaps for both reasons? Some critics of the IMF answer yes.[99] The question itself acquired heightened saliency as world capital markets and multinational financial institutions developed further and as emerging market and other developing nations experienced increased access to those institutions and markets.

Analysts cannot easily make a sensible comparison between IMF interest charges and the market interest rates that a borrowing government would otherwise have to pay. The policy conditions imposed by the IMF on borrowings are an order of magnitude tougher than any conditions associated with private sector lending. A government borrowing from the IMF is also much more likely to be criticized by domestic political opponents than if it attempts to borrow in foreign capital markets. If the subsidized interest charge for IMF lending was a major consideration tipping governments in favor of borrowing from the IMF, one should observe numerous governments quickly approaching the IMF when balance-of-payments difficulties first threaten. In practice, the experience is more the opposite: governments tend to approach the IMF for lending only late in the game, often when recourse to borrowing from private sources may already have dried up. When comparing IMF lending with private sector lending, one would in principle like to compare "conditionality-equivalent" interest rates. If that comparison were possible, it would probably show a much smaller difference between the two rates than a simple comparison of unadjusted interest rates. These considerations suggest that critics

99. The International Financial Institution Advisory Commission (2000) chaired by Allan Meltzer is a prominent example.

of the IMF probably have exaggerated the merits of their argument that governments borrowing from the IMF are given an excessive subsidy that encourages excessive IMF borrowing.[100]

At the time the SRF was created in 1997, these issues were again debated. Concerns were expressed that too low an interest rate would encourage borrowing members to make more than "temporary" use of the facility. The outcome of the discussions was that SRF lending should be subject to a surcharge graduated over time. The surcharge above the basic IMF rate of charge is initially 3 percentage points in the first year; it rises a further 0.5 percentage point in each succeeding six-month period (with the total surcharge rate possibly rising to a level as high as 5.0 percentage points). In concept, this interest rate is like the penalty interest rate for emergency liquidity assistance first recommended by Bagehot.[101]

During 2000, the G-7 finance ministers, the IMFC, and the IMF conducted a general review of all the IMF's nonconcessional lending facilities. The focus was yet again on whether member nations might be making unduly "prolonged use" of IMF resources and thereby also making an insufficient effort to access private capital markets instead. In the event, by September 2000 significant changes had been made in IMF interest charges, repayment terms, and conditions of access. The new Independent Evaluation Office at the IMF conducted an extended review of prolonged use issues, published in 2002.[102]

For all its nonconcessional lending, the IMF restored a policy of graduated rates of charge—that is, the borrower is required to pay increasingly higher rates of interest as its borrowing remains outstanding for longer periods. This policy, already in force for the surcharge on emergency SRF loans, was reintroduced into lending under standby arrangements and in

---

100. Goldstein (2000a) thoughtfully reviews the issues of interest rates and maturities for IMF lending. Developing nation members, especially if they are having balance-of-payments difficulties or encountering precrisis conditions, would have to pay very much more than the IMF basic rate of charge if they were to borrow from world capital markets. In the year 2000, for example, the IMF rate of charge varied between 4 and 5 percent. Spreads of emerging market nations' bonds relative to U.S. Treasury securities were on the order of some 3-1/2 to 6 percentage points, and for some nations they were much higher than that. In 1997–98, at the height of the Asian financial crises, the spreads of emerging market bonds over U.S. Treasuries rose as high as 15 to 17 percentage points! Note, however, that none of these interest rates are adjusted to be "conditionality equivalent."

101. For discussion of Walter Bagehot's (1873) recommendation for a penalty rate charged by a lender of last resort and other issues about emergency lending, see *Crisis Management for the World Financial System.*

102. See IMF (2000a, 2000b, 2000c). The Independent Evaluation Office's analysis is contained in IMF, Independent Evaluation Office (2002).

the EFF. The principle that the basic rate of charge will vary with market interest rates also was reiterated.[103]

Significant changes were also made to the repayment conditions for IMF loans. For SBAs, the new policies specified that a member nation is normally expected to begin repayments after two and a quarter years and to complete repayments by the end of four years (compared with earlier expectations of from three and a quarter to five years). For a loan under the EFF, the new policies stipulated that the borrowing member should begin repayments after four and a half years (the same period as before) and to complete repayments by the end of seven (rather than ten) years. Although borrowing members are expected to repay on these schedules, a member can in some circumstances request and receive an extension if its circumstances have not improved sufficiently to allow repayments on the normal terms.

Additional changes were made in the conditions for access to the Extended Fund Facility. The new 2000 understanding reinforced the original decision setting up the EFF, emphasizing that borrowings under the EFF should be allowed only "where there is a reasonable expectation that the member's balance of payments difficulties will be relatively long-term, including because it has limited access to private capital, and where there is an appropriately strong structural reform program to deal with the embedded institutional or economic weaknesses." The IMF Executive Board's statement observed that "members with meaningful access to capital markets were not likely to suffer from the problems described in the EFF decision, and hence that such members would not normally be expected to seek extended arrangements." Reflecting the differences of view and tensions among member nations, the Board's statement also emphasized that "at the same time, the EFF remains available to all members, and there will be circumstances where it will be the most appropriate instrument to meet a member's needs."[104]

The proponents of the changes to interest charges, repayment terms, and access conditions made during the year 2000 expected them to strengthen the incentives for borrowing members to avoid overly prolonged and unduly large use of IMF resources. Some member nations, reportedly

103. The surcharge above the basic rate of charge for SBAs and EFF loans now begins at a level of 1.0 percentage point at 200 percent of quota and rises to 2.0 percentage points with credit outstanding above 300 percent of quota.

104. The quotations are from the IMF's Public Information Notice 00/79, September 18, 2000 ("IMF Board Agrees to Changes to Fund Financial Facilities"); see IMF (2000b).

including the United States, wanted to go still further, increasing interest charges or shortening repayment terms. A number of developing nations were said to be doubtful about, or even to resist, the tightening of terms. The outcome of the review was a delicate political compromise.

Prequalification for Emergency Lending?

When originally formulated in 1999, the CCL facility for emergency lending emphasized *prequalification*. The United States, supported by some other nations, was a proponent of the underlying concept. Other nations, inside and outside the G-7, voiced reservations. Critics of the concept sought to build features into the CCL that were sufficiently stringent to discourage its use. In particular, eligibility criteria were set to be demanding. A member nation seeking prequalification was required, in effect, to have unambiguously sound policies in place and to have demonstrated a track record of responsible policies in the recent past. Provided the demanding criteria were met, the member could then be prequalified ex ante for quick access to IMF financial resources in the event that contagion might lead to crisis.[105]

Although ex ante prequalification seems attractive in principle, it raises serious difficulties. From the perspective of a member considering a CCL arrangement, uncertainties about market reactions are one source of difficulty. Market participants might interpret application for a CCL commitment as a signal that the member expects trouble ahead, which in turn could be viewed as indicating weakness rather than strength. At worst, market reaction could be sufficiently adverse to provoke the speculative attack that the CCL commitment is supposed to deter. If a nation plans in any event to maintain unambiguously sound policies, it may decide that it has little to gain by requesting prequalification under a CCL arrangement. The IMF has demonstrated that it is capable of moving quickly in a crisis, especially for members whose track record is sufficiently strong to meet the CCL's eligibility requirements. Why not merely wait, therefore, and plan on a quick application for borrowing under the Supplemental Reserve

---

105. The criteria included i) absence of a need for IMF resources at the time a CCL is applied for and committed; ii) a favorable IMF assessment of the nation's policies, "taking into account the extent of a member's adherence to internationally accepted standards" (including subscription to the IMF's Special Data Dissemination Standard); iii) "constructive relations with private creditors, with a view to facilitating appropriate involvement of the private sector, and satisfactory management of external vulnerability"; and iv) "a satisfactory economic and financial program, which the member stands ready to adjust as needed." See IMF (1999d) for further details.

Facility if a crisis should strike? As originally specified in 1999, furthermore, the interest charges and fees for the CCL were identical to those for the SRF. Hence that structure of charges provided no price incentive to prequalify.

Still another difficulty with the prequalification features of the original CCL was that ex ante approval of a member's policies did not guarantee ex post automatic access to CCL funds in an actual crisis. The original rules required the IMF to complete an "activation review" prior to releasing funds at the time of crisis; in that review the IMF had to be satisfied that the member was "committed to adjusting policies to deal with any real economic impact from contagion." A member with a CCL arrangement therefore might worry that it would become involved in a further lengthy negotiation with the IMF about performance conditions before it could gain access to the funds.

The concept of prequalification also poses serious difficulties for the IMF. The greatest of these stems from "exit" situations. As an example, suppose that a member nation has been prequalified and a CCL commitment is in place. Then imagine that new individuals come to power in the government, with the result that the nation's policies shift rapidly from sound to questionable, raising the probability of a financial crisis. If the IMF decides that the member no longer qualifies for the CCL because of the deterioration in its policies, public knowledge of that decision could trigger the very crisis that the CCL arrangement was set up to prevent. Such a situation is a no-win dilemma for the IMF. The IMF needs to be able to withdraw from the CCL commitment if the new circumstances invalidate the original commitment. Yet extrication without stimulating turbulence may not be possible. Even from the perspective of a well-performing nation, exit problems may exist. An advantage of a CCL arrangement at the outset is the favorable effect of the announcement that the member's policies have been certified as sound. If the member believes a CCL arrangement is no longer needed, however, might a decision to terminate the arrangement trigger a reverse announcement effect and unsettle financial markets?

Supporters of the CCL, believing that the original 1999 design incorporated serious flaws, lobbied during 2000 to restructure the facility to make it more appealing to potential users. Several significant changes were in fact made during the general review of IMF facilities completed in September 2000. For example, procedures for the initial activation review and for subsequent IMF monitoring were made more flexible. Those changes ensured that a member would have somewhat more automatic access to the committed CCL resources in an actual crisis. The IMF also reduced the rate of charges for use of the CCL below the rate of charges for the SRF, thereby enhancing the attractiveness of the CCL relative to the SRF.[106] The greatest difficulties with the CCL are inherent in the prequalification concept itself, however, and were not altered by the September 2000 changes.[107] As of the early fall of 2003, it was still the case that no member nation had yet applied for a CCL arrangement. Then, in late November 2003, the IMF executive directors decided to abandon the CCL altogether.

The pros and cons of prequalification for IMF lending should be seen in a larger context. The highest priority for the international financial community, looking ahead, should be a gradual enhancement of the IMF's capacities to conduct supranational surveillance. Surveillance is even more important than sensible lending policies. The concept of prequalification embedded in the CCL—that the IMF can certify the soundness of a member nation's policies, rendering judgments about good or ill health and providing a public seal of approval or disapproval—may acquire greater saliency and stature over future decades. Whether such a gradual strengthening of "certification" should emphasize ex ante prequalification rather than focusing first on improved ex post analysis is a more difficult call. Over the shorter run, the IMF should probably concentrate on continuing to strengthen the annual Article IV consultations process and refine its procedures for public disclosure of consultations documents. The consultations process, like the commitments that would have been made under a CCL arrangement, is essentially motivated by the wish to prevent crises. But the consultations process does not generate market uncertainties and exit dilemmas as complex as those associated with prequalification in the CCL facility. Given the abandonment of the CCL in late 2003, actual crisis lending now depends primarily on speedy and skillful activation of the SRF. This status, though ruling out ex ante prequalification for IMF crisis lending, is probably a satisfactory outcome for the time being.

---

106. The initial surcharge for CCL use was reduced from the 3.0 percentage points applicable to the SRF to 1.50 percentage points; thereafter the surcharge was to rise with the length of the borrowing at the same rate as the surcharge under the SRF, but with a ceiling of 3.50 percentage points (the ceiling for the SRF is 5.0 percentage points). The IMF also reduced the commitment fee on the CCL to 0.25 percentage point on the first 100 percent of quota, with another 0.10 percentage point for amounts committed in excess of 100 percent of quota. (These changes in commitment fees were applied to all IMF lending arrangements, not just to the CCL.) For an overview of the changes in all aspects of the CCL, see the IMF's Public Information Notice 00/79, September 18, 2000 ("IMF Board Agrees on Changes to Fund Financial Facilities").

107. In particular, the eligibility criteria were not changed in the September 2000 review.

Conditionality

The conditionality accompanying IMF lending has been contentious in every decade of the institution's history. It still remains controversial, but the grounds for dispute have changed over time.[108]

Some of the earlier controversy was generated by confusion about basic points. After several decades, those points are now better understood and acknowledged. For example, it is now widely accepted that performance conditions of some sort are a feature in all lending arrangements, private or governmental. For valid reasons, lenders invariably insist that borrowers adhere to performance conditions and subject themselves to some form of monitoring. Performance conditions are forward-looking constraints that attempt to ensure that a borrower's behavior is sound and sustainable, thereby raising the probability that the lender will be repaid according to the terms of the loan contract.[109] IMF lending, as stressed above, is essentially an intergovernmental loan—credit extended from the governments of nations having a balance-of-payments surplus to the government of a nation whose balance of payments is in deficit. Creditor nation governments acting through the mechanism of the IMF justifiably insist on some type of performance conditions and monitoring. Safeguarding the resources of the IMF for operations in future years, moreover, requires conditionality to be imposed on lending extended this year. Conditionality in some form is inescapable.

Recent controversies about conditionality stem from disagreements about which types of a nation's policies should be subject to performance conditions, how the conditions should be decided and designed, and how assertive the IMF should be in its efforts to monitor compliance with the conditions. Many such disagreements are in turn related to differences of view about whether the IMF should or should not be deeply engaged in functional areas outside its core competence of macroeconomics and finance. Debates about the appropriate scope of IMF conditionality, in other words, are in part a rehash of the debates about the IMF's mandate.

108. For the earlier history, see Horsefield and others (1969) and de Vries (1976, 1985). For the last several decades, see, among others, Dell (1981), Guitian (1981), Williamson (1983), Buira (1983), Spraos (1986), Polak (1991), Schadler and others (1993, 1995), Feldstein (1998), Radelet and Sachs (1998), Boughton (2001), Council on Foreign Relations Independent Task Force (1999), International Financial Institution Advisory Commission (2000), U.S. Department of the Treasury (2000), Williamson (2000), Goldstein (2000a, 2000b), and Kenen (2001).

109. *Turbulent Waters* (chapters 2 and 6) discusses why lenders always insist on conditionality and monitoring.

To illustrate, consider the question of whether the IMF's conditionality should be applied only to macroeconomic and financial policies or whether it should be extended further afield to apply also to microeconomic and structural policies. One set of arguments against the extension to micro-economic and structural policies asserts that the IMF, if it does so, will dissipate its effectiveness and credibility in its core areas. Skillful crisis management might be undermined by excessive attention to areas of peripheral concern in an immediate crisis, even if structural reforms are necessary for improved longer-term performance of the economy. The IMF staff, it has been argued, has inadequate competence to assess microeconomic and structural policies and to make recommendations for their reform. If performance conditions become too numerous and too detailed, proliferating into all types of structural as well as macroeconomic and financial policies, both the nation's government and the IMF might lose sight of the highest shorter-run priorities and become confused about how to appraise overall compliance with the performance conditions.

Recall also that the presence of performance conditions in IMF lending packages represents a powerful temptation for non-IMF parties to try to embed compliance with their preferred policies and objectives in the conditions. Legislators, nongovernmental organizations, and other interest groups in creditor nations as well as reform-minded domestic groups within the borrowing nation may attempt to piggyback on IMF lending conditionality. The wider the possible scope of the conditionality, the greater the temptation to piggyback.

Yet another argument against broadening the scope of conditionality focuses on the willingness of a nation to approach the IMF for financial assistance when a balance-of-payments problem or the risk of financial crisis becomes manifest. Even though IMF interest charges and repayment terms may seem lenient relative to those in private markets, nations often postpone approaching the IMF until late in the game because of the performance conditions associated with its financial assistance. The more numerous and onerous the performance conditions, the greater this reluctance. At worst, it has been argued, overly ambitious IMF conditionality could exacerbate the initial crisis conditions and induce increased recourse to the beggar-thy-neighbor policies that the IMF was established to inhibit.

If performance conditions in IMF lending arrangements are to be successful, the borrowing government must "own" them—it must believe in their efficacy and explain and justify them to the nation's citizens. That, in turn, implies that the borrowing government must have an essential, probably dominant, role in their design. The more numerous and complex the conditions, the more problematic it may be for the government and the IMF to achieve consensus and hence to generate the appropriate sense of ownership.

For the reasons just summarized, the IMF should hesitate to apply conditionality broadly and ambitiously. In particular, it should incorporate structural and microeconomic policies into its performance conditions only with caution.

Yet weighty arguments also exist on the other side. A nation's balance-of-payments problems and its susceptibility to crisis turbulence can often be traced to structural weaknesses in the economy or financial system. Imagine a nation, for example, whose balance-of-payments crisis is proximately triggered by a rush of domestic and foreign investors exiting the national financial system. But suppose that the investors' behavior is driven by growing awareness of fundamental deficiencies in the government's fiscal policies. If chronic fiscal deficits have arisen because of large losses by government-owned enterprises, a narrow tax base, and inadequate tax collection procedures, an IMF performance condition that merely specified a reduced overall fiscal deficit for the next three years might not be credible. Effective national policies—and hence effective accompanying conditions for an IMF lending program—might need to specify structural measures for privatizing government enterprises, expanding the tax base, and creating new administrative procedures for improving tax collections.

If the IMF's lending and conditionality were to ignore structural weaknesses entirely, its financial assistance might have a poor chance of turning the troubled nation around. Financial markets are not prepared to ignore structural weaknesses and deficiencies in microeconomic policies once they are brought to light. Indeed, financial herd behavior can put disproportionate emphasis on deficiencies in structural policies after some market participants call prominent attention to them. In some circumstances, therefore, the IMF has no effective choice but to take the structural issues into account in its lending decisions.

The example of financial standards and prudential oversight for the financial system is salutary.[110] If weak financial regulation and prudential oversight surface as a major issue in borrowing nations, IMF conditionality would be flawed if it paid no attention to such deficiencies. IMF recommendations for macroeconomic policies could be undermined by

110. *Prudential Oversight and Standards for the World Financial System* contains a detailed analysis.

financial structural problems such as large nonperforming loans and wide-spread "connected lending" at banks, inadequate bankruptcy courts, and weak prudential oversight from supervisory agencies. Even for emergency crisis lending, the arguments in favor of imposing performance conditions that may include policies outside the macroeconomic area—possibly structural or microeconomic policies, especially in the financial system—are more compelling than the arguments against.[111]

Unfortunately for the simple life, a tension will always exist between two broad guidelines. The IMF needs to keep focused on its core competence, macroeconomics and finance. But it also needs to design lending packages that deal appropriately with nations' heterogeneous balance-of-payments difficulties; doing so sometimes requires extending performance conditions into the functional areas of structural and microeconomic policies. An approach that gives weight to both guidelines is the only sensible way for the IMF to proceed.

If such a balanced approach is to succeed, the World Bank must take the lead in framing recommendations about structural and microeconomic policies for nations that wish to borrow from any of the international financial organizations. (In some specialized areas—for example, standards for legal systems, environmental issues, and labor markets—still other international organizations should have the leadership responsibilities.) The IMF, if and when appropriate, can then apply performance conditions derived from those recommendations as a component of its lending arrangements. The IMF need not have the primary responsibility in functional areas such as structural reforms and microeconomic policies. Its conditionality can support the conditionality of the other international organizations and follow their leadership. This intermediate course can keep the IMF's agenda from becoming bloated with detailed staff work

111. So-called bad fundamentals, including weak financial standards and prudential oversight of financial institutions, played an important role in several of the nations most badly afflicted by the Asian financial turbulence in 1997–98. Goldstein (2000b), citing Roubini's comments in McHale (2000, Korea), emphasizes the example of Korea: "In the run-up to the Korean crisis: 7 of the 30 largest chaebol were essentially bankrupt; there were large terms of trade losses in 1996 (especially for semi-conductors); non-performing loans in the banking system and leverage in the corporate sector were already high; there was a low return on invested capital; capital inflows were biased toward short-term capital and against foreign direct investment; there was a lack of transparency (including on the country's short-term foreign liabilities); and substantial political uncertainty exacerbated the government's credibility problem" (p. 10). Claessens and others (2001), Baliño and others (1999), and Lane and others (1999) emphasize structural weaknesses in the financial systems of Asian nations experiencing financial crises and discuss the role played by IMF performance conditions in trying to resolve those crises.

outside its area of core competence yet permit its conditionality to cover noncore policies when a nation's circumstances make that desirable.

Has the conditionality of IMF lending helped borrowing nations improve their policies? Many critics answer no. Many others think the record points to numerous positive achievements and few notable failures, with the blame for the failures falling more on the governments of the borrowing nations than on the IMF. Unfortunately, observers tend to respond to the evidence in much the same way that individuals respond to a Rorschach test. When a nation that accepts an IMF lending program subsequently performs well, many critics infer that the favorable outcome would have occurred anyway without the IMF program. When a nation's subsequent performance is poor, on the other hand, the same critics infer that the outcome was caused by the IMF's misguided policy advice and its performance conditions. The uncritical friends of the IMF have the converse Rorschach bias: if things go well in a nation after an IMF program has been in effect, the IMF deserves much or all of the credit; if things go badly, the borrowing nation simply failed to follow the IMF's sound advice and comply with its conditionality.

In fact, it is difficult to assess the effects of an IMF lending program and its performance conditions. Many efforts claiming to do so have been superficial and inappropriately designed. To conduct an analytically appropriate assessment, in principle one must compare the actual macroeconomic outcome in a borrowing nation having an IMF program with a counterfactual outcome that would have emerged in the nation with different policies and without the IMF's lending and its performance conditions. Specifying a plausible counterfactual outcome is, of course, extremely difficult. Many studies have thus resorted to simple comparisons of a nation's economic variables in two time periods, before adoption and after adoption of an IMF program. But such comparisons are definitely not satisfactory analytically and provide little insight into whether IMF conditionality in any given situation has on balance been constructive.

The IMF's implementation of conditionality is imperfect. It can doubtless be improved and simplified, in terms of both the general guidelines used and their application in specific cases. Yet the difficulty of the IMF's position deserves empathy. Because the IMF operates in a messy, intermediate world polity, guidelines for its performance conditions—indeed for all the dimensions of its surveillance—pull it in opposite directions. On the one hand, the conditionality of IMF lending has to avoid being overly intrusive. It should be highly sensitive to the legal supremacy of a nation's government as the arbiter for that nation of political, social, and economic priorities. On the other hand, the IMF must be sensitive to the systemic interests of the world community. IMF conditionality and surveillance must avoid being overly lax and too flexible, thereby even failing to facilitate a borrowing nation's self-identified own best interests.

To use Michael Mussa's metaphor, the IMF is called upon to be both a social worker and a policeman.[112] The social worker's advice must be sympathetic, taking into account the political difficulties of implementing needed but perhaps unpopular policies. If the borrowing nation should slip a bit in implementing sound policies, it will want the understanding social worker to give it the benefit of the doubt. Yet a tough cop must use objective criteria for extending assistance, should tightly condition assistance on a rigorously designed adjustment program, and should promptly identify any slippages in a borrower's program no matter what political difficulties may be present.

Japanese culture acknowledges the phenomenon of *gai-atsu*—pressure from outside to implement reforms that can help advance a nation's own best interests. Outside pressure is not invariably constructive. It often is resented, sometimes justifiably. But in some instances it can play a helpful role in fostering needed domestic reforms. The positive nuances of *gai-atsu* are often evident in the IMF's use of performance conditions. Indeed, if exercised cautiously, *gai-atsu* is a partial justification for supranational surveillance more broadly conceived.

Necessarily, the IMF must seek a balanced approach—a skillful compromise—between the conditionality guidelines that pull it in opposite directions. It must guard against overindulgence in its role as a sympathetic social worker while simultaneously eschewing overzealous monitoring as a tough cop. Such an approach, avoiding any drift toward extremes, is just as important for the nurturing of supranational surveillance as for enhancing the effectiveness of IMF lending and for ensuring that individual nations do not use IMF resources excessively or for overly prolonged periods.

In practice, the IMF does seek a balanced, compromise approach. The best studies trying to evaluate the success of IMF programs reach mixed conclusions but point to net favorable influences in a majority of cases. IMF efforts to apply a balanced conditionality have often been a constructive influence on nations experiencing economic and financial difficulties.[113]

112. Mussa (2002).
113. The most informative studies have been carried out by current or former IMF staff members; see, for example, Schadler and others (1993, 1995), Haque and Khan (1998), and Goldstein (2000b).

IMF Lending: An Overview

The preceding discussion omits most details about IMF lending and suppresses several specialized issues of secondary importance. If you are a nonspecialist reader, you may understandably feel unsure even about some of the issues raised above. You may be hesitant, for example, to express a judgment about the appropriate scope and design of the performance conditions accompanying IMF lending. You might be agnostic about the balance of pros and cons of prequalifying IMF member nations for emergency liquidity assistance in a financial crisis. You might or might not believe that the IMF's interest charges and repayment terms have been sufficiently tightened by the changes made in recent years. Your instincts may or may not lead you to the conclusion that some of the IMF's lending facilities should be further simplified and revised.

No matter. Those issues are significant. You should want the IMF and national governments to resolve them thoughtfully, taking due account of objective outside analysis. But nonspecialists can without qualms leave the detailed issues to others who are more knowledgeable and directly engaged.

Basic points about IMF lending intermediation, on the other hand, should be acknowledged and understood by all thoughtful observers, specialists and nonspecialists alike. The discussion that follows summarizes the most important points and puts them in perspective.

Fundamental rationales exist for asking the IMF to serve as a focal point for intergovernmental lending intermediation. As cross-border finance and world economic integration become still more important—and hence as the necessity for international financial governance grows apace—the need for skillful IMF lending intermediation will increase further. Two rationales stand out as valid above all others. First, IMF lending—in noncrisis as well as crisis circumstances—can play a helpful role as a handmaiden and backstop for the supranational surveillance of national economic policies. Second, for the foreseeable future, emergency crisis lending by the IMF coupled with IMF leadership in crisis management is the closest approximation the world community can have to collective governance for coping with financial turbulence that disrupts entire nations' economies and threatens to spill contagiously across national borders.

Notwithstanding the valid rationales for IMF lending and notwithstanding the compromise policies designed to steer a middle course among

---

For external analyses commissioned by the IMF, see IMF (1998a,1998b, 1999a). More recent analyses include those of the IMF Independent Evaluation Office (2002, 2003a, 2003b).

conflicting guidelines, IMF lending does entail risks. IMF recommendations for policy adjustments may occasionally be poorly formulated or take
inadequate account of a member nation's long-run interests. Most notably,
a few member nations may abuse IMF lending by borrowing excessively or
for overly prolonged periods. In a world in which savings generated in one
nation increasingly can be readily transferred across borders to other
nations, IMF noncrisis lending could unfairly compete with private lending to governments. If a borrowing government has reasonable and reliable
access to private capital from foreign financial institutions and markets,
lending from the IMF to that government could constitute the "unwarrantedly cheap" financing at below-market cost about which critics have
complained.

IMF lending should be a backstop for occasions when external borrowing by a nation's government is warranted but private sector financing is
available only on unreasonably expensive terms—or is not available at all.
Potential borrowing governments should certainly not be able to regard
IMF lending merely as a low-cost substitute for private finance. Probably
few if any borrowing governments do hold such an attitude. A "conditionality adjusted" rate of interest for borrowing from the IMF is likely to be
high, perhaps virtually as high as a private market interest rate (if private
lenders are willing to lend at all). Even so, continual IMF vigilance is
required to prevent governments of borrowing nations from perceiving
IMF lending as a subsidized substitute for private capital inflows.

No less important, the world community should not want the IMF to
be a major source of low-cost, below-market funds for "development
finance"—investment programs to promote growth, reduce poverty, and
achieve structural reforms. Yes, the world community should wish to make
large amounts of low-cost development finance available to poorer nations,
especially those that do not have ready access to private capital markets.
That goal is a valid objective for international collective governance. But the
World Bank and regional development banks should be the primary international sources of that development finance, not the IMF. The more that
IMF lending is used to support growth promotion, poverty reduction, and
structural reform, the greater the risks that the IMF's activities will be dis-
sipated across too many functional areas and that its effectiveness will be
compromised in the core areas of macroeconomics and finance. Nurturing
of the IMF's nascent responsibilities as an adjustment referee and coordination catalyst in macroeconomics and finance is most likely to be
successful if the IMF pulls back from rather than trespasses further into the

core competence areas of the World Bank and the regional development banks.

Another major risk has to be avoided. Human nature and politics being what they are, the governments of some nations from time to time either will not or cannot maintain sound economic policies. Imagine that such nations were to succeed in borrowing from the IMF, either during noncrisis periods or because they fall into crisis (a crisis being likely sooner or later if unsound policies continue). Those nations would be unlikely to repay their borrowings promptly, if at all. Greatly delayed payments would be a clear violation of IMF guidelines stipulating that IMF lending should be temporary. To describe the situation in the best possible light, such IMF lending would become de facto long-term development finance. At worst, to use provocative language, the governments of those nations might attempt to stay on "welfare" rather than pull up their socks, reform their policies, and "get off the dole." Such outcomes would be undesirable—for the IMF, for the world community, and ultimately for the individual nations themselves.

When making judgments about an "irresponsible" government, other IMF member nations and the IMF itself should exhibit caution and humility. National governments, just like ordinary mortals, are prone to apply a double standard in appraising behavior. The government of any particular nation judges other nations' governments by their actions but judges itself by its motives. Just as protectionism gets defined as some other nation's trade policies, unsound and irresponsible macroeconomic policies are seen as some other nation's policy stance. When difficulties arise in adopting appropriate policies within one's own nation, delays and shortfalls are readily excused because of binding domestic political constraints. In principle, all governments should try to understand their counterparts' difficulties and not rush too quickly to judgment. The venerable query is pertinent here, too: "Why beholdest thou the mote in thy brother's eye but considerest not the beam in thine own eye?"[114] Nor should the governments of big nations push the IMF to be tough on the governments of small nations but not, heaven forbid, on themselves. Difficult cases—and complex trade-offs—will inevitably arise. The basic principle, nevertheless, is clear: applications to borrow from the IMF should typically be denied to member nations whose governments are pursuing policies that are considered unsound on the basis of objective criteria.

114. Matt. 7:3, King James Bible.

As with IMF surveillance, so it should be with IMF lending: what is needed, again, is a balanced perspective. Allowing lending by the IMF to become an easy substitute for improving national policies or borrowing from private lenders in world financial markets would be wrong. But severely constraining or eliminating IMF lending because of its risks also would be wrong. IMF lending should follow a middle course that shuns the flawed extremes. It is a collective good that, prudently supplied, can underpin the stability and efficiency of the world financial system.

The IMF: Whose Institution?

The drift in IMF activities since the mid-1970s toward increased engagement in growth, structural reform, and poverty reduction in developing nations significantly influenced popular perceptions of the institution. In many quarters today the IMF is seen as an institution whose "clients" are exclusively the developing nations. That impression is badly misinformed and damages efforts to strengthen and improve the IMF.

The damaging impression stems in part from the fact that none of the industrial nations has been a recipient of IMF credit since the early 1980s. For a couple of decades the only recipients have been developing nations. That change in the composition of borrowers in turn gradually transformed the IMF's role as a lending intermediary. The impression that the clients of the IMF are developing nations alone, however, pays attention only to IMF lending. It ignores the other functions of the IMF, most notably the IMF's surveillance of the policies of member nations—industrial as well as developing, borrowers and nonborrowers alike.

When speaking about "clients" of the IMF, one must acknowledge the asymmetries among IMF member nations. Nations differ greatly in size and wealth, and hence in relative political power. Inevitably, these asymmetries have unsurprising consequences for the IMF's surveillance of and other interactions with its members. As discussed earlier, for example, the IMF sometimes assertively pushes smaller members to consider changes in economic policies but is significantly less forceful in recommending changes for the economies of its largest and most powerful members. This difference stems in part from the fact that the IMF has more potential leverage with borrowing than with nonborrowing members. Given the absence of borrowing by industrial nations since the early 1980s, the IMF has influenced the economic policies of developing nation members to a much greater extent than those of industrial nations. Policy outcomes themselves are therefore asymmetric. To summarize again: if a small nation and the IMF disagree, the small nation typically falls into line; if one of the largest nations and the IMF disagree, the IMF characteristically falls into line.

Asymmetry in the relative political power of nations is a fact of life. The wealthiest, most powerful nations have the largest IMF quotas (see below). Because the industrial nations are no longer borrowing from the IMF, on average they are much the most important creditors, accounting for a very high percentage of total IMF resources lent to developing nations. The large, wealthy nations therefore "call the shots" in important IMF decisions.

The inevitable asymmetries contribute to the impression that the only nations benefiting from the existence of the IMF are developing nations. The mistaken corollary of that mistaken impression is that the IMF exists because the large wealthy nations condescend to contribute their resources to it. The simple-minded version of this sloppy caricature is that the IMF is a charity run by the wealthy nations for the benefit of poor nations.

This mistaken caricature of the IMF would not merit discussion if those holding this view had no influence in political discussions of cross-border financial problems. Unfortunately, the caricature is often encountered in the national legislatures of industrial nations. Some members of the U.S. Congress, for example, frequently invoke this characterization of the IMF. A version of this view with its rough edges polished off even permeates the criticisms of the IMF in the report to the U.S. Congress and Treasury Department of the International Financial Institution Advisory Commission (the so-called Meltzer Commission).[115]

The frequently voiced caricature is fundamentally wrong because it fails to appreciate the significance of supranational surveillance and IMF functions other than IMF lending intermediation. Worst of all, it embodies a badly distorted understanding of the selfish interests of the major industrial nations. The wealthiest nations have the most to gain from a healthy, stable evolution of the world economy. They have the most to lose if the world economy and financial system malfunction. The best hope for improved prosperity management—not least for the largest and wealthiest nations—is to nurture a gradual strengthening of collective surveillance over national economic policies. That evolution requires increased and more thoughtful support of the IMF. Informed citizens in the wealthy, powerful nations should regard the IMF as *"our* institution" serving *our*

115. International Financial Institution Advisory Commission (2000).

interests, not as an altruistic charity that drains *our* resources to benefit *other*, poorer nations elsewhere in the world.

IMF Governance: Distribution of Quotas, Voting Power, and Constituencies

The quota of an individual member nation critically determines its rights and responsibilities in the International Monetary Fund. For example, the size of its quota determines the amount of the member's required contribution to the IMF's lendable resources, the amount of its potential access to borrowing from the IMF, and the amount of its share in any new creation of special drawing rights. The share of a member's quota in the aggregate total of quotas of all members is very highly correlated with, although not exactly identical to, its share in voting power. The capital shares and voting rights of a nation in the World Bank depend directly on its quota in the IMF.[116]

The size of a member's IMF quota and its associated voting rights *relative to those of other members* are by far the most significant factors determining its differential ability to influence decisions made by the IMF and the World Bank—decisions about the nation's own interactions with the two institutions, and decisions about all the other operations and policies of the institutions.

The IMF Articles of Agreement require a formal review of the size and distribution of quotas at intervals of not more than five years. Following a review, the IMF Board of Governors decides whether to make adjustments; an 85 percent majority of the total voting power is required for any changes in quotas. A common pattern in the quinquennial reviews (which are called general reviews) has been for all members to receive an equiproportional increment in their individual quota, with a few members receiving a selective, larger-than-equiproportional increase. After the eleventh general review in 1997, for example, the Board of Governors in January 1998 approved a 45 percent increase in the aggregate total of quotas with selective increases for a number of individual members; the revised quotas went into effect in January 1999.

Because of "basic votes," a nation's voting power in the IMF is not exactly proportional to the size of its quota. The Articles of Agreement

116. In the World Bank, a member's share in total capital shares and its relative voting strength also are very highly correlated but not exactly identical.

specify that each member shall have a uniform small number of basic votes plus one additional vote for each part of its quota equivalent to 100,000 special drawing rights. The component of basic votes in a member's total votes was originally intended to give smaller member nations somewhat more influence than they otherwise would have had, thereby protecting their participation in decisionmaking. Some analysts have interpreted the uniformity of basic votes across members as a reflection of the principle that member nations should, at least for some purposes, be treated as equal regardless of their size.

The number of basic votes has remained unchanged, at 250 for each member, since the founding of the IMF. Quotas, on the other hand, are now a large multiple of their original value. The significance of basic votes has accordingly declined greatly. Because of the provision for basic votes, however, large nations still have a slightly smaller share of the total votes than of total quotas. A small nation's share of total votes is slightly larger than its share of quotas.[117] Apart from this qualification due to basic votes, formal "voting strength" in the decisions of the IMF depends directly on the relative size of a member's individual quota.[118]

The Executive Board, the primary decisionmaking entity in the governance structure of the IMF, was composed of twenty-four executive directors appointed or elected by the member nations at the end of 2003. Each executive director (ED) represents a constituency. The original Articles of Agreement stipulated that the five members with the five largest quotas can *appoint* their own ED; that provision was not changed in subsequent amendments. As of end 2003, the five members with the largest quotas and hence with appointed EDs were the United States, Japan, Germany, the United Kingdom, and France. Other member nations, grouped into constituencies, *elect* an executive director. Three members—Saudi Arabia, China, and Russia—had a constituency to themselves in 2003; therefore they, like the five members with the largest quotas, effectively designated their own ED. All other members are grouped into multiple-nation constituencies that elect an ED to represent the constituency on the Executive Board.[119]

117. For example, as of April 2000 the United States had 17.68 percent of total quotas but only 17.30 percent of total votes; comparable figures for both the United Kingdom and France were 5.11 percent of total quotas and 5.02 percent of total votes Senegal had 0.08 percent of total quotas but 0.09 percent of total votes; Seychelles had only 0.004 percent of total quotas but 0.02 percent of total votes.

118. A comparable provision of basic votes, similarly set at 250 for each member, exists in the World Bank governance structure.

119. At its inaugural meeting in 1946, the executive directors were twelve in number; by 1964 the Board had twenty EDs. As amended in the 1970s, the IMF Articles of Agreement provided for a

Except for the nations having their own constituency and their own EDs, the preferences and choices of an individual member nation have to be expressed through the ED of the multiple-member constituency to which the nation belongs. Formal votes are seldom taken on the Executive Board. Rule C-10 of the IMF's rules and regulations, which dates back to the early years of the institution, when the United States and the United Kingdom dominated the IMF's discussions, prescribes that "the Chairman shall ordinarily ascertain the sense of the meeting, in lieu of a formal vote." The tradition of decision by consensus is often praised as fostering a spirit of cooperation among member nations. Its proponents regard it as safeguarding "minority rights" of small nations.[120] Significantly, however, if a formal vote is taken in the Executive Board, the ED is not allowed to split his or her vote. The combination of the consensus tradition, the grouping of all but the biggest members into only sixteen constituencies, and the provision against split votes within constituencies may, it is argued by skeptics, give smaller nations less of a voice and influence in decisionmaking than they might have with the strict application of formal voting rules on a member-by-member basis.

The governance features of the IMF just summarized raise issues of great importance and political difficulty. I argue in the analysis that follows that the existing distribution across member nations of quota shares, voting power, and Executive Board constituencies is not satisfactory and that it will prove to be politically unsustainable over time. Adjustments—major reforms—are needed in those three key structural features. The required adjustments should, among other effects, enhance the influence and "voice" of developing nations and correspondingly reduce somewhat the dominance of the advanced industrial nations. The shifts in influence for the advanced nations will necessarily be largest for European nations belonging

---

Board of twenty EDs but also allowed for flexibility in the number—subject, however, to approval by an 85 percent majority of the total voting power. Each executive director appoints an alternate with full power to act for him when he is not present. When the executive directors appointing them are present, alternates may participate in meetings but may not vote. Germany replaced Taiwan China in 1960 and Japan replaced India in 1970 as members having their own constituency and appointing their own ED. The Executive Board grew to twenty-one members in 1978, with Saudi Arabia gaining its own constituency. In 1980 the People's Republic of (mainland) China replaced Taiwan China as the representative of China in the IMF; China's quota was raised to a level high enough to make it possible for China to have its own constituency and ED. The size of the Board was raised to twenty-four in the early 1990s after Russia, Switzerland, and former centrally planned economies joined the IMF.

120. Van Houtven (2002) discusses constituencies and the tradition of consensus decisionmaking on the IMF Executive Board; he asserts that the tradition of consensus decisions favors developing nations.

to the European Union. Because governance of the World Bank is similar in most respects to that of the IMF, much of the analysis that follows also pertains to the World Bank.

Quota Shares: Calibrated to Relative Position in the World Economy?

From the inception of the IMF to the present, analysts and governments have generally agreed that IMF quotas and voting power should reflect a member nation's "relative position in the world economy." That presumption, however, is too vague to have operational significance. Alternative measures of relative status point in very different directions. At the outset, when quotas were first determined in 1948, no genuine consensus existed about how to define relative position in the world economy. Certainly none exists now.

The initial determination of relative quotas at Bretton Woods was partly shaped by a complex formula incorporating several different macroeconomic variables. Much more important, however, the initial quotas depended on political horse trading, first between the American and British negotiators and then among countries more generally. If a formula and political judgments yielded different verdicts about the appropriate size of a member's quota, the tendency was, understandably, to bend or even ignore the formula. Even the formulas themselves were deliberately "cooked" to produce a politically desired result.[121]

Subsequent quinquennial reviews of quotas were similar in many ways to the initial deliberations. In the beginning stages of a review, IMF staff and then IMF management and the executive directors examined alternative formulas for determining suggested values for members' quotas. Four additional formulas were developed. The values for quotas resulting from the various formulas were known as "calculated quotas." Not surprisingly, the typical final outcome of a quinquennial review was influenced more by

---

121. See Horsefield and others (1969), especially volume 1, pp. 94–100; and Mikesell (1994). Harry Dexter White baldly told Raymond Mikesell, the economist in the U.S. Treasury during World War II charged with creating a formula for determining quotas, that the result of the formula "should yield a quota of about $2.5 billion for the United States, about half this amount for the United Kingdom, and such figures for the U.S.S.R. and China as should assure them third and fourth places, respectively, in the list of quotas" (p. 95). Many countries tried to negotiate a different quota than that suggested by the Americans' formula and the American and British teams; Keynes, for example, complained about the "stonewalling tactics" of the Russians that gave them "too large a quota" (Skidelsky, 2001, chapter 10). See also Gardner (1969).

existing quotas prevailing at the time and by political horse trading than by calculated quotas.[122]

Formulas for calculated quotas remained contentious. Although various revisions of the formulas were considered over time, and sometimes adopted, many member nations continued to be restive with the formulas and the entire process. By the time of the eleventh general review, the underlying issues were more insistently raised and were beginning to command more widespread public attention. The IMF therefore commissioned a group of external experts, chaired by Richard Cooper, to review the quota formulas "with a view to providing the IMF Executive Board with an independent report on their adequacy." The group met during the second half of 1999; their report was made public in September 2000.[123] The Executive Board discussed the issues of relative quota sizes several times in the subsequent three years, and reports were also made by the World Bank and the IMF to the Development Committee.[124]

The broad nature of the dilemma in specifying the "relative position in the world economy" of individual nations can be readily grasped from the data shown in table 1. The table gives the "world" distribution for five variables: output measured as real GDP valued at market exchange rates averaged over the three years from 1997 through 1999; output measured as real GDP valued at purchasing power parity (PPP) prices averaged over the three years from 1997 through 1999; a measure of cross-border trade transactions (average of exports and imports) averaged over the five years from 1995 through 1999; the average value of total international reserves during the year 1999; and the size of population at mid-year 1999. For

122. For the eleventh review, whose proposed quotas went into effect in 1999, for example, the IMF's press release summarized the complex compromise in the following manner: "75 percent of the overall increase will be distributed among all members in proportion to their existing quotas; 15 percent of the overall increase will be distributed in proportion to members shares in calculated quotas (based on 1994 data), so as to better reflect the relative economic positions of members; and the remaining 10 percent of the overall increase will be distributed among those members whose present quotas are out of line with their positions in the world economy (as measured by the excess of their share in calculated quotas over their share in actual quotas), of which 1 percent of the overall increase will be distributed among five members whose current quotas are far out of line with their relative economic positions, and which are in a position to contribute to the IMF's liquidity over the medium term" (IMF, 1997).

123. See IMF (2000d, 2000f). The report is a useful summary document on the historical background as well as the relative merits of different alternative formulas. The review group's mandate, as interpreted by the group, excluded the issues of the total size of IMF quotas and specific relativities among the quotas of individual members.

124. IMF (2001a, 2001b, 2002a, 2002b); World Bank and IMF, Development Committee (2003a, 2003b).

Table 1. *Distribution by Nation of Key Economic Variables*

Percent of world total, ranked by population in descending order

Country	GDP Market exchange rates 1997–99 average	GDP PPP prices 1997–99 average	External trade 1995–99 average	International reserves 1999 average	Population UN data mid-year 1999	IMF quotas eleventh review
World, defined as all IMF member nations	100.00	100.00	100.00	100.00	100.00	100.00
China, People's Republic	3.74	11.17	5.11	9.75	21.15	2.98
India	1.41	4.39	0.73	1.99	16.60	1.95
United States	29.46	21.49	15.31	4.78	4.69	17.38
Indonesia	0.50	1.65	0.74	1.63	3.50	0.97
Brazil	2.37	2.74	0.94	2.45	2.81	1.42
Russia	1.01	2.46	1.19	0.51	2.45	2.78
Pakistan	0.21	0.55	0.18	0.11	2.30	0.48
Bangladesh	0.15	0.35	0.10	0.10	2.25	0.25
Japan	14.25	7.77	7.80	15.83	2.12	6.23
Nigeria	0.34	0.82	0.19	0.33	1.85	0.82
Mexico	1.46	1.90	1.64	2.02	1.63	1.21
Germany	7.13	4.72	8.86	4.20	1.37	6.09
Iran	0.67	1.89	0.24	0.00	1.16	0.70
Egypt	0.29	0.52	0.26	1.05	1.12	0.44
Turkey	0.66	1.04	0.67	1.43	1.10	0.45

United Kingdom	4.68	3.18	6.86	2.01	0.99	5.02
Italy	3.96	3.18	4.34	1.64	0.96	3.30
Korea	1.34	1.58	2.03	3.99	0.78	0.76
Spain	1.88	1.67	2.25	2.47	0.67	1.43
Argentina	0.98	0.96	0.49	1.51	0.61	0.99
Saudi Arabia	0.47	0.53	0.78	0.96	0.33	3.27
Australia	1.31	1.14	1.16	1.01	0.32	1.51
Netherlands	1.27	0.89	3.43	0.75	0.26	2.42
Belgium	0.83	0.61	2.40	0.75	0.17	2.15
Switzerland	0.87	0.48	1.86	2.53	0.12	1.62
Denmark	0.58	0.35	1.10	1.36	0.09	0.77
Industrial nations (24)	76.91	53.40	71.42	47.70	14.19	61.09
European Union nations before May 2004 (15)	28.18	20.08	40.79	20.48	6.29	30.10
Developing nations (160)	23.09	46.60	28.58	52.30	84.90	38.91

Source: Derived from appendix table. The numbers presented here are percentages of the totals for all IMF member nations. The percentages shown in the appendix table, slightly different from those in table 1, are percentages of "World Plus" totals (that is, all IMF member nations plus Cuba, China, and Taiwan).

comparison, the final column in table 1 shows the distribution of IMF quotas agreed to in the eleventh general review, which went into effect for most members during 1999. The figures in the columns are percent shares in the world total for that variable. The rows show a selection of the member nations with large shares in one or more of the variables; rows also are provided for several regional groupings. Table 1 is an abridgment of the larger appendix table, in which more individual IMF members are shown. The appendix table also reports member shares in total voting power and gives the underlying data as well as the percentage shares.[125]

A nation's relative position in the world economy is highly sensitive to the choice of variable used as a yardstick. Table 1 as presented happens to rank countries by their share of the world's population. But the table could equally well have been shown with rows ordered by one of the other variables. Rankings by shares in world GDP or international reserves plainly produce very different results from a ranking by population. The ranking by GDP in terms of market exchange rates, moreover, is different from a ranking by GDP measured at purchasing power parity, with the familiar large differences among industrial and developing nations.[126] And shares of total IMF quotas—relative position in the IMF itself—do not correlate at all closely with any of the rankings based on the macroeconomic variables shown.

Striking comparisons virtually jump out of the table. Consider these five IMF members: India, the People's Republic of China, the United Kingdom, Japan, and the United States. If IMF quota shares were determined solely by shares of world GDP at market exchange rates, the shares in total quotas of these five members would be India 1.4, China 3.75, the United Kingdom 4.7, Japan 14.25, and the United States 29.5 percent. If quota shares were instead determined by shares of world population, the relative shares would be India 16.6, China 21.2, the United Kingdom 1.0, Japan 2.45, and the United States 4.7 percent. If quota shares were determined

125. The dates and averages used in table 1 and the appendix table were chosen to be representative of the most recent period for which comprehensive statistics are available. The underlying data were compiled by the IMF staff in their papers for the Executive Board; see tables 1 and 3 in the statistical appendix of IMF (2002a) and the table in appendix II of IMF (2003e). My table 1 and the appendix table use the higher IMF quota for China agreed to in 2001 that reflected incorporation of Hong Kong in the People's Republic of China (rather than the quota for China initially agreed in the eleventh review before the adjustment for the consolidation of Hong Kong).

126. It is well known that large differences exist between gross domestic products (and gross national products and gross national incomes) calculated at current market exchange rates and those calculated at purchasing power parities. Cross-nation comparisons that convert nominal output and income data to a common currency using market exchange rates understate the outputs of poor nations. Conversions using PPP methods are one way of trying to correct for this bias.

by shares of international reserves, Japan and China would have the two largest shares. Shares in *actual* IMF quotas were India 1.95, China 3.0, the United Kingdom 5.0, Japan 6.2, and the United States 17.4 percent.

Putting the same information another way, if GDP at market exchange rates was the only yardstick for determining relative position in the world economy, the U.S. quota would be almost twenty-one times that of India and nearly eight times that of China. At the opposite extreme with population as the yardstick, the U.S. quota would be only about two-sevenths of India's quota and merely one-fifth of China's quota! In practice, with the complex political decisions that determine actual quota shares, the U.S. quota is nine times larger than India's quota and somewhat less than six times larger than China's.

Comparisons among smaller and mid-sized nations suggest equally striking anomalies. Brazil accounts for 2.4 percent of world GDP at market exchange rates (2.7 percent at purchasing power parities) and for 2.8 percent of world population, but it has only a 1.4 percent share in total IMF quotas. The Netherlands has 1.3 percent of world GDP, only 0.3 percent of the world's population, but more than 2.4 percent of total quotas. Mexico and Korea are two developing nations with a relatively large GDP and population, but their quota shares are only 1.2 and 0.8 percent, respectively. Belgium, Switzerland, and Denmark are three developed nations with a smaller GDP and smaller population than Mexico and Korea, yet their quota shares are 2.2, 1.6, and 0.8 percent, respectively. Can it be appropriate that the Netherlands's IMF quota is much larger than Brazil's or that Belgium, Switzerland, and Denmark have individual quotas larger than those of Mexico and Korea?

The macroeconomic variables whose world distributions are shown in table 1 are, of course, only a few of those that may be deemed pertinent. Analysis of relative position in the world economy should probably take into account the sizes of nations' capital flows, the outstanding stocks of international investment positions (net external asset/liability positions), or both. The "variability" over time of changes in the variables, not merely their relative levels, is in principle a relevant determinant of a nation's ability to contribute resources to the IMF or of its need to borrow such resources. Each of the relevant variables can be measured in different ways. (The differences between measurements of GDP at market exchange rates and purchasing power parity are an especially striking example.)

Plainly, no single macroeconomic variable can be acceptable to all member nations as the sole yardstick of relative position. The most dramatic contrast of all arises when relative positions are judged by focusing on numbers of people instead of by measures of income or wealth. A population yardstick for determining IMF quota shares would accord greater weights and hence substantially more voting power to developing nations, many of which have low per capita incomes but proportionately large populations. A yardstick based only on relative incomes or wealths (for example, GDPs) would accord large quota shares to nations with strong abilities to contribute resources to the IMF usable for lending.

In practice, as even a cursory glance at table 1 makes clear, quota shares in the IMF and hence decisionmaking power reflect relative income and relative trade volume very much more than they reflect relative population.

Formulas for calculating quotas are devices for weighting and combining the various macroeconomic variables to yield a composite measure of relative position. Efforts to find consensus on a composite measure, however, stumble on essentially the same cross-nation differences in vested interests that prevent any single variable from being accepted as a yardstick. Composite measures resulting from formulas that incorporate numerous variables and possibly complex weighting schemes, furthermore, are difficult for most people to understand and accordingly tend not to be transparent.[127]

The IMF expert group that met during 1999, the Quota Formula Review Group, struggled with distribution and formula issues and presented a recommendation for dealing with them in its report (albeit with dissenting opinions from the majority view). Reviewing the history of formula calculations and noting that the five formulas used in the recent past had been based on data for GDP, reserves, current account transactions, variability of current receipts, and the ratio of current account receipts to GDP, the review group suggested instead a simpler formula. It recommended relating quota shares to only two variables, one representing a member's relative ability to contribute to the IMF's resources (which for simplicity would be calibrated by GDP) and the other a measure of the member's external vulnerability (which would be calibrated by the vari-

---

127. Still another complicating factor is that the variables included in quota formulas—for example, the variables shown in table 1 and the appendix table—tend to be correlated with each other to varying degrees. A nation with a large GDP may have a large volume of trade and high reserves; a larger population, other things being equal, is associated with a higher GDP; and so on. These correlations make interpretation of calculated quotas resulting from the formulas tendentious. One cannot interpret the coefficients multiplying a variable in the formula as a definitive indication of the "true" weight given to that variable in calculated quotas. This correlation issue has been extensively discussed within the IMF; see, for example, IMF (2000d, 2000f).

ability of its current account transactions and net long-term capital flows). The review group proposed giving twice as much weight to a nation's ability-to-contribute variable as to the variable measuring external vulnerability.[128]

The 2001, 2002, and 2003 Executive Board discussions generated "broad support for a [quota] formula that is simpler and more transparent than the traditional formulas." The majority sense of the Board as of the summer of 2003 was that a quota formula should be based on updated traditional economic and financial variables and comprise at most four variables, including GDP as the most important indicator of a country's economic size, along with measures of openness, variability of current receipts and net capital flows, and reserves." [129] The Board acknowledged that quota formulas should pay attention to the two general considerations emphasized by the Quota Formula Review Group, namely, the "creditor" perspective (a nation's ability to contribute resources to the IMF usable for lending) and the "debtor" perspective (a nation's need to borrow resources from the IMF for balance-of-payments financing). The specific two-variable recommendation of the review group was not accepted, however, apparently because it would have caused a significant *increase* in the aggregate quota share of the industrial countries.[130]

The 2000 report of the Quota Formula Review Group alluded only in passing to population as a variable to be included in quota formulas. The executive summary of the group's report did indicate that one member of the group "supports population as a third variable to give poor countries relatively greater voting power." An aside in the body of the report noted that "inclusion of a separate population variable would give greater weight to more populous countries, which perhaps [*sic*] could be justified on the grounds that the international community should move toward a system in which individuals begin to count as such in global decision-making."[131] But the report did not seriously focus on population as an indicator of relative position in the world economy. As far as the public documents reveal, moreover, the possibility of including population as a formula variable received no attention at all in the subsequent Executive Board discussions.

Notwithstanding neglect of this issue in IMF documents and public discourse, a fundamental rationale exists for according some weight to pop-

128. IMF (2000d, 2000f).
129. IMF (2003f).
130. Van Houtven (2002, p. 8).
131. IMF (2000d), paragraphs 8 and 100d; see also paragraph 109 and its footnote.

ulation in measures of relative position in the world economy. When considering the geographical allocation of votes or political influence among jurisdictions *within an individual nation*, citizens—not to mention politicians and philosophers—all tend to accept the premise that the primary criterion should be the number of people residing in a jurisdiction, not its aggregate income or output or wealth. Nations whose cultures and government structures are not conditioned by democratic presumptions may be a partial exception to that presumption. Nonetheless, within a large majority of nations the principle if not always the practice of "one person, one vote" is now widely accepted. Imagine asking a typical American whether the number of votes cast in federal elections in Vermont relative to those cast in New York should depend on the relative incomes of Vermont and New York residents rather than on the numbers of adults living in those states.[132]

The fact that the principle of one person, one vote is widely accepted within nations today does not, of course, constitute a convincing rationale that the same principle should determine the allocation of IMF quota and voting shares. As discussed below, in today's world polity it would be neither politically feasible nor economically desirable to give dominant weight to relative populations in formulas for allocating voting power within international institutions such as the IMF and World Bank. To rationalize a *zero* weight for relative populations, however, requires complete neglect of the principle of one person, one vote. Eventually, reflecting its gradually increasing salience within nations, that principle is certain to become increasingly relevant even on a world level.

Concurrently with their study of alternative quota formulas during 2002, the executive directors were required to make a recommendation to the Board of Governors to conclude the twelfth general review of quotas. Their recommendation, announced in January 2003, was for no increase in total quotas and no selective adjustments in members' quotas. The deci-

132. Of course the principle of one person, one vote is not fully respected in practice today within individual nations. For all nations it has a complex, checkered history. In the early history of the United States, the Constitutional Convention of 1787–88 was able to reach the so-called great compromise among small and large states only by agreeing that each state would have two senators regardless of the size of the state's population; the heart of the so-called "sectional compromise" among slavery and antislavery states was to count slaves as three-fifths of a person for the computation of populations governing the allocation among states of seats in the House of Representatives. The size-of-Senate compromise endures to this day. Slavery and its implications for the federal government became the central problem for the next seventy, turbulent years of U.S. history, and the sectional compromise was ultimately amended only after the bloody Civil War of 1861–65.

sion not to increase aggregate quotas was justified by stating that "the IMF's current liquidity position remains adequate by historical standards" and hence "there is no need for a quota increase."[133] The United States opposed any increase; the U.S. effective veto ensured that no agreement for an increase could be reached. The decision not to increase total quotas was doubtless also influenced by the political difficulty of reaching agreement on appropriate selective adjustments in quota shares.

Adjustments in Quota Shares

The distribution of IMF quota shares existing in 2004 and the closely related distribution of shares in voting power, essentially unchanged from the shares prevailing in 1999–2000, cannot be defended—at least not plausibly defended—as a satisfactory reflection of members' relative positions in the world economy. Nor will trends in world politics allow the 2004 quota shares to be sustained over time. Ultimately, adjustments in shares will be required as part of reforms in the governance of the IMF and the World Bank.

No governance problem for the IMF and World Bank is politically more contentious. Member nations whose incomes are growing rapidly or that have large populations argue for increases in their quota shares. Members with already high relative shares, especially those countries whose shares are high today because they received initially generous shares at the outset in 1948, drag their feet and resist decreases. Sophisticated rationalizations, horse trading among members that leads to side bargains, and the exercise of raw political power all play a part in the discussions of prospective changes in shares. Changes in shares force member nations to play a zero-sum game: an increase in one member's share necessarily requires a reduction in the share of one or more other members.

The contention that quota shares for some nations are inappropriate—"out of line"—is strongly suggested by the simple comparisons in table 1 and in the appendix table.[134] Examination of the results for actual quotas relative to quotas calculated from various existing or proposed formulas

133. IMF (2003f, 2003g).

134. IMF quotas were not changed between 1999 and 2004 (apart from a selective adjustment in the People's Republic of China's quota because of the consolidation of Hong Kong into China and apart from very small adjustments for new member nations and the delay of a few small nations in taking up their proposed quotas from the eleventh general review). Hence the distribution of quota shares in 2004 was essentially the same as that shown in the last column of table 1 and the quota columns of the table in the appendix table.

provides more detailed evidence.[135] The official IMF documents discussing this matter contain numerous references to (and examples of) members whose calculated quotas are substantially above their actual quotas. Given the political sensitivities, the official documents tend to be silent about members whose calculated quotas are substantially *less* than their actual quotas.[136]

The selective adjustments in quotas and voting power that ultimately will be required are easy to state in broad terms, albeit inordinately challenging to negotiate. For developing nations in the aggregate, the share of total quotas should increase. Among the developing nations, some individual members' quota shares should increase much more than those of others. Many developing nations in Asia should be among the group receiving large share increases. The biggest diminutions in quota shares and voting power should come out of nations in western Europe. The shares of the United States, and probably also of Canada, also should decline.

The aggregate share of developing nations in total IMF quotas did rise significantly beginning in the 1960s. From a level of 23 to 24 percent before the 1960s, the share rose to 30.7 percent by the end of 1972, 36.3 percent by year-end 1984, 37.5 percent by year-end 1992, and 38.5 percent by year-end 2001.[137] Much of that increase stemmed from the surge of new member nations being assigned a quota for the first time. Another part resulted from selective increases in the shares of rapidly growing emerging market and developing nations. Notwithstanding that upward adjustment over time, there exists a widespread perception, especially among the developing countries themselves, that actual quota shares give too much weight to past historical quotas and that quota shares calculated from the quota formulas give too much weight to relative incomes and relative trade volumes and not enough weight to other variables—notably, relative populations—that would raise the share of developing nations.

---

135. See, for example, IMF (2000d; 2001a, particularly table 6; 2002a).

136. One exception is an August 2003 Public Information Notice (IMF, 2003f) which included the following: "[Executive Directors] underscored that a new quota formula would make a significant difference in measuring the out-of-lineness of the quotas of individual countries. Many Directors also observed that, for a number of countries, actual quota shares are considerably lower than calculated quota shares, *almost regardless of specific formulas, whereas the opposite appears to be true for many other countries*" [emphasis added].

137. *Turbulent Waters*, table 4-1. Table 1 in this essay uses quotas as *proposed* in the eleventh quinquennial review; among other minor complexities, not all IMF members had taken up their eleventh review quota increases by the end of 2001.

That perception is essentially correct. Although no definitive method exists of calibrating the relative positions of nations in the world economy, all objective methods point to the existence of significant anomalies between the quota shares of the industrial and the developing nations. Significant anomalies in relative quota shares are also present within the groups of the industrial and the developing nations.

The quota shares of European nations, especially those belonging to the European Union, raise complicated issues that lie at the heart of the quota adjustment problem. After the quota increase approved in the eleventh general review, the combined quota share of the fifteen pre-enlargement European Union members was 30.1 percent. Their shares of world GDP at market exchange rates and world population were only 28.2 percent and 6.3 percent, respectively. The actual quotas of numerous European industrialized nations as of 2004 substantially exceeded their quotas as calculated on the basis of most existing or proposed quota formulas. If quota formulas were to give any weight to population, the "out-of-lineness" of several European members would be more prominent still.

In principle, IMF members can agree to a selective adjustment of quota shares outside the context of a quinquennial general review. When a new member joins the IMF and World Bank, for example, it typically has been possible to arrange for a straightforward adjustment in all members' quota shares.[138] And on a few occasions selective adjustments were made to an existing member's quota outside of a general review. A special adjustment was made in Saudi Arabia's quota in 1981 to improve the IMF's liquidity in conjunction with a borrowing agreement with Saudi Arabia. The quota for the People's Republic of China was selectively increased in early 2001 following the consolidation of Hong Kong (not a formal IMF member and hence without a quota) into China, which created a strong case at the time for raising China's quota by some amount. To agree on the exact size of the increase for China's quota required delicate negotiations. Once that increase was agreed on, however, total quotas were increased by that amount; China's quota share was increased from 2.22 percent to 2.98 percent, and every other member's quota share correspondingly declined slightly.[139]

138. A new member must be given a quota. Determining an appropriate size for its quota vis-à-vis those of other members (making a judgment in practice about that nation's position in the world economy relative to existing members) is politically contentious. Once a compromise is reached on that issue, however, all the other members recognize that their quota shares will decline very slightly, reflecting the entrance of the new member.

139. The agreement with China was reported in the *IMF Morning Press* (January 5, 2001). For a complete listing of selective quota increases that have occurred outside the context of general reviews,

Although selective adjustments in quota shares could in principle be agreed to outside the context of a general review, it has proven less difficult to implement selective adjustments in combination with general quota increases for all members. When a "package" including a general increase in quotas is negotiated, each member can still perceive that it receives some benefit even though its quota share may decline as a result. Some benefit may be believed to occur because the IMF as a whole is perceived to be able to operate more efficiently with generally larger resources. More important, members who are borrowers or potential borrowers can perceive a tangible benefit to themselves if their quotas and hence their potential access to IMF lending increase (the larger absolute size of their quota offsetting at least to some extent any reduction in their quota share).

Quota adjustments occurring during general reviews typically have had three components. An equiproportional component has been allocated to every member according to its existing quota share. A second component, also resulting in a change in the quota of every member, has consisted of selective increases with the distribution of those increases made in proportion to the calculated quota shares resulting from the quota formulas. The third component of the total increase has been a negotiated amount of ad hoc, special increases, selectively allocated to particular members whose quotas are deemed to be especially far "out of line."[140]

In most general reviews, the largest part of the total increase in quotas has been allocated equiproportionally to existing quotas. In the seventh review (agreed to in 1978), fully 98 percent of the total increase was equiproportional; the equiproportional element in the Eleventh Review (1999) was 75 percent. The average equiproportional element in past quota increases was 70 percent of the total. Plainly, when the largest part of quota increases is allocated in proportion to existing quotas, inertia from the past guarantees that changes in quota shares will remain minor. Accordingly, "actual shares have converged only a little toward calculated shares over time and, for countries that have experienced relatively rapid growth, actual quotas continue to lag behind economic developments."[141]

If more rapid progress in adjusting quota shares is to be made in future general reviews, a key requirement of that progress will be to hold the equiproportional element to a markedly smaller fraction of the total increase

---

see IMF (2003e, table A.2). Any change in quotas requires an 85 percent majority of the total voting power and no member's quota can be changed without the member's consent.

140. The details of the quota increase for the eleventh review are given in a preceding footnote.

141. IMF (2001a, paragraph 59).

than in the past. Ideally, the equiproportional component might be as little as 10 to 20 percent of the total. Tentative indications from IMF
executive directors about the thirteenth general review, scheduled for com-
pletion not later than January 2008, can be interpreted as favoring a quota
increase with characteristics that lean in that direction but that probably will
not reduce the equiproportional component by a large enough amount.[142]

If agreement could be reached to make selective (non-equiproportional)
increases the largest fraction of total increases, the formulas for calculating
quotas and for allocating the selective increases would play a more influential role than in the past. The IMF's executive directors said in June 2002
that they had reached an understanding on "broad principles for arriving
at an alternative quota formula." They described further general progress in
2003.[143] Unfortunately, the understanding as of 2003 appeared not to go
far enough. In particular, as discussed above, the EDs appeared unwilling
to give population any role in the quota formulas.

Any quota formula that includes as variables only GDP at market
exchange rates, trade values, and reserves cannot yield calculated quotas that
will lead to reductions in the quota shares of the industrial countries and
corresponding increases in the quota shares of developing nations. This
conclusion is abundantly clear from the analyses and illustrative calculations
conducted by the Quota Formula Review Group and subsequently by IMF
staff. Many of the formulas containing exclusively these variables in fact lead
to calculated *increases* in the quota shares of industrial countries and
decreases in the shares of developing nations. If a quota formula were to use
GDP on a purchasing power parity basis rather than at market exchange
rates, the calculated shares for some developing nations could show an
increase. But most executive directors, following the leanings of the review
group, reject the inclusion of PPP-based GDP in the quota formulas.

The status of quota formulas as of 2004 was therefore quite unsatisfac-
tory. It was not possible, on the basis of the existing formulas or the revised

142. The August 2003 Public Information Notice about quota distribution issues (IMF 2003f)
contains the following language: "In discussing how best to move forward toward achieving adjustments in quota shares, Directors recognized the potential benefits that a package of changes in quotas,
based on a new quota formula, could confer. They observed that significant adjustments in quota
shares have tended to take place in the context of general quota increases, given the opportunity that
general quota increases have provided to include elements that benefit the membership as a whole.
Most Directors therefore saw considerable merit in a package that would involve—in the context of the
next general quota increase—the following elements: a general increase with a relatively large selective
element allocated by means of a new quota formula; [and] ad hoc quota increases aimed at addressing
the clearest cases of out-of-lineness."

143. IMF (2002a, 2002b, 2003e, 2003f).

formulas that the EDs were considering, to obtain calculated quotas that would significantly increase the aggregate quota share of the developing nations and the individual quota shares of the most populous developing nations. A desirable revision of the formulas would have included population as an additional variable. The EDs, however, apparently had ruled out such a change.

To repeat, it would be inadvisable—and of course politically infeasible—to go so far as to make population the dominant variable in a new quota formula. The resources needed to fund lending by the IMF and World Bank are broadly available in the world more or less in proportion to the incomes and wealths, not the populations, of contributing members. The IMF and World Bank are world *financial* institutions. They cannot perform several of their key functions without adequate financial resources. Thoughtful analysts all tend to agree, therefore, that a variable such as GDP has to be a major—perhaps *the* major—variable in quota formulas. GDP measured at market exchange rates, moreover, is probably a better indicator of ability to contribute usable financial resources than GDP measured on the basis of purchasing power parity.

To agree that population cannot be the variable with the most important weight in quota formulas, however, is not to agree that a population variable should be excluded altogether. And if GDP at market exchange rates or variables highly correlated with that measure continue to be the dominant or only variables included in quota formulas, the interests of wealthy and creditor nations will continue to receive excessive emphasis.

My view is that population should be one of the variables in any quota formula and should have a significant but not dominant weight in the formula calculations. According some weight to population would marginally help in the short run to increase quota shares for many individual developing nations and for developing nations in the aggregate.

Over a much longer run, the relative emphasis on population in quota formulas should even rise further from an initial modest beginning. Pressures to adjust the governance of international institutions to reflect more fully the widely professed democratic principle of one person, one vote will push the IMF and its shareholder governments in that direction. The world in the first few decades of the twenty-first century is certainly not ready for a form of governance of international financial institutions based primarily on that principle. But if the experiences of the democracies in western Europe, North America, and Japan are any guide, global decisionmaking over the very long run will need to accord gradually increasing weight to individual persons regardless of their geographical jurisdiction and regardless of their incomes and wealths.

Selective adjustments in quota shares based on a new quota formula should be an important component of quota increases decided in future quinquennial reviews. But ad hoc selective adjustments for some individual members also will continue to be needed. Such adjustments will, as in the past, require complex political horse trading.[144] But such negotiations are probably the only way to make substantial progress in correcting the quota shares that are most egregiously out of line. Ideally, such selective adjustments in quota shares might include decreases as well as increases in quotas themselves. It may well prove to be too demanding politically, however, to require members whose actual quota shares are substantially higher than their calculated quota shares to accept an absolute decline in the non-equiproportional component of a general quota increase. That would be, nevertheless, an appropriate policy in principle.

Adjustment in Basic Votes

Adjusting the quota shares of developing nations upward over time is the surest method of enhancing the "voice" of smaller nations and developing nations in the governance of the IMF and the World Bank. But a complementary—not substitute—action would be to increase the number of basic votes allocated to each IMF member independently of increases in quotas, thereby augmenting the voting strength of the members with the smallest quotas.

When the Bretton Woods institutions were first established, basic votes in the IMF were a significant factor in the voting strength of member states. In 1944–45, for example, the basic votes of all IMF members were 11.3 percent of total voting power. With many new members joining the IMF and total quotas being increased only moderately in the 1950s and early 1960s, basic votes as a proportion of total votes even rose, reaching 14 percent by 1965. The number of basic votes per member, however, has never been changed. After the mid-1960s, the total of quotas increased substantially, exerting much greater influence on total voting power than did

144. On the sensitive point of ad hoc selective increases, the July 2003 document reviewing quota issues (IMF, 2003e) blandly observes: "Ad hoc increases for particular countries have been used to address the most serious disparities in the quota distribution. However, determining the eligibility of members for ad hoc increases in their quotas is difficult since such increases tend to change the ranking of countries in the Fund; they are borne proportionally by all other members; and they inevitably create issues of comparability with other members not considered eligible but whose quotas do not adequately reflect their position in the world economy" (paragraph 57).

increases in basic votes associated with adding new members. Thus basic votes declined sharply in significance after the 1960s. Quotas themselves became the dominant determinant of voting strength. Basic votes as a proportion of total votes fell to 5.6 percent by 1983 and to only 2.1 percent by 1998–2003. The waning significance of basic votes has had the effect of reducing the voting power of smaller members and hence their ability to influence IMF decisionmaking.[145]

Executive directors and IMF staff have from time to time discussed the erosion in significance of basic votes. Smaller members have complained about the erosion. But up through 2004, no steps had been agreed on to address the issue. The primary reason for inaction was the lack of interest or outright opposition of larger members. The number of basic votes for each member cannot be changed without an amendment to the Articles of Agreement, and such an amendment requires the approval of three-fifths of the members and an 85 percent majority of total votes.

If sufficient support for an amendment of the articles could be obtained, an increase in basic votes could be implemented at any time. But as with other aspects of quotas and voting power, the likelihood of generating broad support for an increase in basic votes would be enhanced by incorporating a proposed change into a "package" agreement negotiated as part of a general review of quotas.[146]

Making selective upward adjustments in the quotas for medium-sized or small IMF members without changing the quotas of the largest IMF members would alter the ability of the largest members to exercise a veto over key IMF decisions, which require an 85 percent majority of the total voting power. If changes in basic votes could be implemented, they also would somewhat diminish the ability of the largest members to veto key decisions. But the size of that diminution would be small unless basic votes were increased by a large amount. Correspondingly, changes in basic votes would

145. Basic votes in the World Bank as a share of total votes declined from 9.01 percent in 1945 to 2.84 percent in 2002. For discussion, see World Bank and IMF, Development Committee (2003a, 2003b), IMF (2003e), and Buira (2002, 2003).

146. Past discussions in the Executive Board and elsewhere about the erosion in relative importance of basic votes suggest that remedial action is unlikely to be adequate if sought through use of the existing or new quota formulas. In July 2003, for example, an IMF staff paper observed that "in principle, the erosion . . . could be addressed by providing a 'compensating' increase in the quotas of those members that are affected by the declining importance of basic votes. However, this approach would involve difficult judgments about the eligibility and size of compensating quota increases" (IMF, 2003e, para. 36). If executive directors sought to mitigate the erosion in importance of basic votes through adjustments in quota formulas, they would find it still more difficult to achieve consensus on a new quota formula. These aspects of possible changes in basic votes are discussed in IMF (2002a, 2002d).

not dramatically raise the aggregate voting strength of developing nations unless the changes were large.

As of 2003, developing nations other than transition economies had, in the aggregate, 31.7 percent of the total voting power and a slightly lower share of total quotas. The largest member, the United States, had 17.1 percent of votes (17.4 percent of quotas); the fifteen members of the European Union had 29.8 percent of the votes (30.1 percent of quotas). If basic votes for each member were doubled from 250 to 500 votes, that action would raise the proportion of basic votes in total votes from 2.1 percent to 4.1 percent; the aggregate share of nontransition developing countries in voting power would rise to 32.5 percent; the U.S. share in votes would fall to 16.7 percent. Suppose agreement could be reached to restore the relative significance of basic votes to 11.3 percent of the total, the fraction prevailing at the outset when the IMF was established in 1948. In that hypothetical scenario, the required basic votes for each member would have to rise to 1,488; nontransition developing nations would have 35.3 percent of the votes (compared with their current 31.7 percent); and the voting strength of the United States would fall to 15.5 percent.[147]

Such illustrative calculations suggest that an increase in basic votes could help raise the voting strength of developing nations in the aggregate. Moreover, such an increase need not arouse sharp opposition from the largest IMF members because of fears that their voting shares would fall so far as to endanger their ability to organize vetoes of decisions inimical to their interests. Even from the perspective of developing nations, however, an increase in basic votes could be a mixed blessing. A large stand-alone increase in basic votes would probably displease the biggest developing countries. Although such a change would raise the voting power of developing nations as a group, the benefits would accrue primarily to the smallest developing nations. If given an either-or choice, nations such as China, India, Brazil, and Mexico would prefer selective increases in their quotas and quota shares rather than an across-the-board large increase in basic votes.

The thirteenth general review of quotas (to be concluded by January 2008, if not before) will be a felicitous opportunity to reverse the gradual erosion of the importance of basic votes. A proposed increase in basic votes should be packaged with a general increase in quotas and a set of ad hoc selective increases more ambitious than those attempted in recent reviews.

147. These calculations of the effects of hypothetical increases in basic votes are reported in IMF (2002a, table 10).

The general increase in quotas should itself be dominated by selective adjustments allocated in proportion to deviations of actual quotas from calculated quotas, with the calculated quotas stemming from a revised quota formula. The published views of the executive directors in 2003 about a possible prospective package of changes for the thirteenth general review indicated support for alterations in basic votes.[148]

The secretariat of the Group of Twenty-Four, speaking for the bulk of developing nations, supports a one-time reversal of the erosion of the relative importance of basic votes. Thereafter, as a long-run measure for improving governance of the IMF and the World Bank, the G-24 secretariat suggests that subsequent general reviews of quotas should include an adjustment in basic votes that would increase basic votes by the same proportion as total quotas.[149] This constructive suggestion could help to prevent a recurrence of the past tendency for the salience of basic votes to decline. (That policy, just as any form of change in basic votes, cannot be implemented without amending the IMF Articles of Agreement.)

Adjustments in Executive Directors and Constituencies

A further complementary approach to enhance the voice of smaller and developing nations in the governance of the IMF and the World Bank is to implement structural and procedural changes to provide greater opportunities for such nations to present their views and effectively advocate their interests.

One class of ideas is to augment support for the multination constituencies in the executive boards of the IMF and the World Bank. It has been suggested, for example, that the executive directors of multination constituencies might be given extra technological support to facilitate communication with national capitals. They might be given further technical, research, and administrative support—for example, by increasing the staff in the constituency offices. Still another proposal has been to add a second alternate executive director to some or all of the multination constituencies. These suggestions seem likely to have positive though probably only mod-

148. The Public Information Notice of August 29, 2003 (IMF 2003f), for example, mentions "an increase in basic votes specifically aimed at correcting the erosion of the voting power of the smallest members." The PIN also observed, "Most Directors indicated their willingness to consider an increase in basic votes outside the context of a general quota increase, as a direct means of responding to calls for enhancing the voice of developing countries, in particular of the smallest members, although it was acknowledged that, at this stage, the required majority does not exist." Similar remarks are included in World Bank and IMF, Development Committee (2003b).

149. Buira (2002).

est net benefits. The costs of implementing them probably also would be small. Some of the suggestions were already being put into practice as of 2003. They merit continued study and implementation.

A second group of suggestions focuses on strengthening the effectiveness of the constituency system. Increased communication and interaction across the multination constituencies might enhance consensus building on issues of interest and thereby increase the influence of these constituencies in Board decisions. For individual constituencies, the rotation of the executive director's chair among the members of the constituency could be speeded up or slowed down. The composition of the twenty-four constituencies themselves also could be reorganized. Numerous developing nations are part of a "mixed" constituency containing both developed and developing members. Some developing nations in mixed constituencies may believe that their influence would be less diluted in a constituency composed only of developing nations. Reshuffling of the constituencies, either toward fewer or more mixed constituencies, is possible with no change in the Articles of Agreement, but it would require the mutual agreement of a large number of member nations.

A third, more radical suggestion is to increase the existing number of executive directors—and hence constituencies—while substantially altering the composition of the multination constituencies. Increasing the size of the IMF Executive Board would reduce the number of members in some multination constituencies. And, depending on how it was carried out, it could slightly or moderately raise the number of constituencies headed by a developing nation or composed exclusively of developing nations. Decisions in the IMF to increase the number of executive directors require an 85 percent majority of the total voting power (decisions in the World Bank require an 80 percent majority). The potential benefits from raising the number of executive directors in the IMF and the World Bank, in particular the greater opportunity for developing nations to exercise "voice," need to be weighed against the potential costs. Costs from enlarging the Boards include the budgetary expenses and a possible loss in efficiency and effectiveness of decisionmaking.

The executive boards existing in 2004, with their twenty-four constituencies, were already large. In the abstract, a strong case might be made for reducing rather than increasing their size. In practice, however, an actual reduction in the number of executive directors would be difficult to achieve politically.[150] The overriding political obstacle stems from the existing posi-

150. Because the United States has enough votes to prevent attainment of an 85 percent majority of the voting power, the United States could vote against any change in the Executive Board of which

tion of European nations in the IMF and the World Bank, and in particular those nations belonging to the European Union. The issue of the representation of European nations in international institutions, because it is so thorny, was effectively kept under wraps in general public discussions in recent years. But that issue cannot be postponed indefinitely.

The Problem of Europe and the European Union

Several European nations are, as discussed earlier, among the most prominent IMF members whose quota shares and voting powers are "out of line" on the high side. As of the eleventh and twelfth reviews of quotas, the fifteen members of the European Union had 29.8 percent of the total voting power in the IMF, a very much larger share than, for example, the United States (17.1 percent) or all ninety-eight developing nations in Asia, the Middle East, and Africa (23.7 percent). Yet the fifteen-member EU share of world GDP at market exchange rates, 28.2 percent, was slightly less than the U.S. share of 29.5 percent and only about one-fifth to one-fourth greater than the share of all 160 developing and transition nations combined (23.1 percent).

An analogous imbalance exists in the numbers of Executive Board constituencies dominated by European nations. At least eight of the twenty-four IMF constituencies are regularly headed by a western European nation (Germany, the United Kingdom, France, Italy, Belgium, the Netherlands, Denmark, and Switzerland). In 2003–04, nine of the twenty-four constituencies—three-eighths—were headed by a western European nation.[151] The executive directors for these nine constituencies together controlled 40.8 percent of the total votes. When members belonging to a given multi-nation constituency hold differing views on a subject, the executive director can and often does put the differing views in the record. As noted earlier, however, the executive director cannot split his or her vote. That practice and the related tradition of consensus decisionmaking in the Board mean that the voices of the developing nation or non-European

---

it disapproves provided it is willing to incur the political displeasure of other nations. Because the Articles of Agreement specify a twenty-member Board, the United States with its effective veto even has the power (by withholding its vote) to force the number of Board constituencies back to twenty from the existing twenty-four. Such an action by the United States, however, would have grave political repercussions.

151. The constituency headed by Spain in 2003–04 contains Mexico, Venezuela, and several Central American countries. When the executive director chair for that constituency rotates in the biannual elections, the ED is sometimes a Mexican or Venezuelan national.

members of the nine constituencies headed by western European nations tend to be diluted.

The political difficulties with the status of European nations go even deeper because of the European Union. Given the existence of the evolving European Union, the issue of quota shares for European nations belonging to the union is entangled with the issue of how European Union countries should be represented in the IMF and the World Bank. The key representation issues concern the appropriate world total of separate constituencies in the Executive Board, the number of constituencies dominated by EU members, and which EU members should have a constituency and executive director to themselves.

Should the European Union be represented by just one executive director, with EU members belonging to just one constituency (with an extra-large quota share and share of the total votes)? That status may be appropriate several decades into the future, but it is not now politically feasible and probably not even desirable for the short or medium runs. Yes, European monetary union with its common currency has been implemented for twelve of the EU nations. Monetary policy for the monetary union is now determined by the European Central Bank. Yes, the euro area now has a common short-term interest rate. For many aspects of financial supervision and prudential oversight, EU nations are gradually adopting common standards. Notwithstanding progress toward economic and financial integration, however, *political* integration has proceeded slowly, even for the fifteen EU members existing in 2003 and early 2004. The enlargement of the European Union to twenty-five member nations in May 2004 will make it that much more difficult for the union to act with unanimity in international financial matters. The unresolved issues in the Treaty of Nice, negotiated painfully in December 2000, and the failure to move forward on a new draft constitution at the meeting in December 2003, underscore the fact that for the shorter run it is premature—on political grounds—to expect European Union members to agree to be represented in the IMF and the World Bank through a single constituency.

Something less sweeping, however, should be done about the position of European Union members in the IMF, even in the shorter run. There is a strong case on economic and financial grounds for adjusting downward the aggregate quota shares of the twelve EU members participating in the European monetary union. And the U.K. quota is still relatively high judged against the variables in existing or proposed new quota formulas. The long-standing tradition of parity between the French and U.K. quota shares should probably be abandoned. Denmark and Sweden, the other two non-EMU nations of the fifteen-member pre-enlargement European Union, should perhaps see a downward adjustment in their quota shares, as should some other non-EU European nations. The United States, Canada, and Japan should be willing to make adjustments in their quota shares in conjunction with the adjustments in European quota shares.

For the Executive Boards of the IMF and World Bank, the case seems especially persuasive for reducing the number of constituencies dominated by western European members relative to the total number of constituencies. The first best method for accomplishing this adjustment would be to keep the Executive Boards at their existing size of twenty-four members (or even to reduce the number slightly) while reshuffling the constituencies so that European members would dominate several fewer than the existing nine. Efficiency and cost arguments would justify a reduction in the number of executive directors. But negotiating a reduction in the size of the Boards would be extremely difficult. Smaller European members would fight it doggedly. A second-best approach would be to acknowledge the probability that European members will not budge from holding on to their constituencies and therefore to negotiate an increase in the size of the Board by a few executive directors, say two to four more. Either the first or second-best approach would entail delicate negotiations among all members, not least among developing nations, to ensure an appropriate agreed-on regrouping of constituencies.[152]

Aggregate Size of IMF Resources

The distribution of quotas and voting rights across nations is the most important and certainly the most difficult governance issue facing the IMF

---

152. Decisions to change the size of the Executive Board and the existing constituencies require at least an 85 percent majority of the total voting power. Given the existing distribution of voting power, the United States has a de facto veto on changes in the size of the Board. If the political will could be mustered to resize the Board and regroup the constituencies, it would be beneficial at the same time to reconsider the now somewhat anomalous provision in the Articles of Agreement that the members with the five largest quotas can *appoint* their own executive director whereas the other members grouped together in constituencies must *elect* their ED. As noted already, as of 2003–04 there were eight single-member constituencies, three of which (Saudi Arabia, China, and Russia) were deemed "elected" rather than appointed. An amendment of the articles might specify that any IMF member with a quota share larger than some cut-off percentage (say, 3 percent) would be presumed to select its own executive director and to have a constituency entirely to itself. Getting political agreement for such an amendment would, of course, be difficult and could eventually cause one or more of the existing single-member constituencies (for example, Russia) to lose that preferred status.

and the World Bank today. The linked issue of the aggregate size of quotas, however, also is important and contentious.

The IMF lends funds contributed to it by members in proportion to their quotas. The amounts that members can borrow are functions of their quotas. Therefore the aggregate amount of financial resources that can be used in IMF lending intermediation is critically dependent on the aggregate total of IMF quotas. Under appropriate conditions, the IMF can supplement its quota resources by borrowing under the contingent commitments of the New Arrangements to Borrow (NAB) and the General Arrangements to Borrow (GAB). But quotas remain the dominant source of funds.[153]

The IMF Articles of Agreement emphasize that an important purpose of the IMF is "to give confidence to members by making the general resources of the Fund temporarily available to them under adequate safeguards, thus providing them with opportunity to correct maladjustments in their balance of payments without resorting to measures destructive of national or international prosperity." The articles also require a general review of quotas at intervals of not more than every five years. Neither the articles nor the IMF's established procedures, however, specify clearly how the size of aggregate quotas should be determined. Guidance in quantitative terms is lacking. Throughout the IMF's history, the appropriate size of quotas has always been controversial. When the IMF looks ahead beyond the short run, therefore, the aggregate amount of financial resources available to lend to member nations with balance-of-payments difficulties is always somewhat uncertain.

One rough way that analysts have tried to gauge the appropriate size of total IMF quotas is to compare total quotas to various measures of world economic variables. The presumption implicit in this method is that IMF quotas should grow secularly over time pari passu with growth in the world economy and financial system. But views invariably differ about which world variables are appropriate benchmarks for comparison. Accordingly, judgments about the needed size of IMF quotas depend critically on the choice of those variables.

---

153. In 1962 the largest industrial nations established the General Arrangements to Borrow, a contingent mechanism permitting the IMF to buttress its resources by borrowing funds from them in defined emergency circumstances. The General Arrangements to Borrow were effectively expanded to include Saudi Arabia in 1983. A second borrowing option for the IMF, known as the New Arrangements to Borrow (NAB), was negotiated among twenty-five IMF member nations in 1996 and became operational in November 1998.

The differing growth rates for world macroeconomic variables suggest how difficult the analytical comparisons can be. Since World War II, cross-border transactions have grown faster than domestic transactions. Financial activity has grown faster than real sector activity in goods and services. Over the period 1964–89, for example, several measures of cross-border financial activity grew at a compound rate of roughly 25 percent per year; for industrial nations, nominal trade grew at a 12.4 percent annual rate while nominal output grew at a 10.8 percent rate. For later years, 1989 through 2001, the differences in growth rates were somewhat less dramatic, but cross-border trade in goods and services still increased faster than output and cross-border financial activity still increased more rapidly than cross-border trade.[154]

If quotas since the establishment of the IMF should have grown as fast as cross-border financial transactions, they would have had to increase very rapidly indeed. Was such rapid growth needed for robust growth in the world economy? Probably not.

In the first several decades of the IMF's existence, national financial systems were still fairly segmented and numerous border restraints inhibited capital flows. In more recent decades, private multinational institutions and private capital markets developed rapidly and cross-border transfers of savings from one national financial reservoir to another could be made much more readily than before. Therefore the relative need for IMF lending—which is, again, *intergovernmental* lending intermediation—probably did not grow nearly as rapidly. Many more nations than before, including their governments, now have access to foreign savings through private capital markets and private financial institutions located abroad. That access has been, and should have been, a substitute for borrowing through the IMF.

An argument working in the opposite direction, however, maintains that the increasing financial integration of the world economy has heightened the volatility of cross-border capital flows and hence raised the probability of occasional financial turbulence. To that extent, the needs for occasional borrowing from the IMF could have increased rather than decreased in relative importance. Certainly the increasing openness of national economies has exposed them relatively more to external shocks. We know from the Latin American debt crises of the 1980s, the so-called Tequila Crisis set off by Mexico in 1994–95, and the Asian financial crises

154. *Turbulent Waters* (chapter 5, especially pp. 135–45).

of the late 1990s that financial turbulence today can more easily be spread by contagion and can threaten to become systemic.

Weighing the various arguments is problematic. There is no sound basis for a conclusion. No consensus exists. Nonetheless I am inclined to believe that there was no compelling need in recent decades for IMF quotas to grow as fast as international financial activity.

Perhaps IMF quotas, and hence the resources available for IMF lending, should have grown only as fast as cross-border trade in goods and services? That more moderate presumption, too, could conceivably suggest too high a secular growth rate for quotas. Yes, to the extent that nations have become gradually more exposed to external shocks while payments imbalances have become more variable, IMF quotas perhaps should have kept pace with cross-border trade for current account transactions. Yes, the possibility of financial contagion and systemic crises cannot be judged well by focusing on secular trends in cross-border transactions. Even so, to err on the conservative side, suppose we presume that IMF quotas need not have grown as rapidly as cross-border trade.

A still more modest presumption for the secular growth in IMF quotas would argue that total quotas, adjusted for inflation, should have kept pace with secular growth in the real (inflation-adjusted) value of world output (GDP). Such a presumption begs some significant issues about the appropriate level of quotas in periods of severe worldwide price inflation. The same uncertainties and lack of consensus apply to that guideline. But might it serve as a rough and ready benchmark for analytical comparisons?

A broad sense of the historical relationships between IMF quotas, GDP at market exchange rates, cross-border trade, and international reserves can be gleaned from table 2. The columns report figures for the four variables associated with selected general reviews of quotas. The data for earlier reviews are taken from the 2000 report of the Quota Formula Review Group; the data in the final column, which pertain to the twelfth general review (concluded in early 2003), come from the IMF documents used in preparing table 1. In addition to the aggregate data, the table reports various ratios—for example, quotas as a percent of world GDP. Figure 1 shows graphically the development over time of the ratios of quotas to GDP and to external payments for cross-border trade.

The table and figure document the facts that IMF quotas in the six decades since the establishment of the IMF have grown less rapidly than the nominal value of world output—and much less rapidly than the nominal value of cross-border trade. No measures of aggregate cross-border financial

Table 2. *Aggregate IMF Quotas and Global Indicators for GDP, Cross-Border Trade, and International Reserves*

	Original 1944[a]	First review completed 1950[a]	Fourth review completed 1965[a]	Fifth review completed 1970[a]	Seventh review completed 1978[a]	Ninth review completed 1990[a]	Eleventh review completed 1998[a]	Twelfth review completed 2003[b]	World economic outlook projection for 2004[c]
Levels (billions of SDRs)									
Total IMF quotas	8.0	8.0	21.0	29.0	61.1	135.2	212.0	213.7	213.7
World GDP at market exchange rates	214	439	1,031	1,505	4,253	11,083	17,884	21,828	27,431
External payments (imports)	14	46	139	213	718	2,168	3,700	5,777	9,925
International reserves	27	36	57	65	185	391	768	1,152	1,687
Ratios (percent)									
Quotas as percent of GDP	3.74	1.82	2.04	1.93	1.44	1.22	1.19	0.98	0.78
Quotas as percent of external payments	57.14	17.39	15.11	13.62	8.51	6.24	5.73	3.70	2.15
Quotas as percent of reserves	29.63	22.22	36.84	44.62	33.03	34.58	27.59	18.55	12.67
External payments as percent of GDP	6.54	10.48	13.48	14.15	16.88	19.56	20.69	26.47	36.18
Reserves as percent of external payments	192.86	78.26	41.01	30.52	25.77	18.04	20.77	19.94	17.00

Sources: International Monetary Fund (2000d, 2002a, 2002c).

a. Data for GDP, external payments, and international reserves refer to the most recent period for which data were compiled for use during that quota review. See IMF (2000d, table 7).

b. Quotas were not increased in the Twelfth General Review. The difference between the Eleventh and Twelfth Review totals for quotas is explained by the fact that the People's Republic of China received a selective increase in its quota in 2001 and several small nations joined the IMF during 1999–2002.

c. Data are from IMF (2002a, statistical appendix annex table 1). The figure for GDP is for an average of the years 1997–99. The figure for external payments refers to an average for the years 1995–99 and is one-half of the sum of current receipts plus payments shown in the IMF source. The figure for international reserves refers to an average of end-month data during the year 1999. Data are taken from the final column of table 1 in IMF (2002c).

Figure 1. *IMF Quotas as Percent of Nominal World GDP and External Payments*

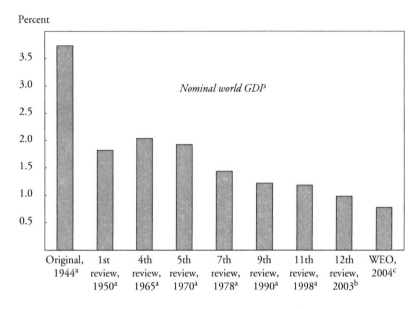

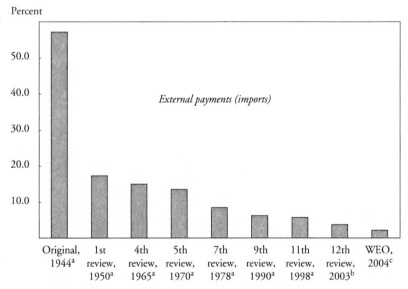

Sources and notes: See table 2, facing. Note that bars in these graphs correspond to columns in the table.

activity are readily available for the entire six decades. Were any such variable available, the decline in the ratio of quotas to that yardstick would have been, as emphasized earlier, still more dramatic than the declines evident in figure 1.

IMF quotas since the organization's inception, therefore, have fallen well short of even a modest interpretation of the presumption that quotas should increase proportionately with secular growth in the world economy and financial system. One way of dramatizing the point is to ask how large the total of IMF quotas would be if the presumption of growth in proportion to world GDP had been followed. If quotas in 2003 had been of the same size relative to world GDP (at market exchange rates) as at the creation of the IMF, they would have been nearly four times their actual value. Had quotas grown at the faster pace of aggregate world trade, they would have been some thirteen to fifteen times larger in 2003 than they actually were.

The preceding rough comparisons do not, of course, take into account many relevant considerations. For one thing, as earlier sections of this essay emphasize, the IMF itself has evolved with the world economy and has strengthened its capacities for surveillance and for the prevention of financial crises. Surveillance of individual members' policies through Article IV consultations and of systemic developments through supranational surveillance has, it is hoped, reduced some instances of payments imbalances that otherwise might have required borrowing from the IMF. Greater surveillance attention is now focused on nations' vulnerability to capital account stresses and financial instability. The transparency of many members' policies and of the IMF's own activities and assessments has been improved. In cooperation with other international financial institutions, the IMF has facilitated the development and use of international standards and codes of good practice—for example, for the prudential oversight of financial systems and fiscal and monetary policies. The strengthening of supranational surveillance has, other things being equal, reduced the need for increases in total IMF quotas.

For another thing, the IMF has modestly improved its capacities to handle balance-of-payments and financial crises when they occur. As discussed earlier, the IMF has somewhat streamlined and refocused the conditionality associated with members' borrowing. The facilities for borrowing were reviewed. Access policies were clarified. The Supplemental Reserve Facility and the Contingent Credit Lines facility were instituted (though the CCL was abandoned in 2003 as unsuccessful). The New Arrangements to Borrow were created to supplement the General Arrangements to Borrow, and both have enhanced the IMF's ability to mobilize additional funds quickly. These developments, like the gradual strengthening of surveillance, reduced the need for total IMF quotas to increase as fast as might otherwise have seemed preferable.

Analysis of the desirable size of increases in IMF quotas must also confront often-mentioned fears about the "moral hazard" associated with IMF lending. A number of IMF critics have argued that increases in IMF quotas could exacerbate moral-hazard incentives by encouraging member governments to borrow excessively from the IMF and encouraging private financial institutions to lend in an excessively risky manner because they believe that IMF lending in crises will create an undesirable "bail out" option. Such critics have also asserted that increases in IMF resources will undercut the efforts of the official world community to encourage greater and more constructive private sector involvement in crisis resolution.[155]

There is merit in carefully examining moral hazard aspects of the IMF's activities. Moral hazard difficulties inevitably arise from the collective-governance provision of management leadership and emergency lending during a financial crisis by a lender of last resort. But should society therefore forswear the provision of lender-of-last-resort support to the financial system? A few misguided individuals are tempted to answer yes. But the appropriate answer is, unambiguously, no. Private insurance companies do not accept the pervasiveness of moral hazard as a valid reason for not providing any insurance. Rather, the optimal behavior is to supply the insurance, combined with incentives designed to limit moral hazard. Vigilance is always needed to ensure that moral hazard incentives are kept within reasonable bounds. But the appropriate goal of sound public policy is to contain moral hazard, not to eliminate it completely.

Too often the critics of the IMF raise the moral hazard issues in a one-sided fashion. They fail to acknowledge that inadequate provision of resources to the IMF could curtail IMF lending that would prevent disorderly balance-of-payments adjustments and that would thereby avoid serious potential costs. An important purpose of the IMF, again, is to enable members "to correct maladjustments in their balance of payments *without resorting to measures destructive of national or international prosperity*" [emphasis added]. There also exists a tendency to overstate greatly the moral hazard incentives associated with increases in IMF quotas. "Moral hazard" should not become a bugaboo. Michael Mussa, who analyzed such

---

155. These issues are discussed in *Turbulent Waters* and in more detail in *Crisis Management for the World Financial System.*

problems for many years from within the IMF, argues correctly, I believe, that "concerns about moral hazard have been vastly exaggerated, and most of the proposals to deal with this purported problem . . . are unnecessary, unworkable, or fundamentally misguided."[156]

To judge the adequacy of quotas and the usability of its resources for lending, the IMF conducts monthly reviews of its "liquidity position." These reviews are a focused way of trying to determine prospective needs for members' borrowings. The reviews produce estimates of "forward commitment capacity" (FCC) for future periods. At the time of the twelfth general review of quotas during 2002, the Executive Board concluded, based on the then-current *World Economic Outlook* baseline scenario, that the IMF's liquidity position appeared "adequate for the period immediately ahead, barring unforeseen developments that could result in large new demands for Fund resources. However, . . . the demand for Fund resources is increasingly difficult to predict and a deterioration in the global economy could result in potential spikes in new commitments and credit outstanding that could exhaust the FCC from own resources and require possible activation of the borrowing arrangements."[157]

The regular reviews of the IMF's liquidity position provide a better guide to the need for resources over short runs than any comparisons of secular growth in quotas relative to world macroeconomic variables. But the uncertainties about prospective needs are great. The shorter-run analyses of liquidity cannot anticipate contingencies such as a sudden, unexpected financial crisis that spreads quickly and contagiously, resulting in a widespread systemic crisis. Such low-probability events, if they were to occur, could require IMF commitments for prompt disbursements of funds in potentially very large cumulative amounts. Erosion in the size of total quotas relative to the world economy and financial system runs the risk of undermining the credibility of the institution to respond appropriately.

My personal inclination is to give considerable weight to the uncertainties about possible sudden surges in vulnerability to crises and in members' needs for emergency borrowing. That emphasis, together with the persistent secular decline in quotas relative to world GDP and cross-border trade, persuades me that substantial increases in quotas will be needed in the future. At the very least, it seems to me, there ought to be widespread agree-

156. Mussa (2002, p. 74).
157. IMF (2002e). See also IMF (2002c, 2002d). The Executive Board approved the renewal of the New Arrangements to Borrow and General Arrangements to Borrow for a further five years on November 12, 2002.

ment that IMF quotas in recent decades did not expand at too rapid a pace. The opposite—inadequate expansion—is much more likely to have been true. Prospectively, during the thirteenth general review (to be concluded by January 2008 if not before), a large increase in total quotas will almost certainly be justified.

That conclusion is reinforced by a point made in the preceding discussion. The distribution and total size of quotas are linked together politically. The least difficult circumstances in which to try to make selective adjustments in quota shares is at the time of an across-the-board increase in quotas. Quite apart from the underlying need to increase IMF resources as a whole as the world economy and financial system grow, therefore, the world community should favorably consider increases in total quotas at the time of general reviews in order to lubricate the process of making selective adjustments in quota shares.

Uncertainties about sudden surges in members' needs for emergency borrowing in financial crises should also lead to periodic reviews of the desirability of increases in backup resources in the IMF's contingent borrowing arrangements. Increases in those contingent credit lines are a partial substitute for increases in quotas. At the very least, from time to time the official world community should consider increases in the General Arrangements to Borrow or of the New Arrangements to Borrow so that those backup lines do not decline excessively relative to the size of the world economy. Eventually, moreover, the world official community may even want to provide for possible emergency increases in the allocation of SDRs as a supplementary way of cooperatively supplying liquidity to the world financial system in times of financial crisis.

Concluding Perspective

This essay addresses a wide range of issues that are important to the robust and stable evolution of the world economy and financial system. The common underlying theme is collective cross-border governance actions to foster crisis prevention and prosperity management.

Unlike many other commentaries on reform of the so-called international financial architecture, the analysis here gives pride of place to supranational surveillance of macroeconomic policies and exchange rates. To buttress the general case for multilateral surveillance made in the book *Turbulent Waters*, this essay gives further details of pragmatic and incremental steps that can lead to the strengthening of surveillance by international institutions and intergovernmental consultative groups. The second main part of the essay reviews intergovernmental lending interme- diation through international institutions, again providing more details about the policy issues and pointing the way toward their balanced resolu- tion. Finally, the essay highlights governance issues themselves, in particular the distribution across nations of decisionmaking rights and responsibilities in international institutions. The International Monetary Fund is the sin- gle most important international institution having surveillance and lending functions. Accordingly it is the IMF that has featured most promi- nently in the analysis.

My analysis emphasizes pragmatic incrementalism because the world community essentially has no other effective choice but to proceed prag- matically. The laissez-faire views of those who advocate untrammeled markets are not politically realistic. The hope that markets and individual national governments can cope resiliently with all cross-border problems without any efforts at collective international governance is bound to be dis- appointed. Crisis-generated political pressures cause the untrammeled markets position to buckle (usually, appropriately so).

But the opposite extreme position, that the world community must engage in sweeping institutionalist reform, badly misjudges the relevant political constraints and therefore is equally unrealistic. It is just not possi- ble to proceed so rapidly. The delegation of radically increased powers for collective surveillance to existing international institutions or intergovern- mental consultative groups is not yet feasible. The world is not politically ready for a genuine supranational lender of last resort, much less a world central bank. It would be no easier to establish additional international institutions with greatly enhanced authority. Such radically increased authority would probably not even be desirable.

More modest steps, however, are feasible and desirable. Incremental improvements to strengthen surveillance and intergovernmental lending should be a top priority for the next several decades. The IMF can gradu- ally put more muscle into its Article IV consultations and its nascent systemic surveillance analyses, increasing their effectiveness marginally here and there. Other international institutions such as the Bank for International Settlements and the OECD and consultative groups such as the G-7, the G-20, the G-24, and the Financial Stability Forum can nurture gradual improvements in their contributions to surveillance. Policymakers and ana- lysts can recognize that hard guidelines cannot be agreed on and can focus on soft guidelines for the shorter run. Analytical foundations to underpin surveillance can be improved one step at a time. Governments can be open to opportunities for the fruitful coordination of macroeconomic policies but can avoid efforts that are too ambitious or that underestimate the uncertainties. The existing international financial institutions can incrementally enhance their cooperation with each other while avoiding unnecessary duplication of efforts and the blurring of areas of core competence. National governments and the IMF itself can avoid defining the IMF's mission too narrowly while also resisting an expansion of its mandate that dissipates its core effectiveness in macroeconomics and finance. The IMF can gradually improve the efficacy and transparency of the conditionality attached to its loans. It can be sensitive to and seek to mitigate the moral hazard dimensions of cross-border finance but not permit them to be exaggerated or to inhibit lending in circumstances when it is needed and can be constructive.

Incrementalism can be overdone. It remains a fact that collective governance problems with cross-border dimensions have been evolving so rapidly that progress in strengthening international financial governance has lagged behind. If governments had been more determined and farsighted, incremental progress could have been more substantial than it has been. One side of pragmatic incrementalism, it is true, demands caution and gradual progress. But the other side often requires decisions that are expeditious and even ambitious, not protracted and fainthearted. As stressed in *Turbulent Waters*, the complete motto of pragmatic incrementalism reads: *Don't ask too much, too soon. But don't be too timid either!* The world community needs to proceed cautiously rather than precipitously. But it does need, unambiguously, to proceed. Caution should not slip into procrastination.

The final sections of this essay emphasize messy details of governance issues for the international financial institutions. It should be acknowledged once again that those governance issues are complex and contentious. But it will not do to pretend that they are unimportant, or that the existing situation can be sustained indefinitely. Pragmatic incrementalism does not justify sweeping them under the rug.

Large asymmetries in resources and power among the world's nations are an awkward but ineluctable fact of life. They obviously shape decisions and events. They inevitably dominate politics. Accordingly, at every layer of governance—for both government and nongovernmental organizations, within nations and at the regional and world levels—some realistic acknowledgment of asymmetric power is inevitable. For international institutions, it is inevitable that the largest and wealthiest nations will have disproportionate influence, reflecting their disproportionate relative power.

At the same time, some sort of balance has to be struck, one way or another, between acknowledging the greater relative power of large wealthy nations and giving smaller and poorer nations an adequate voice and influence. It also needs to be remembered that asymmetries in resources and power shift over time in response to changing circumstances, to differences in economic growth rates, and to altered political configurations within regions and in the world as a whole. As the asymmetries do shift, accommodations eventually have to be made. International institutions—and notably the IMF—will be sorely challenged to devise improved governance mechanisms for responding to the shifts. A key example is that in the next several decades, the voice and influence in international institutions of developing nations in the aggregate, especially those with large populations, will need to rise still further. The industrial nations, most notably those in western Europe, will have to find ways of reducing somewhat their relative dominance of decisionmaking.

The enlightened selfish interests of the major industrial nations should lead them to encourage a robust evolution and strengthened governance for international financial institutions. Again, the wealthiest nations have the most to gain from a healthy, stable evolution of the world economy. They have the most to lose if the world economy and financial system malfunction. The best hope for improved prosperity management—for the world as a whole, and certainly for the largest and wealthiest nations—is to nurture a gradual strengthening of collective surveillance over national economic policies.

Some critics unfriendly to the international financial institutions disparage them as somehow not politically accountable. Silly and impractical notions of national sovereignty often underlie the criticisms. Inconsistently, the critics blame the international institutions first if sufficient progress is not made in resolving cross-border problems.

But it is unreasonable to pick on the international institutions in such fashion. It is, for example, a hopelessly wild and misleading exaggeration to assert that the IMF and the World Bank are not politically accountable. The international institutions are directly and tightly accountable to their members' national governments. When international institutions fail in their exercise of collective governance, the explanation is virtually always that national governments, typically elected and accountable to their own citizens, have failed to demand and support more appropriate policies. It is the major shareholders in the international institutions—in particular the governments of the nations of North America, Europe, and Japan—that warrant criticism and need to be nudged to do better.

International institutions are not independent entities with unconstrained powers. Far from it. They are relatively new, fragile seedlings in the gardens of collective governance. One should think of them as graft cuttings, or at most saplings, that serve as extensions of the governments that planted them. When the day comes that the saplings have grown into mature trees, pruning may be required. In the meantime, gardeners should not confuse saplings with deep-rooted trees and should be at least as concerned with judicious applications of fertilizer as with wielding the pruning shears.

Appendix Table. Distribution by Nation of Key Economic Variables, Levels, and Percent of World Total

Country and grouping	GDP[a] 1997–99 average SDRs millions	%	PPP-GDP[a] 1997–99 average SDRs millions	%	Cross-border trade 1995–99 average SDRs millions	%	International reserves[d] 1999 SDRs millions	%	Population[e] 1999 Thousands	%	IMF quota[f] December 2003 SDRs millions	%	IMF voting power December 2003 Number of votes	%
World, defined as all														
IMF member nations	21,941,253.05	99.17	29,481,633.06	99.43	11,582,963.99	98.43	1,210,864.44	94.14	5,945,477.84	99.44	213,719.20	100.00	2,173,940	100.00
"World plus"[c]	22,124,895.85	100.00	29,651,086.82	100.00	11,768,262.62	100.00	1,286,216.77	100.00	5,978,725.84	100.00				
Industrial nations	16,788,209.83	75.88	15,688,313.65	52.91	8,252,234.34	70.12	549,345.43	42.71	848,311.56	14.19	130,566.60	61.09	1,311,666	60.34
United States	6,430,333.42	29.06	6,314,954.34	21.30	1,769,304.09	15.03	55,025.77	4.28	280,433.88	4.69	37,149.30	17.38	371,743	17.10
Canada	462,302.92	2.09	571,073.58	1.93	391,460.51	3.33	18,678.95	1.45	30,492.03	0.51	6,369.20	2.98	63,942	2.94
Australia	285,304.10	1.29	334,839.62	1.13	134,010.43	1.14	11,582.51	0.90	18,933.13	0.32	3,236.40	1.51	32,614	1.50
Japan	3,110,063.00	14.06	2,281,852.43	7.70	901,050.67	7.66	182,273.83	14.17	126,820.54	2.12	13,312.80	6.23	133,378	6.14
New Zealand	42,766.58	0.19	50,200.25	0.17	30,429.94	0.26	2,936.61	0.23	3,747.44	0.06	894.60	0.42	9,196	0.42
Austria	152,980.94	0.69	139,621.17	0.47	153,847.41	1.31	11,572.47	0.90	8,085.32	0.14	1,872.30	0.88	18,973	0.87
Belgium	181,245.18	0.82	180,180.88	0.61	276,802.31	2.35	8,686.10	0.68	10,232.42	0.17	4,605.20	2.15	46,302	2.13
Denmark	126,781.39	0.57	102,000.24	0.34	126,561.79	1.08	15,650.64	1.22	5,304.77	0.09	1,642.80	0.77	16,678	0.77
Finland	92,651.86	0.42	84,277.17	0.28	71,949.10	0.61	5,306.85	0.41	5,163.55	0.09	1,263.80	0.59	12,888	0.59
France	1,047,810.70	4.74	951,880.85	3.21	619,991.02	5.27	30,894.90	2.40	59,026.05	0.99	10,738.50	5.02	107,635	4.95
Germany	1,555,512.75	7.03	1,385,505.91	4.67	1,023,683.67	8.70	48,385.93	3.76	82,026.13	1.37	13,008.20	6.09	130,332	6.00
Greece	89,981.21	0.41	112,493.69	0.38	40,788.94	0.35	15,020.75	1.17	10,590.95	0.18	823.00	0.39	8,480	0.39
Iceland	5,893.68	0.03	5,276.06	0.02	4,270.10	0.04	326.89	0.03	277.07	0.00	117.60	0.06	1,426	0.07
Ireland	63,696.05	0.29	61,410.62	0.21	124,577.38	1.06	3,884.89	0.30	3,762.80	0.06	838.40	0.39	8,634	0.40
Italy	864,376.33	3.91	935,499.02	3.16	501,555.93	4.26	18,911.45	1.47	57,530.52	0.96	7,055.50	3.30	70,805	3.26
Luxembourg	13,447.45	0.06	11,285.14	0.04	88,178.03	0.75	46.97	0.00	431.46	0.01	279.10	0.13	3,041	0.14
Netherlands	277,408.32	1.25	260,420.68	0.88	396,074.26	3.37	8,681.80	0.67	15,792.95	0.26	5,162.40	2.42	51,874	2.39
Norway	110,954.50	0.50	89,468.62	0.30	90,264.48	0.77	13,466.81	1.05	4,448.97	0.07	1,671.70	0.78	16,967	0.78
Portugal	78,723.13	0.36	107,461.86	0.36	69,136.77	0.59	6,573.68	0.51	9,995.59	0.17	867.40	0.41	8,924	0.41
San Marino	563.75	0.00	563.75	0.00	2,678.06	0.02	3.36	0.00	26.20	0.00	17.00	0.01	420	0.02
Spain	411,077.68	1.86	491,504.82	1.66	260,515.38	2.21	28,403.59	2.21	39,892.49	0.67	3,048.90	1.43	30,739	1.41
Sweden	174,139.61	0.79	142,932.29	0.48	167,302.96	1.42	10,788.42	0.84	8,850.40	0.15	2,395.50	1.12	24,205	1.11
Switzerland	189,451.03	0.86	139,709.95	0.47	215,098.42	1.83	29,131.62	2.26	7,170.43	0.12	3,458.50	1.62	34,835	1.60
United Kingdom	1,020,744.23	4.61	933,900.68	3.15	792,702.69	6.74	23,110.63	1.80	59,276.46	0.99	10,738.50	5.02	107,635	4.95
European Union, EMU[h]	4,828,911.61	21.83	4,721,541.83	15.92	3,627,100.19	30.82	186,369.39	14.49	302,530.23	5.06	49,562.70	23.19	498,627	22.94
European Union (15)[i]	6,150,576.85	27.80	5,900,375.05	19.90	4,713,667.62	40.05	235,919.09	18.34	375,961.86	6.29	64,339.50	30.10	647,145	29.77
European Union (25)[j]	6,390,777.96	28.89	6,426,285.28	21.67	4,931,774.93	41.91	281,136.03	21.86	450,991.37	7.54	68,733.20	32.16	693,582	31.90
Total developing nations	5,336,686.021	24.12	13,962,773.17	47.09	3,516,028.28	29.88	736,871.35	57.29	5,119,202.24	85.62	83,152.60	38.91	862,274	39.66

Western Hemisphere	**1,417,620.13**	**6.41**	**2,503,934.85**	**8.44**	**566,344.29**	**4.81**	**113,121.42**	**8.79**	**505,687.37**	**8.46**	**15,933.90**	**7.46**	**167,339**	**7.70**
Antigua & Barbuda	451.10	0.00	526.66	0.00	709.77	0.01	43.75	0.00	64.64	0.00	13.50	0.01	385	0.02
Argentina	213,563.52	0.97	283,310.44	0.96	56,616.49	0.48	17,433.44	1.36	36,577.03	0.61	2,117.10	0.99	21,421	0.99
Bahamas	2,708.73	0.01	2,264.80	0.01	3,351.06	0.03	314.96	0.02	300.29	0.01	130.30	0.06	1,553	0.07
Barbados	1,725.43	0.01	2,466.41	0.01	1,951.71	0.02	240.32	0.02	266.55	0.00	67.50	0.03	925	0.04
Belize	471.97	0.00	791.34	0.00	557.02	0.00	45.90	0.00	221.54	0.00	18.80	0.01	438	0.02
Bolivia	6,016.81	0.03	17,774.79	0.06	2,798.65	0.02	604.51	0.05	8,142.21	0.14	171.50	0.08	1,965	0.09
Brazil	518,221.26	2.34	805,783.57	2.72	108,129.63	0.92	28,162.77	2.19	168,246.36	2.81	3,036.10	1.42	30,611	1.41
Chile	52,685.33	0.24	145,287.36	0.49	31,945.87	0.27	10,866.16	0.84	15,018.75	0.25	856.10	0.40	8,811	0.41
Colombia	70,817.19	0.32	210,026.99	0.71	24,287.13	0.21	6,117.47	0.48	41,400.27	0.69	774.00	0.36	7,990	0.37
Costa Rica	10,197.79	0.05	19,017.89	0.06	9,321.96	0.08	987.33	0.08	3,933.15	0.07	164.10	0.08	1,891	0.09
Cuba[k]	15,863.88	0.07	na	na	5,498.42	0.05	na	na	11,158.00	0.19	0	0.00	0	0.00
Dominica	186.97	0.00	250.18	0.00	245.58	0.00	21.82	0.00	70.63	0.00	8.20	0.00	332	0.02
Dominican Republic	11,775.20	0.05	31,791.81	0.11	12,397.54	0.11	402.05	0.03	8,237.38	0.14	218.90	0.10	2,439	0.11
Ecuador	8,682.79	0.04	13,310.01	0.04	6,086.71	0.05	1,420.48	0.11	12,410.74	0.21	302.30	0.14	1,963	0.09
El Salvador	12,972.35	0.06	43,825.08	0.15	9,106.80	0.08	1,201.68	0.09	6,155.93	0.10	171.30	0.08	3,273	0.15
Grenada	254.56	0.00	380.63	0.00	336.89	0.00	34.56	0.00	93.23	0.00	11.70	0.01	367	0.02
Guatemala	13,537.29	0.06	34,200.87	0.12	6,070.02	0.05	884.26	0.07	11,089.89	0.19	210.20	0.10	2,352	0.11
Guyana	519.04	0.00	1,982.73	0.01	1,282.70	0.01	187.41	0.01	757.42	0.01	90.90	0.04	1,159	0.05
Haiti	2,705.59	0.01	7,303.02	0.02	1,369.58	0.01	199.86	0.02	8,015.85	0.13	81.90	0.04	1,069	0.05
Honduras	3,757.83	0.02	10,300.26	0.03	3,778.49	0.03	756.61	0.06	6,257.90	0.10	129.50	0.06	1,545	0.07
Jamaica	5,342.06	0.02	6,722.39	0.02	6,245.29	0.05	480.18	0.04	2,554.52	0.04	273.50	0.13	2,985	0.14
Mexico	317,614.24	1.44	558,834.41	1.88	189,590.63	1.61	23,248.16	1.81	97,356.44	1.63	2,585.80	1.21	26,108	1.20
Nicaragua	1,524.36	0.01	7,402.66	0.02	2,501.40	0.02	348.10	0.03	4,938.09	0.08	130.00	0.06	1,550	0.07
Panama	6,723.21	0.03	15,481.23	0.05	13,930.43	0.12	707.64	0.06	2,811.73	0.05	206.60	0.10	2,316	0.11
Paraguay	6,327.88	0.03	14,793.56	0.05	6,648.46	0.06	614.26	0.05	5,358.36	0.09	99.90	0.05	1,249	0.06
Peru	40,854.44	0.18	88,458.63	0.30	15,314.58	0.13	6,763.51	0.53	25,229.51	0.42	638.40	0.30	6,634	0.31
St. Vincent & Grenadines	228.73	0.00	379.19	0.00	308.73	0.00	27.79	0.00	112.55	0.00	8.30	0.00	333	0.02
St. Kitts & Nevis	208.82	0.00	262.69	0.00	277.80	0.00	31.61	0.00	38.76	0.00	8.90	0.00	339	0.02
St. Lucia	455.74	0.00	665.68	0.00	676.76	0.01	52.46	0.00	146.14	0.00	15.30	0.01	403	0.02
Suriname	580.78	0.00	1,821.94	0.01	728.26	0.01	55.72	0.00	415.38	0.01	92.10	0.04	1,171	0.05
Trinidad & Tobago	4,566.22	0.02	7,084.04	0.02	4,528.86	0.04	569.23	0.04	1,288.62	0.02	335.60	0.16	3,606	0.17
Uruguay	15,853.13	0.07	23,230.42	0.08	6,622.78	0.06	1,539.08	0.12	3,313.16	0.06	306.50	0.14	3,315	0.15
Venezuela	70,225.90	0.32	148,203.15	0.50	33,128.29	0.28	8,758.32	0.68	23,706.36	0.40	2,659.10	1.24	26,841	1.23
Middle East	**586,841.73**	**2.65**	**1,315,058.25**	**4.44**	**373,948.69**	**3.18**	**66,906.12**	**5.20**	**238,667.58**	**3.99**	**16,162.90**	**7.56**	**158,535**	**7.29**
Bahrain	4,671.47	0.02	7,855.02	0.03	13,418.45	0.11	960.27	0.07	627.42	0.01	135.00	0.06	1,600	0.07
Iran	145,455.00	0.66	556,115.69	1.88	27,184.54	0.23	12.97	0.00	69,243.56	1.16	1,497.20	0.70	15,222	0.70
Iraq	24,332.80	0.11	24,332.80	0.08	9,848.00	0.08	660.00	0.05	22,335.32	0.37	1,188.40	0.56	5,290	0.24

Appendix Table. *Distribution by Nation of Key Economic Variables, Levels, and Percent of World Total (continued)*

Country and grouping	GDP[a] 1997–99 average SDRs millions	%	PPP-GDP[b] 1997–99 average SDRs millions	%	Cross-border trade[c] 1995–99 average SDRs millions	%	International reserves[d] 1999 SDRs millions	%	Population[e] 1999 Thousands	%	IMF quotas[f] December 2003 SDRs millions	%	IMF voting power December 2003 Number of votes	%
Israel	74,699.73	0.34	75,686.33	0.26	60,921.77	0.52	16,149.10	1.26	5,909.55	0.10	928.20	0.43	9,532	0.44
Jordan	5,699.31	0.03	11,774.44	0.04	8,312.48	0.07	1,704.95	0.13	4,785.29	0.08	170.50	0.08	1,955	0.09
Kuwait	20,744.94	0.09	23,177.79	0.08	26,414.72	0.22	3,197.18	0.25	1,847.81	0.03	1,381.10	0.65	14,061	0.65
Lebanon	11,626.64	0.05	18,970.55	0.06	7,127.72	0.06	5,347.29	0.42	3,437.88	0.06	203.00	0.09	2,280	0.10
Oman	11,102.43	0.05	18,435.38	0.06	10,984.59	0.09	1,720.67	0.13	2,457.25	0.04	194.00	0.09	2,190	0.10
Qatar	8,230.29	0.04	12,294.99	0.04	8,050.40	0.07	853.77	0.07	555.40	0.01	263.80	0.12	2,888	0.13
Saudi Arabia	101,877.47	0.46	156,452.11	0.53	90,022.55	0.76	11,012.65	0.86	19,644.49	0.33	6,985.50	3.27	70,105	3.22
Syria	51,231.04	0.23	156,164.22	0.53	9,077.09	0.08	29.24	0.00	15,777.67	0.26	293.60	0.14	3,186	0.15
United Arab Emirates	36,212.69	0.16	37,379.12	0.13	55,572.74	0.47	7,096.64	0.55	2,558.18	0.04	611.70	0.29	6,367	0.29
Egypt	62,876.57	0.28	154,078.80	0.52	29,604.34	0.25	12,147.71	0.94	66,693.17	1.12	943.70	0.44	9,687	0.45
Yemen	4,678.94	0.02	9,665.53	0.03	5,763.10	0.05	820.42	0.06	17,619.79	0.29	243.50	0.11	2,685	0.12
Libya	23,402.41	0.11	52,675.48	0.18	11,646.19	0.10	5,193.26	0.40	5,174.82	0.09	1,123.70	0.53	11,487	0.53
Asia	**2,215,553.08**	**10.01**	**6,987,120.09**	**23.56**	**1,800,425.41**	**15.30**	**449,870.52**	**34.98**	**3,193,170.21**	**53.41**	**22,046.80**	**10.32**	**228,468**	**10.51**
Afghanistan	1,651.00	0.01	1,651.00	0.01	569.80	0.00	112.00	0.01	21,201.52	0.35	161.90	0.08	1,869	0.09
Bangladesh	32,851.62	0.15	103,056.15	0.35	11,606.68	0.10	1,170.43	0.09	134,584.18	2.25	533.30	0.25	5,583	0.26
Bhutan	303.03	0.00	990.19	0.00	290.21	0.00	198.49	0.02	2,028.94	0.03	6.30	0.00	313	0.01
Brunei Darussalam	3,372.07	0.02	3,372.07	0.01	5,645.50	0.05	38.56	0.00	321.79	0.00	215.20	0.10	2,402	0.11
Myanmar	4,833.80	0.02	50,550.42	0.17	3,468.70	0.03	243.39	0.02	47,113.89	0.79	258.40	0.12	2,834	0.13
Cambodia	2,177.74	0.01	10,451.89	0.04	1,898.57	0.02	266.77	0.02	12,766.15	0.21	87.50	0.04	1,125	0.05
China, People's Republic[l]	930,436.66	4.21	3,384,148.45	11.41	618,346.20	5.25	171,514.16	13.33	1,271,514.40	21.27	6,369.20	2.98	63,942	2.94
China, Taiwan[m]	167,778.92	0.76	169,453.75	0.57	179,800.20	1.53	75,352.33	5.86	22,090.00	0.37	0	0	0	0
Sri Lanka	11,353.87	0.05	36,517.31	0.12	9,574.68	0.08	1,275.66	0.10	18,747.16	0.31	413.40	0.19	4,384	0.20
India	307,643.42	1.39	1,290,953.14	4.35	84,622.87	0.72	22,924.08	1.78	992,686.19	16.60	4,158.20	1.95	41,832	1.92
Indonesia	110,165.51	0.50	484,798.21	1.64	85,758.88	0.73	18,807.40	1.46	209,287.32	3.50	2,079.30	0.97	21,043	0.97
Korea	292,334.40	1.32	463,196.41	1.56	234,661.78	1.99	45,998.33	3.58	46,403.25	0.78	1,633.60	0.76	16,586	0.76
Laos	1,092.51	0.00	5,391.24	0.02	971.70	0.01	82.06	0.01	5,156.18	0.09	52.90	0.02	779	0.04
Malaysia	61,310.32	0.28	129,201.53	0.44	130,829.91	1.11	21,732.45	1.69	21,790.97	0.36	1,486.60	0.70	15,116	0.70
Maldives	384.36	0.00	738.59	0.00	619.11	0.01	96.74	0.01	282.30	0.00	8.20	0.00	332	0.02
Nepal	3,701.92	0.02	19,760.64	0.07	2,340.93	0.02	582.43	0.05	22,501.20	0.38	71.30	0.03	963	0.04
Pakistan	45,522.55	0.21	161,812.12	0.55	20,481.60	0.17	1,273.74	0.10	137,556.15	2.30	1,033.70	0.48	10,587	0.49
Palau	95.05	0.00	95.05	0.00	149.21	0.00	16.70	0.00	19.00	0.00	3.10	0.00	281	0.01
Philippines	54,527.65	0.25	197,922.07	0.67	61,696.14	0.52	9,095.61	0.71	74,183.56	1.24	879.90	0.41	9,049	0.42

Singapore	63,695.95	0.29	68,995.44	0.23	213,425.63	1.81	54,448.56	4.23	3,918.39	0.07	862.50	0.40	8,875	0.41
Thailand	280.85	0.00	690.97	0.00	382.50	0.00	39.09	0.00	62,007.83	1.04	1,081.90	0.51	354	0.02
Vietnam	93,865.49	0.42	287,881.34	0.97	106,641.61	0.91	22,542.68	1.75	77,117.64	1.29	329.10	0.15	11,069	0.51
Solomon Islands	20,181.44	0.09	100,761.49	0.34	19,042.56	0.16	1,201.63	0.09	432.43	0.01	10.40	0.00	3,541	0.16
Fiji	1,363.69	0.01	2,166.78	0.01	1,840.58	0.02	297.12	0.02	804.56	0.01	70.30	0.03	953	0.04
Kiribati	34.65	0.00	101.61	0.00	127.44	0.00	190.30	0.01	81.77	0.00	5.60	0.00	306	0.01
Vanuatu	172.41	0.00	517.27	0.00	299.52	0.00	31.58	0.00	191.75	0.00	17.00	0.01	420	0.02
Papua New Guinea	2,983.75	0.01	8,344.85	0.03	3,732.23	0.03	93.67	0.01	4,700.70	0.08	131.60	0.06	1,566	0.07
Samoa	171.27	0.00	464.54	0.00	204.88	0.00	45.77	0.00	158.41	0.00	11.60	0.01	366	0.02
Tonga	117.28	0.00	295.05	0.00	134.11	0.00	20.34	0.00	98.69	0.00	6.90	0.00	319	0.01
Marshall Islands	69.57	0.00	69.57	0.00	114.00	0.00	9.00	0.00	50.44	0.00	3.50	0.00	285	0.01
Micronesia	153.62	0.00	153.62	0.00	251.29	0.00	98.37	0.01	119.63	0.00	5.10	0.00	301	0.01
Mongolia	702.63	0.00	2,617.34	0.01	896.39	0.01	71.07	0.01	2,509.48	0.04	51.10	0.02	761	0.04
Timor-Leste	224.07	0.00	na	na	na	na	na	na	744.36	0.01	8.20	0.00	332	0.02
Africa	**363,582.08**	**1.64**	**1,085,587.19**	**3.66**	**219,263.82**	**1.86**	**28,406.83**	**2.21**	**702,162.99**	**11.74**	**11,738.90**	**5.49**	**127,731**	**5.88**
Djibouti	378.83	0.00	1,179.66	0.00	462.20	0.00	46.73	0.00	616.67	0.01	15.90	0.01	409	0.02
Algeria	35,050.54	0.16	103,922.66	0.35	17,623.70	0.15	3,789.40	0.29	29,755.00	0.50	1,254.70	0.59	12,797	0.59
Angola	4,943.23	0.02	14,634.85	0.05	8,824.58	0.07	155.93	0.01	12,758.61	0.21	286.30	0.13	3,113	0.14
Botswana	3,701.25	0.02	9,599.04	0.03	4,811.03	0.04	4,303.90	0.33	1,524.44	0.03	63.00	0.03	880	0.04
Burundi	658.96	0.00	3,377.66	0.01	257.60	0.00	45.50	0.00	6,255.44	0.10	77.00	0.04	1,020	0.05
Cameroon	6,819.10	0.03	21,868.71	0.07	3,354.04	0.03	1.86	0.00	14,552.61	0.24	185.70	0.09	2,107	0.10
Cape Verde	396.72	0.00	997.73	0.00	425.16	0.00	9.53	0.00	417.38	0.01	9.60	0.00	346	0.02
Central African Republic	751.13	0.00	3,626.47	0.01	573.58	0.00	101.08	0.01	3,648.84	0.06	55.70	0.03	807	0.04
Chad	1,167.18	0.01	5,390.12	0.02	793.43	0.01	79.67	0.01	7,640.62	0.13	56.00	0.03	810	0.04
Comoros	158.56	0.00	602.61	0.00	127.46	0.00	27.23	0.00	685.41	0.01	8.90	0.00	339	0.02
Congo, Rep. of the	1,582.29	0.01	3,484.97	0.01	2,926.88	0.02	5.08	0.00	2,930.08	0.05	84.60	0.04	1,096	0.05
Congo, Democratic Rep. of the	5,431.25	0.02	28,450.84	0.10	2,561.79	0.02	102.10	0.01	49,580.61	0.83	533.00	0.25	5,580	0.26
Benin	1,660.83	0.01	5,822.19	0.02	1,166.51	0.01	208.91	0.02	6,107.89	0.10	61.90	0.03	869	0.04
Equatorial Guinea	484.63	0.00	1,193.33	0.00	829.60	0.01	0.38	0.00	444.35	0.01	32.60	0.02	576	0.03
Eritrea	590.18	0.00	590.18	0.00	738.97	0.01	108.10	0.01	3,523.97	0.06	15.90	0.01	409	0.02
Ethiopia	4,309.27	0.02	21,139.26	0.07	3,068.77	0.03	292.56	0.02	61,388.05	1.03	133.70	0.06	1,587	0.07
Gabon	3,610.75	0.02	6,781.84	0.02	4,073.67	0.03	2.02	0.00	1,199.00	0.02	154.30	0.07	1,793	0.08
Gambia	255.95	0.00	1,116.14	0.00	416.21	0.00	78.97	0.01	1,266.73	0.02	31.10	0.01	561	0.03
Ghana	5,383.69	0.02	23,369.45	0.08	4,074.57	0.03	287.58	0.02	18,893.26	0.32	369.00	0.17	3,940	0.18
Guinea-Bissau	166.50	0.00	820.57	0.00	132.51	0.00	26.74	0.00	1,173.28	0.02	14.20	0.01	392	0.02
Guinea	2,634.61	0.01	10,088.93	0.03	1,504.61	0.01	150.73	0.01	8,020.73	0.13	107.10	0.05	1,321	0.06
Côte d'Ivoire	8,188.21	0.04	20,945.88	0.07	7,790.49	0.07	571.81	0.04	15,684.92	0.26	325.20	0.15	3,502	0.16
Kenya	7,984.51	0.04	26,440.26	0.09	5,264.01	0.04	514.40	0.04	30,029.01	0.50	271.40	0.13	2,964	0.14

Appendix Table. *Distribution by Nation of Key Economic Variables, Levels, and Percent of World Total*

Country and grouping	GDP[a] 1997–99 average SDRs millions	%	PPP-GDP[b] 1997–99 average SDRs millions	%	Cross-border trade[c] 1995–99 average SDRs millions	%	International reserves[d] 1999 SDRs millions	%	Population[e] 1999 Thousands	%	IMF quotas[f] December 2003 SDRs millions	%	IMF voting power December 2003 Number of votes	%
Lesotho	671.47	0.00	2,456.45	0.01	1,392.32	0.01	390.66	0.03	2,007.60	0.03	34.90	0.02	599	0.03
Liberia	714.49	0.00	2,048.04	0.01	1,377.68	0.01	0.39	0.00	2,709.46	0.05	129.20	0.06	963	0.04
Madagascar	2,684.23	0.01	10,385.88	0.04	1,608.28	0.01	136.43	0.01	15,511.94	0.26	122.20	0.06	1,472	0.07
Malawi	1,511.31	0.01	5,777.86	0.02	1,239.79	0.01	186.93	0.01	11,029.65	0.18	69.40	0.03	944	0.04
Mali	1,915.83	0.01	5,960.85	0.02	1,395.31	0.01	280.94	0.02	11,039.03	0.18	93.30	0.04	1,183	0.05
Mauritania	719.55	0.00	3,253.99	0.01	829.75	0.01	151.92	0.01	2,582.31	0.04	64.40	0.03	894	0.04
Mauritius	3,073.38	0.01	8,577.41	0.03	3,990.84	0.03	467.75	0.04	1,152.24	0.02	101.60	0.05	1,266	0.06
Morocco	25,390.48	0.11	71,538.25	0.24	17,726.03	0.15	3,682.53	0.29	29,333.51	0.49	588.20	0.28	6,132	0.28
Mozambique	2,737.75	0.01	10,042.68	0.03	2,217.66	0.02	469.65	0.04	17,936.46	0.30	113.60	0.05	1,386	0.06
Niger	1,228.79	0.01	5,665.09	0.02	683.26	0.01	36.47	0.00	10,454.62	0.17	65.80	0.03	908	0.04
Nigeria	73,803.65	0.33	239,751.06	0.81	22,051.63	0.19	3,826.80	0.30	110,844.77	1.85	1,753.20	0.82	17,782	0.82
Zimbabwe	4,818.42	0.02	19,771.58	0.07	4,563.60	0.04	168.53	0.01	12,400.36	0.21	353.40	0.17	3,784	0.17
Rwanda	1,410.09	0.01	4,321.15	0.01	714.09	0.01	113.04	0.01	7,086.54	0.12	80.10	0.04	1,051	0.05
Sao Tomé & Principe	32.12	0.00	127.73	0.00	36.46	0.00	6.51	0.00	135.26	0.00	7.40	0.00	324	0.01
Seychelles	423.97	0.00	612.13	0.00	612.86	0.00	18.57	0.01	79.40	0.00	8.80	0.00	338	0.02
Senegal	3,377.78	0.02	12,235.97	0.04	2,713.18	0.02	323.38	0.03	9,184.38	0.15	161.80	0.08	1,868	0.09
Sierra Leone	534.62	0.00	1,489.07	0.01	251.43	0.00	21.05	0.00	4,271.79	0.07	103.70	0.05	1,287	0.06
Somalia	343.40	0.00	343.40	0.00	249.50	0.00	13.90	0.00	8,417.71	0.14	81.70	0.04	692	0.03
South Africa	100,364.10	0.45	232,253.71	0.78	52,853.51	0.45	3,892.55	0.30	42,753.86	0.72	1,868.50	0.87	18,935	0.87
Namibia	2,378.49	0.01	6,393.14	0.02	3,298.06	0.03	191.38	0.01	1,724.42	0.03	136.50	0.06	1,615	0.07
Sudan	7,239.27	0.03	33,724.11	0.11	2,241.62	0.02	101.76	0.01	30,423.49	0.51	315.10	0.15	1,947	0.09
Swaziland	1,028.18	0.00	2,677.27	0.01	2,071.66	0.01	266.61	0.02	909.00	0.02	50.70	0.02	757	0.03
Tanzania	6,108.87	0.03	13,841.65	0.05	3,052.33	0.03	471.00	0.04	34,285.47	0.57	198.90	0.09	2,239	0.10
Togo	1,055.86	0.00	4,845.61	0.02	1,005.22	0.01	87.30	0.01	4,388.10	0.07	73.40	0.03	984	0.05
Tunisia	14,520.67	0.07	37,430.12	0.13	13,615.75	0.12	1,368.19	0.11	9,360.50	0.16	286.50	0.13	3,115	0.14
Uganda	4,881.38	0.02	19,586.03	0.07	2,325.56	0.02	535.87	0.04	22,610.91	0.38	180.50	0.08	2,055	0.09
Burkina Faso	1,787.17	0.01	8,153.57	0.03	1,123.29	0.01	234.93	0.02	11,246.36	0.19	60.20	0.03	852	0.04
Zambia	2,518.59	0.01	6,880.02	0.02	2,221.76	0.02	51.45	0.00	10,186.95	0.17	489.10	0.23	5,141	0.24
Europe (excluding industrial nations)	**753,089.00**	**3.40**	**2,071,072.79**	**6.98**	**556,046.07**	**4.72**	**78,566.46**	**6.11**	**479,514.09**	**8.02**	**17,270.10**	**8.08**	**180,201**	**8.29**
Armenia	1,311.81	0.01	6,128.75	0.02	1,149.24	0.01	230.70	0.02	3,787.51	0.06	92.00	0.04	1,170	0.05
Azerbaijan	3,169.00	0.01	12,699.00	0.04	2,238.80	0.02	451.79	0.04	7,981.57	0.13	160.90	0.08	1,859	0.09
Belarus	10,120.78	0.05	48,134.83	0.16	10,321.22	0.09	237.17	0.02	10,224.89	0.17	386.40	0.18	4,114	0.19
Albania	2,203.49	0.01	7,184.43	0.02	1,455.25	0.01	263.83	0.02	3,131.22	0.05	48.70	0.02	737	0.03
Georgia	2,439.44	0.01	16,148.07	0.05	1,590.26	0.01	93.19	0.01	5,281.78	0.09	150.30	0.07	1,753	0.08
Kazakhstan	15,001.41	0.07	55,993.86	0.19	10,852.48	0.09	943.39	0.07	16,258.13	0.27	365.70	0.17	3,907	0.18
Kyrgyz Republic	1,135.84	0.01	8,176.23	0.03	1,105.07	0.01	147.53	0.01	4,848.07	0.08	88.80	0.04	1,138	0.05

Bulgaria	8,491.96	0.04	30,290.03	0.10	9,555.26	0.08	1,972.95	0.15	8,038.85	0.13	640.20	0.30	6,652	0.31
Cyprus	6,537.03	0.03	7,292.60	0.02	6,775.72	0.06	1,136.84	0.09	777.08	0.01	139.60	0.07	1,646	0.08
Malta	2,560.15	0.01	3,903.88	0.01	5,356.74	0.05	1,241.39	0.10	387.95	0.01	102.00	0.05	1,270	0.06
Moldova	1,170.19	0.01	5,562.95	0.02	1,625.75	0.01	141.68	0.01	4,305.08	0.07	123.20	0.06	1,482	0.07
Russia	220,326.23	1.00	724,146.56	2.44	137,506.31	1.17	5,909.59	0.46	146,210.94	2.45	5,945.40	2.78	59,704	2.75
Tajikistan	861.88	0.00	4,400.89	0.01	1,180.12	0.01	4.48	0.00	6,029.66	0.10	87.00	0.04	1,120	0.05
Turkey	144,713.88	0.65	306,335.33	1.03	77,620.79	0.66	16,439.61	1.28	65,674.24	1.10	964.00	0.45	9,890	0.45
Turkmenistan	2,155.63	0.01	15,502.78	0.05	2,644.43	0.02	1,076.63	0.08	4,636.37	0.08	75.20	0.04	1,002	0.05
Ukraine	29,943.64	0.14	121,779.59	0.41	28,217.70	0.24	662.85	0.05	50,021.94	0.84	1,372.00	0.64	13,970	0.64
Uzbekistan	11,607.71	0.05	38,227.25	0.13	6,122.05	0.05	291.98	0.02	24,487.22	0.41	275.60	0.13	3,006	0.14
Czech Republic	40,131.48	0.18	99,062.51	0.33	48,845.45	0.42	8,926.71	0.69	10,285.14	0.17	819.30	0.38	8,443	0.39
Slovak Republic	14,985.61	0.07	40,024.44	0.13	18,864.94	0.16	2,105.36	0.16	5,394.41	0.09	357.50	0.17	3,825	0.18
Estonia	3,642.11	0.02	8,331.15	0.03	5,549.98	0.05	555.62	0.04	1,410.52	0.02	65.20	0.03	902	0.04
Latvia	4,484.77	0.02	10,295.21	0.03	4,528.85	0.04	600.78	0.05	2,435.46	0.04	126.80	0.06	1,518	0.07
Hungary	34,349.89	0.16	78,569.14	0.26	37,334.50	0.32	7,070.15	0.55	10,019.69	0.17	1,038.40	0.49	10,634	0.49
Lithuania	7,562.49	0.03	17,632.98	0.06	7,334.89	0.06	953.85	0.07	3,701.14	0.06	144.20	0.07	1,692	0.08
Croatia	15,113.99	0.07	23,369.83	0.08	14,283.38	0.12	1,972.28	0.15	4,653.11	0.08	365.10	0.17	3,901	0.18
Slovenia	14,115.98	0.06	21,742.68	0.07	16,148.91	0.14	2,487.07	0.19	1,990.69	0.03	231.70	0.11	2,567	0.12
Macedonia	2,593.80	0.01	6,305.54	0.02	2,861.65	0.02	258.42	0.02	2,021.89	0.03	68.90	0.03	939	0.04
Bosnia & Herzegovina	2,668.38	0.01	2,864.38	0.01	4,013.08	0.03	179.90	0.01	3,846.03	0.06	169.10	0.08	1,941	0.09
Yugoslavia	10,458.90	0.05	10,458.90	0.04	7,049.20	0.06	209.50	0.02	10,567.19	0.18	467.70	0.22	4,927	0.23
Poland	111,831.60	0.51	239,055.65	0.81	67,367.34	0.57	20,139.18	1.57	38,627.43	0.65	1,369.00	0.64	13,940	0.64
Romania	27,399.94	0.12	101,453.36	0.34	16,546.71	0.14	1,862.06	0.14	22,478.90	0.38	1,030.20	0.48	10,552	0.49

Sources: Most data in the table are taken from data underlying the Appendix II table in the IMF's *Quota Distribution—Selected Issues* (IMF, 2003c); the IMF staff kindly made the underlying data available to the author. See also IMF (2002d). Regional subtotals were created by the author. Minor adjustments are described in the footnotes. Other data sources include the United Nations (for population), Asian Development Bank (for Taiwan), and the World Bank's *World Development Indicators 2004*.

a. "World Plus" in this table is defined as all IMF member nations plus Cuba and China,Taiwan. Data for Hong Kong are included with the data for People's Republic of China.

b. Measured at market prices, converted into SDRs at current market exchange rates.

c. Data at purchasing power parity prices as included in the IMF's *World Economic Outlook* database. For eleven small IMF member nations for which PPP-GDP data are not available, GDP at market prices is used instead.

d. Data for cross-border trade are measured as the average sum of current external receipts and current external payments, not adjusted for official transfers, re-exports, and international banking interest.

e. Average international reserves during the year 1999 based on end-month data.

f. UN population data reported in *World Population Prospects: The 2000 Revision* (published by the United Nations in February 2001).

g. IMF quotas are actual quotas as of end-2003, except that for the few countries that had not yet consented to and paid for their quota increases from the Eleventh General Review of Quotas, the proposed Eleventh Review quotas are used instead.

h. The twelve members of the European Monetary Union as of 2004 (Austria, Belgium, Finland, France, Germany, Greece, Ireland, Italy, Luxembourg, Netherlands, Portugal, and Spain).

i. The fifteen members of the European Monetary Union as of 2004 (see note h) plus Denmark, Sweden, and the United Kingdom.

j. The ten nations that acceded to the EU in May 2004 (Poland, Hungary, Czech Republic, Slovak Republic, Estonia, Latvia, Lithuania, Slovenia, Malta, and Cyprus). The ten nations joining the Union in May 2004 were not labeled as "industrial nations" in the IMF statistics used for this table.

k. Data for Cuba are estimated from Economic Commission for Latin America and the Caribbean, *Statistical Yearbook for Latin America and the Carribean 2002*, and from the World Bank's *World Development Indicators 2004*.

l. Data include Hong Kong (which became a special administrative region of China in July 1997) as well as mainland China.

m. Data for China, Taiwan are taken from the Asian Development Bank's *Key Indicators 2003*.

References

Abbott, Kenneth W., and Duncan Snidal. 2000. "Hard and Soft Law in International Governance." In *Legalization and World Politics*, a special issue of *International Organization* 54 (Summer): 421–56.

Abbott, Kenneth W., and others. 2000. "The Concept of Legalization." In *Legalization and World Politics*, a special issue of *International Organization* 54 (Summer): 401–20.

Artis, Michael, and Mark Taylor. 1995. "The Effect of Misalignment on Desired Equilibrium Exchange Rates: Some Analytical Results." In *European Currency Crises and After*, edited by C. Bordes, E. Girardin, and J. Melitz. Manchester University Press.

Artus, Jacques R., and Andrew Crockett. 1978. *Floating Exchange Rates and the Need for Surveillance.* Princeton Essay in International Finance No. 127 (May). International Finance Section, Princeton University.

Artus, Jacques R., and Malcolm Knight. 1984. *Issues in the Assessment of the Exchange Rates of Industrial Countries.* Occasional Paper No. 29 (July). Washington: International Monetary Fund.

Asian Development Bank. 2003. *Key Indicators 2003.* Manila, Philippines.

Bagehot, Walter. 1873. *Lombard Street: A Description of the Money Market.* London: Kegan, Paul. Reprinted by John Murray, 1924.

Baliño, Tomás J. T., and others. 1999. *Financial Sector Crisis and Restructuring: Lessons from Asia.* September. Washington: International Monetary Fund.

Balls, Edward. 2003. "Preventing Financial Crises: The Case for Independent IMF Surveillance." Remarks at the Institute for International Economics, Washington, D.C., March 6.

Boughton, James M. 1997. *Modeling the World Economic Outlook at the IMF: A Historical Review.* Working Paper WP/97/48. Washington: International Monetary Fund.

_____. 2000. "From Suez to Tequila: The IMF as Crisis Manager." *Economic Journal* 110 (January): 273–91.

_____. 2001. *Silent Revolution: The International Monetary Fund, 1979–89.* Washington: International Monetary Fund.

Brainard, William C. 1967. "Uncertainty and the Effectiveness of Policy." *American Economic Review* 57 (May): 411–25.

Brau, Eduard. 1981. "The Consultations Process of the Fund." *Finance and Development* 18 (December): 13–16.

Bryant, Ralph C. 1980a. *Financial Interdependence and Variability in Exchange Rates.* Brookings.

_____. 1980b. *Money and Monetary Policy in Interdependent Nations.* Brookings.

_____. 1987. *International Financial Intermediation.* Brookings.

_____.1995. *International Coordination of National Stabilization Policies.* Integrating National Economies series. Brookings.

_____. 2003. *Turbulent Waters: Cross-Border Finance and International Governance.* Brookings.

_____. 2004a. *Prudential Oversight and Standards for the World Financial System. Pragmatic Choices for International Financial Governance, II.* Brookings.

_____. 2004b. *Crisis Management for the World Financial System. Pragmatic Choices for International Financial Governance, III.* Brookings.

Bryant, Ralph C., Peter Hooper, and Catherine L. Mann, eds. 1993. *Evaluating Policy Regimes: New Research in Empirical Macroeconomics.* Brookings.

Buira, Ariel. 1983. "IMF Financial Programs and Conditionality." *Journal of Development Economics* 12 (1983): 111–36.

_____. 2002. "A New Voting Structure for the IMF." Paper prepared by the G-24 Secretariat for the Intergovernmental Group of Twenty-Four. Washington: G-24 Secretariat (October).

_____. 2003. "The Governance of the International Monetary Fund." In *Providing Global Public Goods: Managing Globalization,* edited by Inge Kaul and others, pp. 225–44. Oxford University Press.

Calomiris, Charles W. 1998a. *Blueprints for a New Global Financial Architecture.* Washington: American Enterprise Institute.

_____. 1998b. "The IMF's Imprudent Role as Lender of Last Resort." *The Cato Journal* 17 (Winter): 275–94.

Calvo, Guillermo A., and Carmen M. Reinhart. 2001. "Fixing for Your Life." *Brookings Trade Forum 2000:* 1–58.

_____. 2002. "Fear of Floating." *Quarterly Journal of Economics* 117 (May 2002): 379–408.

Claessens, Stijn, Simeon Djankov, and Daniela Klingebiel. 2001. "Financial Restructuring in East Asia: Halfway There?" In *Resolution of Financial Distress,* edited by S. Claessens, S. Djankov, and A. Mody, pp. 229–59. Washington: World Bank.

Clark, Peter, Leonardo Bartolini, Tamim Bayoumi, and Steven Symansky. 1994. *Exchange Rates and Economic Fundamentals: A Framework for Analysis.* IMF Occasional Paper No. 115. Washington: International Monetary Fund (December).

Collins, Susan M., and Barry P. Bosworth. 1994. *The New GATT.* Brookings.

Council on Foreign Relations Independent Task Force. 1999. *Safeguarding Prosperity in a Global Financial System: The Future International Financial Architecture.* Washington: Institute for International Economics for the Council on Foreign Relations (September).

Crockett, Andrew. 1989. "The Role of International Institutions in Surveillance and Policy Coordination." In *Macroeconomic Policies in an Interdependent*

World, edited by Ralph C. Bryant and others, pp. 343–64. Washington: International Monetary Fund.

Dam, Kenneth W. 1970. *The GATT: Law and the International Economic Organization.* University of Chicago Press.

De Vries, Margaret Garritsen. 1976. *The International Monetary Fund, 1966–1971: The System under Stress.* 2 vols.: I, Narrative, and II, Documents. Washington: International Monetary Fund.

_____. 1985. *The International Monetary Fund 1972–1978: Cooperation on Trial.* Washington: International Monetary Fund.

_____. 1987. *Balance of Payments Adjustment, 1945 to 1986: The IMF Experience.* Washington: International Monetary Fund, 1987.

Dell, Sidney. 1981. *On Being Grandmotherly: The Evolution of IMF Conditionality.* Princeton Essay in International Finance No. 144 (October). International Finance Section, Princeton University.

Dobson, Wendy. 1991. *Economic Policy Coordination: Requiem or Prologue?* Policy Analyses in International Economics No. 30. Washington: Institute for International Economics (April).

_____. 1994. "Economic Policy Coordination Institutionalized? The G-7 and the Future of the Bretton Woods Institution." In *Bretton Woods: Looking to the Future,* Bretton Woods Commission report, staff review, and background papers. Washington: Bretton Woods Commission (July).

Driver, Rebecca, and Simon Wren-Lewis. 1997. *Real Exchange Rates for the Year 2000.* Washington: Institute for International Economics.

Economic Commission for Latin America and the Caribbean. 2002. *Statistical Yearbook for Latin America and the Caribbean 2002.* Santiago, Chile.

Eichengreen, Barry. 1994. *International Monetary Arrangements for the 21st Century.* Integrating National Economies series. Brookings.

_____. 1999a. "Policy Making in an Integrated World: From Surveillance to . . . ?" In *Rethinking the International Monetary System,* edited by J. Little and G. Olivei, pp. 205–26. Conference Series No. 43. Federal Reserve Bank of Boston.

_____. 1999b. *Toward a New International Financial Architecture: A Practical Post-Asia Agenda.* Washington: Institute for International Economics, 1999.

Feldstein, Martin S. 1998. "Refocusing the IMF." *Foreign Affairs* (March–April): 20–33.

Financial Stability Forum. 2000. *Report of the Working Group on Capital Flows.* Presented at the March 2000, meeting of the Financial Stability Forum. Basel: Financial Stability Forum and the Bank for International Settlements (April).

Finch, C. David. 1983. "Adjustment Policies and Conditionality." In *IMF Conditionality,* edited by John Williamson. Washington: Institute for International Economics.

Fischer, Stanley. 1994. "The Mission of the Fund." In *Bretton Woods: Looking to the Future.* Commission report, staff review, and background papers. Washington: Bretton Woods Commission (July).

_____. 1998. "Capital-Account Liberalization and the Role of the IMF." In *Should the IMF Pursue Capital-Account Convertibility?* edited by Stanley Fischer and others. Princeton Essays in International Finance No. 207 (May). International Finance Section, Princeton University.

_____. 1999. "Reforming the International Financial System." *Economic Journal* 109 (November): F557–76.

_____. 2000. "Globalization: Valid Concerns?" In *Global Economic Integration: Opportunities and Challenges.* Federal Reserve Bank of Kansas City.

Frankel, Jeffrey A. 1999. *No Single Currency Regime Is Right for All Countries or at All Times.* Princeton Essays in International Finance No. 215 (August). International Finance Section, Princeton University.

Frankel, Jeffrey A., Sergio Schmukler, and Luis Serven. 2001. "Verifiability and the Vanishing Intermediate Exchange Rate Regime." *Brookings Trade Forum 2000:* 59–124.

Friedman, Thomas L. 1999. *The Lexus and the Olive Tree.* New York: Farrar, Straus & Giroux.

Gardner, Richard N. 1969. *Sterling-Dollar Diplomacy: The Origins and the Prospects of Our International Economic Order.* New York: McGraw Hill (original edition published in 1956).

Ghosh, Atish R., and Paul R. Masson. 1994. *Economic Cooperation in an Uncertain World.* Oxford: Basil Blackwell, 1994.

Gold, Joseph. 1977. *International Capital Movements under the Law of the International Monetary Fund.* Pamphlet Series No. 21. Washington: International Monetary Fund.

_____. 1979a. "The Fund's Interim Committee—An Assessment." *Finance and Development* 16 (September): 32–35.

_____. 1979b. "The Structure of the Fund." *Finance and Development* 16 (June): 11–15.

_____. 1984. *Legal and Institutional Aspects of the International Monetary System: Selected Essays.* 2 vols. Washington: International Monetary Fund.

Goldstein, Morris. 1984. *The Exchange Rate System: Lessons of the Past and Options for the Future.* IMF Occasional Paper No. 30. Washington: International Monetary Fund (July).

_____. 1995. *The Exchange Rate System and the IMF: A Modest Agenda.* Washington: Institute for International Economics.

_____. 2000a. "Strengthening the International Financial Architecture: Where Do We Stand?" Working Paper No. 00-8. Washington: Institute for International Economics (October).

_____. 2000b. "IMF Structural Programs." Paper prepared for NBER Conference on Economic and Financial Crises in Emerging Market Economies, Woodstock, Vt., October.

Group of 24 Secretariat. 2003. "Adjustment of European Quotas to Enhance the Voice and Participation of Developing and Transition Countries." Paper prepared by the G-24 Secretariat for the Intergovernmental Group of Twenty-Four. Washington: G-24 Secretariat (August 25).

Group of Twenty Two (Willard Group). 1998. *Report of the Working Group on Transparency and Accountability.* Released in Washington, October.

Guitian, Manuel. 1981. *Fund Conditionality: Evolution of Principles and Practices.* Fund Pamphlet Series No. 38. Washington: International Monetary Fund.

Haque, Nadeem Ul, and Mohsin Kahn. 1998. "Do IMF-Supported Programs Work? A Survey of the Cross-Country Empirical Evidence." IMF Working Paper No. WP/98/169. Washington: International Monetary Fund (December).

Harper, Richard. 1998. *Inside the IMF: An Ethnography of Documents, Technology, and Organizational Action.* San Diego: Academic Press.

Hausmann, Ricardo. 1999. "Should There Be Five Currencies or One Hundred and Five?" *Foreign Policy* 116 (Fall): 65–79.

Hausmann, Ricardo, and Andres Velasco. 2003. "Hard Money's Soft Underbelly: Understanding the Argentine Crisis." *Brookings Trade Forum 2002:* 59–104.

Hinkle, Lawrence E., and Peter J. Montiel. 1999. *Exchange Rate Misalignment: Concepts and Measurement for Developing Countries.* Oxford University Press (September).

Hoekman, Bernard, and Michel Kostecki. 1995. *The Political Economy of the World Trading System: From GATT to WTO.* Oxford University Press.

Horsefield, J. Keith, and others. 1969. *The International Monetary Fund, 1945–1965.* 3 vols.: I, Chronicle; II, Analysis; and III, Documents. Washington: International Monetary Fund.

International Financial Institution Advisory Commission. 2000. *Report to the US Congress and US Department of the Treasury.* Government Printing Office (March).

International Monetary Fund (IMF). 1977. "Surveillance over Exchange Rate Policies." In *Annual Report 1977.* Washington.

_____. 1997. "IMF Board Submits Resolution to Governors for 45 Percent Quota Increase." Press Release No. 97/63. Washington (December 23).

_____. 1998a. *External Evaluation of the ESAF. Report of a Group of Independent Experts* (Kwesi Botchwey, Jan Willem Gunning, Yusuke Onitsuka, and Koichi Hamada, authors). Washington (June). [EBS/98/32, 3/2/98]

_____. 1998b. *Annual Report of the Executive Board for the Financial Year 1998.* Washington (October).

_____. 1999a. *External Evaluation of IMF Surveillance*. Report of a Group of Independent Experts (Chairman, John Crow; Ricardo Arriazu, and Niels Thygesen, authors). Washington (September). [EBAP/99/86. 7/15/99]

_____. 1999b. *External Evaluation of the Fund's Economic Research Activities*. Report of the External Evaluation Committee on the IMF's Economic Research Activities. Washington (June). [EBAP/99/85, 7/15/99]

_____. 1999c. *International Standards and Fund Surveillance—Progress and Issues*. Prepared by IMF Staff. Washington (August 16).

_____. 1999d. "IMF Tightens Defenses against Financial Contagion by Establishing Contingent Credit Lines." Press Release No. 99/14. Washington (April 25).

_____. 2000a. "Review of Fund Facilities—Preliminary Considerations." Staff Report, March 2. Washington.

_____. 2000b. "Review of Fund Facilities—Further Considerations." Staff Report. Washington, July 10. (See also Public Information Notice 00/79 of September 18, 2000, "IMF Board Agrees on Changes to Fund Financial Facilities.")

_____. 2000c. "Review of Fund Facilities—Further Considerations. Supplementary Information on Rates of Charge." Staff Report, July 18. Washington.

_____. 2000d. *External Review of Quota Formulas: Report to the IMF Executive Board of the Quota Formula Review Group*. Report of a Group of Independent Experts (Richard Cooper, chairman). Washington (April).

_____. 2000e. *Statement and Report of the Managing Director to the International Monetary and Financial Committee on Progress in Strengthening the Architecture of the International Financial System and Reform of the IMF*. Washington (September 19).

_____. 2000f. *Annual Report 2000*. Washington (September).

_____. 2000g. "Staff Commentary on External Review of the Quota Formulas." Paper prepared in response to the report of the Quota Formula Review Group. Washington (June 6).

_____. 2000h. "IMF Reviews the Experience with the Publication of Staff Reports and Takes Decisions to Enhance the Transparency of the IMF's Operations and the Policies of Its Members." Public Information Notice No. 00/81. Washington (September 20).

_____. 2001a. "Alternative Quota Formulas: Considerations." Paper prepared by the Treasurer's and Statistics Department. Washington (September 27).

_____. 2001b. *IMF Executive Board Informally Discusses Quota Formulas*. Public Information Notice No. 01/118. Washington (November 7).

_____. 2002a. *Alternative Quota Formulas—Further Considerations* and *Alternative Quota Formulas—Further Considerations: Statistical Appendix*. Washington (May 3).

_____. 2002b. *IMF Executive Board Discusses Quota Formulas*. Public Information Notice No. 02/59. Washington (June 14).

_____. 2002c. *Twelfth General Review of Quotas—Preliminary Considerations and Next Steps*. Washington (January 22).

_____. 2002d. *Twelfth General Review of Quotas—Further Considerations*. Washington (August 9).

_____. 2002e. *Twelfth General Review of Quotas—Draft Report of Executive Directors to Board of Governors*. Washington (November 18).

_____. 2003a. *Enhancing the Effectiveness of Surveillance: Operational Responses, the Agenda Ahead, and Next Steps*. Report prepared by the Policy Development and Review Department. Washington (March).

_____. 2003b. *Report of the Managing Director to the International Monetary and Financial Committee on the IMF's Policy Agenda*. Washington (April 2003).

_____. 2003c. *Report of the Managing Director to the International Monetary and Financial Committee on the IMF's Policy Agenda*. Washington (September 16).

_____. 2003d. *Annual Report 2003*. Washington (September).

_____. 2003e. *Quota Distribution—Selected Issues*. Paper prepared by the Finance Department in cooperation with other departments. Washington (July 17).

_____. 2003f. "IMF Executive Board Discusses Quota Distribution Issues." Public Information Notice No. 03/106. Washington (August 29).

_____. 2003g. "IMF Executive Board Recommends to Governors Conclusion of Quota Review." Public Information Notice No. 03/02. Washington (January 10).

IMF, Independent Evaluation Office. 2002. *Evaluation of the Prolonged Use of IMF Resources*. Washington (September).

_____. 2003a. *Fiscal Adjustment in IMF-Supported Programs*. Washington (September).

_____. 2003b. *The IMF and Recent Capital Account Crises: Indonesia, Korea, Brazil. Evaluation Report*. Washington (September).

_____. 2003c. *IEO Annual Report 2003*. Washington (September).

Isard, Peter, and Hamid Faruqee, eds. 1998. *Exchange Rate Assessment: Extensions of the Macroeconomic Balance Approach*. IMF Occasional Paper No. 167. Washington: International Monetary Fund.

Isard, Peter, Hamid Faruqee, G. Russell Kincaid, and Martin Fetherston. 2001. *Methodology for Current Account and Exchange Rate Assessments*. IMF Occasional Paper No. 209. Washington: International Monetary Fund.

Jackson, John H. 1997. *The World Trading System: Law and Policy of International Economic Relations.* 2nd ed. MIT Press.

_____. 1998. *The World Trade Organization: Constitution and Jurisprudence.* Chatham House Papers. London: Royal Institute of International Affairs.

Jadresic, Esteban, Paul R. Masson, and Paolo Mauro. 2001. "Exchange Rate Regimes of Developing Countries: Global Context and Individual Choices." *Journal of the Japanese and International Economies* 15 (1): 68–101.

James, Harold. 1995. "The Historical Development of the Principle of Surveillance." *IMF Staff Papers* 42 (December): 762–91.

Kenen, Peter B. 2001. *The International Financial Architecture: What's New? What's Missing?* Washington: Institute for International Economics (November).

Keynes, John Maynard. 1980a. *The Collected Writings of John Maynard Keynes.* Vol. 25: *Activities 1940–1944: Shaping the Post-War World: The Clearing Union,* edited by Donald Moggridge. New York and London: Macmillan and Cambridge University Press for the Royal Economic Society.

_____. 1980b. *The Collected Writings of John Maynard Keynes.* Vol. 26: *Activities 1941–1946: Shaping the Post-War World: Bretton Woods and Reparations,* edited by Donald Moggridge. New York and London: Macmillan and Cambridge University Press for the Royal Economic Society.

Krueger, Anne O., with Chonira Aturupane. 1998. *The WTO as an International Organization.* Chicago University Press.

Lane, Timothy, and others. 1999. *IMF-Supported Programs in Indonesia, Korea, and Thailand: A Preliminary Assessment.* IMF Occasional Paper No. 178. Washington: International Monetary Fund.

Masson, Paul R. 2000. "Exchange Rate Regime Transitions." IMF Working Paper No. WP/00/134. Washington: International Monetary Fund (July).

McHale, John. 2000. "The Korean Currency Crisis: A Report on the Third Country Meeting of the NBER Project on Exchange Rate Crises in Emerging Market Economies." Cambridge, Mass.: National Bureau of Economic Research.

Mikesell, Raymond F. 1994. *The Bretton Woods Debates: A Memoir.* Princeton Essays in International Finance No.192 (May). International Finance Section, Princeton University.

Minton Beddoes, Zanny. 1999. "From EMU to AMU? The Case for Regional Currencies." *Foreign Affairs* 78 (July–August): 8–13.

Mussa, Michael. 2002. *Argentina and the Fund: From Triumph to Tragedy.* Policy Analyses in International Economics No. 67. Washington: Institute for International Economics (July).

Mussa, Michael, and others. 2000. *Exchange Rate Regimes in an Increasingly Integrated World Economy.* IMF Occasional Paper No. 193. Washington: International Monetary Fund (August).

Nurkse, Ragnar, and others. 1944. *International Currency Experience: Lessons of the Inter-War Period.* Report of the League of Nations Economic, Financial, and Transit Department. Princeton University Press.

Polak, Jacques J. 1991. *The Changing Nature of IMF Conditionality.* Princeton Essays in International Finance No. 184 (September). International Finance Section, Princeton University.

Radelet, Steven, and Jeffrey D. Sachs. 1998. "The East Asian Financial Crisis: Diagnosis, Remedies, Prospects." *Brookings Papers on Economic Activity*, no.1: 1–90.

Rodrik, Dani. 1999. "Governing the Global Economy: Does One Architectural Style Fit All?" *Brookings Trade Forum 1999:* 105–40.

Rojas-Suarez, Liliana. 2000. "What Exchange Rate Arrangement Works Best for Latin America?" *World Economic Affairs* (October).

Roubini, Nouriel. 2000. "Bail-In, Burden-Sharing, Private Sector Involvement (PSI) in Crisis Resolution and Constructive Engagement of the Private Sector. A Primer: Evolving Definitions, Doctrine, Practice, and Case Law." Manuscript, New York University (September).

Sachs, Jeffrey D. 1995. "Do We Need an International Lender of Last Resort?" Frank D. Graham Memorial Lecture, Princeton University (April 20). Unpublished ms.

Sachs, Jeffrey D., and Felipe Larrain. 1999. "Why Dollarization Is More Straitjacket than Salvation." *Foreign Policy* 116 (Fall): 80–92.

Schadler, Susan M., and others. 1995. *IMF Conditionality: Experience under Stand-By and Extended Arrangements. Part I: Key Issues and Findings. Part II: Background Papers.* Occasional Paper No. 128. Washington: International Monetary Fund.

Schadler, Susan M., and others. 1993. *Economic Adjustment in Low-Income Countries: Experience under the Enhanced Structural Adjustment Facility.* Occasional Paper No. 106. Washington: International Monetary Fund (September).

Skidelsky, Robert. 2001. *John Maynard Keynes. Volume Three: Fighting for Freedom, 1937–1946.* London and New York: Viking.

Solomon, Robert. 1991. "Background Paper." In *Partners in Prosperity: The Report of the Twentieth Century Fund Task Force on the International Coordination of National Economic Policies.* New York: Priority Press.

Spraos, John. 1986. *IMF Conditionality: Ineffectual, Inefficient, and Mistargeted.* Princeton Essays in International Finance No.166 (December). International Finance Section, Princeton University.

Stein, Jerome L., and others. 1995. *Fundamental Determinants of Exchange Rates.* Oxford: Clarendon Press.

Summers, Lawrence H. 1999a. "Building an International Financial Architecture for the 21st Century." *Cato Journal* 18, no. 3: 321–30.

_____. 1999b. "Reflections on Managing Global Integration." *Journal of Economic Perspectives* 13 (Spring): 3–18.

_____. 1999c. "The Right Kind of IMF for a Stable Global Financial System." Remarks at the London School of Business, December 14.

_____. 1999d. Testimony before the Subcommittee on International Economic Policy and Export-Trade Promotion of the Senate Committee on Foreign Relations. 106 Cong. 1 sess. January 27.

_____. 2000a. "Rising to the Challenge of Global Economic Integration." Remarks at the School for Advanced International Studies, Johns Hopkins University, Washington, September 20.

_____. 2000b. Statement by the U.S. Treasury Secretary Lawrence H. Summers to the International Monetary and Financial Committee. April 16.

_____. 2000c. Statement by Treasury Secretary Lawrence H. Summers to the Senate Committee on Foreign Relations, 106 Congress 2 sess. February 29.

Talbott, Strobe. 2002. *The Russia Hand: A Memoir of Presidential Diplomacy.* New York: Random House.

United Nations. 2001. *World Population Prospects: The 2000 Revision.* New York (February).

U.S. Department of the Treasury. 2000. *Response to the Report of the International Financial Institution Advisory Commission.* Washington (June).

Van Houtven, Leo. 2002. *Governance of the IMF: Decision Making, Institutional Oversight, Transparency and Accountability.* Pamphlet Series No. 53. Washington: International Monetary Fund (August).

Williamson, John, ed. 1983. *IMF Conditionality.* Washington: Institute for International Economics and MIT Press.

_____. 1994. *Estimating Equilibrium Exchange Rates.* Washington: Institute for International Economics.

_____. 2000. *Exchange Rate Regimes for Emerging Markets: Reviving the Intermediate Option.* Policy Analyses in International Economics No. 60. Washington: Institute for International Economics (September).

World Bank. 2004. *World Development Indicators 2004.* Washington.

World Bank and International Monetary Fund, Development Committee. 2003a. *Enhancing the Voice and Participation of Developing and Transition Countries in Decisionmaking at the World Bank and IMF.* Document DC2003-0002. Washington: World Bank (March 27).

_____. 2003b. *Enhancing Voice and Participation of Developing and Transition Countries: Progress Report by the Boards of the World Bank and IMF.* Document DC2003–0012. Washington: World Bank (September 12).

Index

Accountability, 9, 37, 146–47
Adenauer, Konrad, 46
Adjustment referee function, 18, 25, 26
Analytical models: agreement on, 65; international staff support, 31; of national economies, 28–29; need for, 32; research needed, 32–33; role of academic community, 31–32; statistical data supporting, 33; support for supranational surveillance, 30–31, 33–34, 62, 67
Argentina: controls on cross-border financial transactions, 54; G-*20* membership, 13
Article IV consultations: confidentiality, 34; disclosure of information, 35–36; IMF staff roles, 25; importance, 11; influence, 22; number of, 36; procedures, 20–23; proposed changes, 77; Public Information Notices, 35–36; staff reports, 36
Asian financial crisis, 41, 54, 88, 136–37

Bagehot, Walter, 93
Bank for International Settlements (BIS): disclosure of information, 35, 37; lending, 10; surveillance role, 16, 25, 27, 59, 144
Basle Committee on Banking Supervision, 37, 59
Belgium, IMF quota, 117
BIS. *See* Bank for International Settlements
Brazil: controls on cross-border financial transactions, 54; exclusion from consultative groups, 13; G-*20* membership, 13; IMF loans, 88; IMF quota, 117
Britain. *See* United Kingdom
Canada: G-*7* membership, 12; IMF quota, 122, 134
Capital flows. *See* Cross-border financial transactions
CCL. *See* Contingent Credit Lines
Central banks: consultative groups of governors, 13–14; European, 133. *See also* Bank for International Settlements
Chile, controls on cross-border financial transactions, 54
China: exchange-rate policies, 27; G-*20* membership, 13; IMF constituency,